The Amazing Foot Race

OF 1921

D1714746

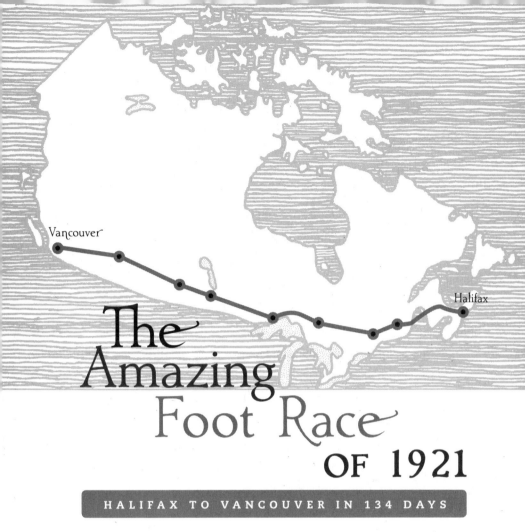

The Amazing Foot Race

OF 1921

HALIFAX TO VANCOUVER IN 134 DAYS

Shirley Jean Roll Tucker

VICTORIA · VANCOUVER · CALGARY

Heritage House Publishing Company Ltd.
www.heritagehouse.ca

LIBRARY AND ARCHIVES CANADA CATALOGUING IN PUBLICATION

Tucker, Shirley Jean Roll
The amazing foot race of 1921 / Shirley Jean Roll Tucker.

Issued also in electronic format.
ISBN 978-1-926936-05-5

1. Running races—Canada—History—20th century.
2. Runners (Sports)—Canada—History—20th century. I. Title.

GV1061.23.C3T83 2011   796.42´5097109042   C2011-900215-9

Edited by Audrey McClellan
Proofread by Karla Decker
Cover, book design and maps by Jacqui Thomas
Front-cover photo of the Dills courtesy of the *Halifax Herald*
Back-cover photo of Frank Dill, Jenny Dill, Jack Behan, Clifford Behan and Charles Burkman,
posing in front of the *Vancouver Sun*, Library and Archives Canada NL-22182

 The interior of this book was produced using 100% post-consumer recycled paper, processed chlorine free and printed with vegetable-based inks.

Heritage House acknowledges the financial support for its publishing program from the Government of Canada through the Canada Book Fund (CBF), Canada Council for the Arts and the province of British Columbia through the British Columbia Arts Council and the Book Publishing Tax Credit.

Printed in Canada

A tribute to:

Clyde W. Tucker
My husband, an exemplary Canadian;
My parents Freda, Paul and Ted Roll, proud Canadians;
My grandparents, Wilhelm and Justine (Schattle) Paul,
and Adam and Louisa (Becker) Roll,
Immigrants with dreams of becoming Canadians

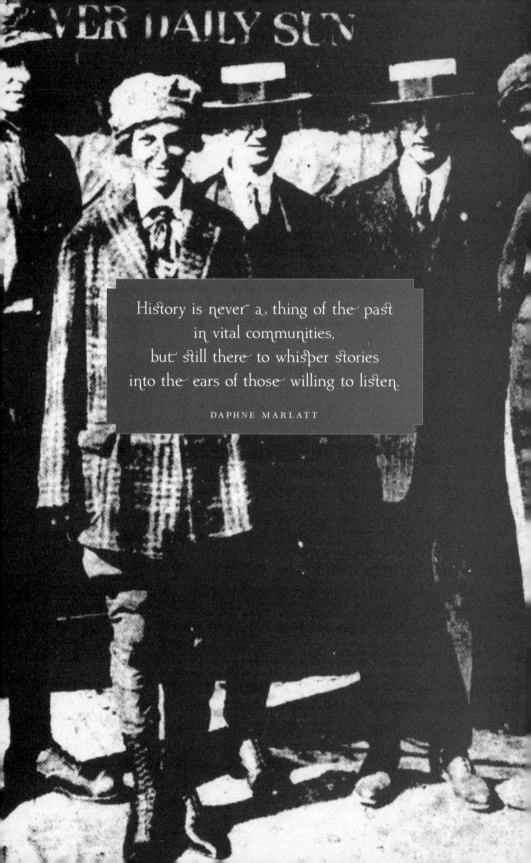

History is never a thing of the past
in vital communities,
but still there to whisper stories
into the ears of those willing to listen.

DAPHNE MARLATT

Introduction

L ike most flag-waving Canadian writers, I am a sucker for an old-fashioned, made-in-Canada adventure story with genuine Canuck heroes. In pursuit of such tales, I devour newspapers, peruse magazines and scour archival records.

In 2005 I came across a story dated June 9, 1921, on microfilm in the Nova Scotia Archives. Written for the *Halifax Herald*'s sister paper, the *Evening Star*, it celebrated the success of five transcontinental foot racers from Nova Scotia—one of them a woman—under the headline "The Greatest Contest in History of Pedestrianism Will Close Monday [June 11]." Maybe I hadn't struck gold, but this journalistic nugget, revealing the Olympian determination, fortitude and endurance of five plucky people who crossed the young Dominion from sea to sea on foot, and in record time, bolstered my faith in the spirit of the Canadian ideal.

The hikers set out from Halifax in mid-winter, and for three months they battled intermittent snow, sleet, freezing rain and high winds as they made 20 to 35 miles a day over slippery ties and rails. Charles Burkman, the lone hiker, announced from Kenora on April 22 that he had, in fact, completed 45 miles that day.

They did not have the high-tech gear that modern hikers possess: no "breathable waterproof anti-slip" boots with shock-absorbing heels, no "hyper-dri HD3 parkas with T-Max insulation," no "thermal medical socks" for extra comfort and support. For their "cross-Canada trudge," the five supplemented personal gear with outfits purchased from Munnis in Halifax or solicited from supporters. Shoe packs, heavy golf stockings, flannel shirts, mackinaws, slickers, caps with ties and wool-lined leather mitts were the order of the day. The hikers replaced worn boots regularly and received gifts of clothing (such as underwear from Stanfield's) and Larrigans (a Cape Breton Island footwear consisting of cowhide moccasins and calfskin leggings) along the way.

There were many other examples of public generosity extending beyond the purchase of the hikers' 10-cent postcards and the offer of free meals and lodging. In Cavers, Ontario, two public-spirited wives of CPR operators drove 11 miles to cook the Dills a delicious dinner, then sent them on their way with a large basket of fruit to eat on the road. A Russian immigrant family, living in the wilderness of Thunder Bay, toasted Burkman and the Behans with homemade potato vodka, and both the Behans and the lone hiker shared the Norwegian staples of pancakes and Rogers' golden syrup, washed down with coffee and a spoonful of milk, at Tache, Ontario. Chocolates and cigarettes were regularly handed out to all the racers, all across the country.

A fine representation of the 6 million Canadians populating the towns, villages and hamlets along the 3,645-mile route from Halifax to Vancouver celebrated and assisted the hikers. Mobs of schoolchildren were released for half-day holidays to cheer them on, and many isolated country folk, scattered along the railroad, raised their spirits and provided a few hours of fellowship, which the pedestrians returned in kind. Some supporters even attempted to entice the often tired and dispirited walkers with invitations to ride in automobiles, hop aboard passenger trains, or extend their visits to avoid adverse weather conditions, but no hiker succumbed to the temptation.

Although there is no evidence to suggest that money was ever paid to any of the contestants by the *Halifax Herald*, the newspaper did support the event with ingenuity and finesse. It even used the hike to bully Haligonians into taking responsibility for their lives and health. By publishing the accounts dispatched to the newspaper by the transcontinental adventurers from railroad stations along their route, the *Herald* whetted the public appetite for more information. Maps, run at least bimonthly in the newspaper, illustrated the hikers' progress and effectively involved readers of all stripes in tracking the competitors, offering them a vicarious opportunity to travel beyond the communities in which they were born. As the event gained in popularity, letters of advice, remedies for physical ills, tribute poems and a general outpouring of moral support appeared in the *Herald* and many other newspapers across the country. The dramatic events of the five-month odyssey endeared the walkers to the people who read the daily accounts in the newspaper, chose their favourites and cheered them on.

The ambitious editor of the *Herald* handled the competition skillfully, encouraging the participation of dignitaries, in various communities, who called in favours from other officials, including fire chiefs, law-enforcement officers, clergymen, train officials working along the lines, parliamentarians and even Prime Minister Arthur Meighen. In some instances, as in Truro, almost the entire community turned out to gawk, applaud and buy postcards, the financial mainstay of the pedestrians.

There were many reasons for the race's success. The country's contribution to the First World War, both on the battlefields and in industry, propelled the colony into national maturity that challenged public and social policies. At the same time, Canadians were poised uncertainly on the edge of recession, the result of too few people and too small an economic base, high unemployment exacerbated by thousands of "returned men," and a collapsed demand for military production. Women left the jobs they had filled when 450,000 men went into uniform; almost simultaneously they received the right to vote, federally and provincially, which represented a major cultural change. Unrest became endemic in the west ("the milch cow of Confederation," according to many prairie editors). In this uncertain climate, distractions were the order of the day. "Cheap" sports like foot racing helped satisfy armchair sporting folk whose ability to participate was limited by money, diet and the physical geography of the second-largest country in the world. This "great transcontinental hike" became a common and benign cause that brought together a nation clearly in search of an identity.

The Amazing Race of 1921 is a social history presented in journalistic form. It is intended to encourage readers to search out family roots, conscious of the spirit of the five Olympian phantoms racing from Halifax to Saint John to Montreal... Ottawa...Port Arthur...Winnipeg...Calgary...Banff...Revelstoke...Salmon Arm... Ashcroft...Spuzzum...Vancouver, and all the places in between that represent our heritage. The CPR line is still there, but it no longer stretches over wild, desolate countryside. Few are the narrow trestle bridges crossing perilous canyons. The majority of railway stations have been torn down or replaced with other forms of real estate like casinos, museums, art galleries or libraries, and signposts indicating where railroad towns once existed have been relegated to archival records or historic postcards.

With the co-operation of the *Halifax Herald*, and the support of Heritage House publisher Rodger D. Touchie, managing editor Vivian Sinclair and editor Audrey McClellan, I have pieced together a true Canadian adventure, that celebrates those remarkable folk-heroes Charles Burkman, the lone hiker; John (Jack) and Clifford Behan, a father-son duo; and Frank and Jenny Dill (a husband-and-wife team): ordinary people who achieved extraordinary results. No previous sporting event had sparked the imagination of the country the way this one did, uniting it in a common voice, and my book is a tribute to what is best about the Canadian spirit, as described by the *Herald*:

All the old time contests pale before [the transcontinental hike]. A few seconds' test of speed or a few hours of endurance are nothing in comparison. The determination and endurance of this competition were phenomenal...They have excelled all the records of antiquity.

NOTE Place-name spellings in quotations and newspaper excerpts from the time have been left unchanged—for example, "St. John" was how "Saint John" was spelled—but modern spellings are used in this text.

For the Cause
That Lacks Assistance

On December 13, 1920, local musician William Leighton's pledge to walk from Halifax to Vancouver sometime after Christmas was front-page news in the *Halifax Herald*. The naive young musician boasted to reporters that he could complete the 4,000-mile journey in seven months—provided he followed the Canadian Pacific Railway (CPR) tracks for the entire journey.

"Of course, I will encounter hardships if I start out on the journey in midwinter," he admitted. "But the upside is that I will be close to Fort William by early spring. Besides, it's not like I'll be shouldering these hardships alone. Dozens of west coast men stranded here without work would be happy to accompany me."

Local sporting men of all stripes—city fathers, business elites and regular blokes—read the article with enthusiasm. After all, it was the dead of winter and the country was reeling from a postwar economic readjustment. More than 3,000 "returned men" from the Great War swelled the ranks of the unemployed of Nova Scotia in the early 1920s, one symptom of a grim economic situation made worse as iron and steel industries in the province were no longer fuelled by wartime demand. What with massive unemployment, the enactment of prohibition legislation and speculation that a federal election would be called in the new year adding to a general feeling of uncertainty, stunts and cheap sporting competitions were the chief distractions of the day.

CITY MAN TO HIKE TO COAST

WILLIAM LEIGHTON, a 21-year-old Halifax musician, intends to walk to Vancouver.

Young Leighton said last night that he is confident that he can complete the 4,000 mile journney in seven months, providing he followed the C. P. R. tracks for the entire journey.

Leighton says that a number of Vancouver men in the city are ready to accompany him and that he will probably make a start shortly after Christmas. He admits that he will encounter many hardships should he start the journey in the winter, but he points out that by starting in the winter, he could be close to Fort William when Spring opened up. This would give him a chance to get through the colder part of Canada in the summer.

The first article on the hike. *Halifax Herald*, December 13, 1920, p. 1

If there was optimism to colour the grey mood of the time, it was to be found in the yellow journalism of newspapers working to inspire young men to take the initiative in solving their own problems. Leighton's announcement fit well with the *Herald*'s warnings about the dangers of becoming too "soft."

IN SOFT, YOUNG NOVA SCOTIANS ?--BEWARE!

An example of how the newspapers were used to motivate youngsters to be physically active. *Halifax Herald*, December 20, 1920, p. 1

HALIFAX, December 20.—…The young man in this picture, congratulating himself because he is "IN SOFT," would look at life very differently in a gymnasium. If he saw on a sofa in the gymnasium one man lying down, congratulating himself while the others worked and developed muscles, he would say: "You poor fool, being in a gymnasium will do you no good unless you exercise. Get up; run around the track, stretch your muscles…or you will stay all your life a soft good-for-nothing." Every young man knows that if he wants to win a race he must run, and run HARD and OFTEN. The difficult thing is to make the young understand that what applies to racing and athletics applies with even more force to the real success of life…

Tavern and pool hall speculation about Leighton's proposed transcontinental hike was further fuelled three days later, on December 16, when a picture appeared on the *Herald's* "Sports News and Reviews" page, confirming that William Leighton and pal Charles Burkman would attempt to walk across the continent to Vancouver.

Herald readers familiar with the story of John Hugh Gillis knew that a walk to Vancouver, although formidable, was not impossible and had in fact already been done. In 1906 the 22-year-old Gillis and two companions set out "on a bet and a dare" to walk from North Sydney, Nova Scotia, to San Francisco and back within a year with $200 in hand. Their only means of support were 10-cent souvenir postcards that they would peddle en route. The bet and a dare agreement was never honoured. John Hugh made it to Vancouver, but the other two swells only got as far as Montreal. There they had a falling out, leaving Gillis on his own. Charles Jackman, a retired Toronto lacrosse player, read about the transcontinental misadventure and set off after John Hugh, catching up with him at Ignace, Ontario. The two hikers became fast friends and walked to Vancouver together. It took Gillis almost eight months to cover the distance.

Christmas 1920 came and went, and although rumours of an impending transcontinental hike persisted, it wasn't until January 15, 1921, that the *Herald* once again picked up the story and ran it on the front page, along with a photograph of two hikers on page three.

Charles Burkman's first walking partner was William Leighton, whose reasons for defecting were unclear. It's been suggested he left the race to take up rum-running.
Halifax Herald,
December 16, 1920, p. 6

HIKERS OFF TO COAST ON MONDAY

Men To Walk From Halifax To Vancouver And To Write Exclusive Stories For *Herald*. EXPECT TO TAKE SEVEN MONTHS TO MAKE TRIP Charles Burkman And Sid Carr Will Carry Letter From Mayor Parker To Mayor Of Vancouver.

TO HIKE FROM HALIFAX TO VANCOUVER
Plan To Walk 4,000 Miles In Seven Months.

Charles Burkman and his
second partner, Sid Carr.
Halifax Herald,
January 15, 1921, p. 2

The paper gave no explanation for Leighton's defection from the hike, but there were murmurs that the young entrepreneur had a more than passing interest in the provincial referendum on prohibition—the motion to ban booze in Nova Scotia had passed in December 1920 by a vote of 59,000—suggesting that Leighton's love of drink might have encouraged him to abandon the hardships of hiking for a more lucrative pursuit: rum-running.

Nor did the *Herald* give much information about Leighton's replacement, Sid Carr, save to say that he, like Burkman, had lived in Vancouver for a short time and was one of the former soldiers who was now unemployed in Nova Scotia.

The *Halifax Herald* had a reputation for backing causes and events, which was re-enforced by a bold credo printed in the masthead at the top of page six:

SETS THE PACE AND FIRST IN EVERYTHING
The *Halifax Herald* Forty-Seven Years In The Public Service…For the cause that lacks assistance, For the wrong that needs resistance, For the future in the distance, And the good that we can do.

The editors recognized that Burkman and Carr's derring-do proposal was more than just an opportunity to entertain readers. It was also a chance to support two young athletes whose daily reports from the road had the potential to create national interest in Halifax newspapers while adding revenue to the *Herald*'s coffers—an ingenious win-win situation. The *Herald* agreed to sponsor Burkman and Carr in return for the exclusive right to publish accounts of their adventures, which the men would send back to Halifax by regular night letters from telegraph station houses along the route. Many writers in the 19th century had earned a living by writing stories in serial form for popular magazines—Charles Dickens is perhaps the most famous example—and the concept of serialization continued to be well received.

The hikers intended to leave Halifax on Monday January 17 at 10 a.m., and they gave the public an enthusiastic overview of their itinerary. There was no cross-country highway, and roads tended to be muddy, rutted and ill-constructed, so they chose to follow the train tracks that ran through all major and minor communities across the Dominion. They would follow the Canadian National Railway line to Saint John, New Brunswick, and then switch to the CPR tracks for the rest of the journey to Vancouver, stopping nightly wherever lodging was offered. Since they expected to encounter the worst weather conditions of the journey in Nova Scotia and New Brunswick, the two men planned to tramp along the CPR line in the state of Maine, thus bypassing the greater part of Quebec and reaching Ontario en route to the western provinces, by spring. Because neither man was in a hurry to get to the west coast, they aimed to hike 15 miles a day until reaching Ontario, where they expected to increase their daily output. Both men claimed to be acquainted with the western provinces and speculated that walking 30 miles a day on prairie sod was a realistic goal. "We are confident that the journey can be safely completed by August 1921," they said. As John Hugh Gillis had done, they would pay their expenses with money earned from selling 10-cent souvenir postcards imprinted with their images. The *Herald*'s reputation and sponsorship was also expected to encourage the generosity of hoteliers and CPR employees along the route.

Despite a downpour of rain and tempestuous winds on Monday January 17, the *Halifax Herald* succeeded in rallying a small but enthusiastic crowd of spectators in front of Halifax City Hall to ensure Charles Burkman and Sidney Carr received a proper send-off on their great transcontinental trek.

The grounds of Halifax City Hall would be the location of a huge send-off for Burkman and Carr in 1921.
Nova Scotia Archives and Records Management, Walter Deinger Collection, 1995-4 no. 21

John S. Parker, mayor of Halifax, gave them his best wishes and presented the hikers with a letter of introduction to Robert Henry Otley Gale, the mayor of Vancouver.

Dear Mr. Mayor,

I am handing this greeting to you for two young men, Charles Burkman and Sid Carr, who are leaving Halifax at 10 o'clock this morning on a tramp across Canada, Halifax to Vancouver. They propose, I understand, to make the attempt to accomplish the feat in seven months, reporting their adventures enroute to the Halifax Herald and the Evening Mail. We wish them good luck and trust to hear from you on the receipt of this letter.
Yours very truly,
✠ J.S. PARKER, MAYOR.

E.W. Savage, who was in the province shooting films for the Canadian government and Pathé newsreels, was invited to the official start, ensuring that the very latest in camera technology rolled and clicked as Charles Burkman and Sidney Carr, buffeted by coastal winds and drenched in icy rain, proceeded north along Barrington Street away from the city centre on the first leg of their seven-month cross-country journey. "The feat is already attracting attention, and Burkman and Carr have received several flattering offers should they make their destination," trumpeted the *Herald*.

The dreadful winter weather discouraged most well-wishers from following Burkman and Carr beyond the city limits; however, a scattering of youthful enthusiasts trailed them to Rockingham Station, where a group of boisterous locals fairly swept them off their feet. The doors of the Florence Hotel were

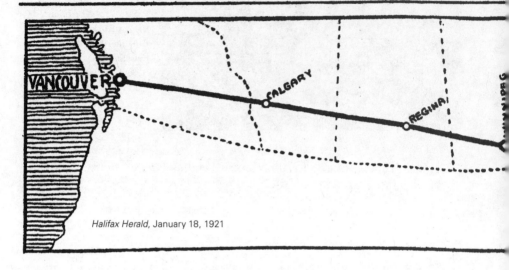

Halifax Herald, January 18, 1921

thrown wide for the pedestrians; their muddy boots and dripping mackinaws were draped in front of a huge grate fire, and they were invited to tuck into an old-fashioned midday dinner prepared especially for them. Burkman and Carr, not used to such generosity, were overwhelmed. "You're good sports, and this is your reward," hotel management declared when the men offered to pay for the dinner. "May you get many more before you reach Vancouver!"

The men experienced quite a different reception at Windsor Junction later in the afternoon, since no accommodations for travellers existed in the village. "Here is an excellent opportunity for a hotel," Burkman telegraphed the *Herald* from the Junction station that evening. After knocking on a few doors, the pedestrians found a family willing to feed them on condition that their names not be printed in the newspaper. With thousands of itinerants roaming the country in search of work, it was not a surprising request.

The coastal storm was intensifying, so Burkman and Carr, tired and sore after their 14-mile hike from Halifax, gratefully accepted the family's offer to spend the night, even though it meant sharing a bed. Enfield, four miles down the road, had been their destination, but they decided that with a good sleep and an early start they could reach Shubenacadie without disrupting their schedule.

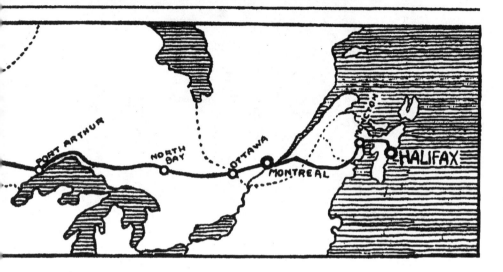

There was no improvement in the weather on day two of the hike, but the pedestrians left Windsor as planned. Again they were uplifted by the many good-hearted people who assembled to watch them slip and slide in the mud along the ties.

"Amazing, isn't it," said Burkman.

"Beyond comprehension," snorted Carr, "given the bloody weather!"

The weather conditions made the men late for dinner at the Pleasant View Hotel in Enfield, but, according to Sidney Carr, "It didn't faze the host who started in immediately to get the works going again and handed out one of the finest spreads you ever stuck your teeth into." The feast boasted roast of venison stuffed with apples and raisins, fried potatoes topped with pan gravy, and molasses-ginger cake with farm cream for dessert.

"Most miraculous of all, the proprietor wouldn't take a cent, same as at the Florence Hotel the previous day," Sidney Carr said.

Hours later, stiff and exhausted from battling the sheets of rain and the gale blowing off Grand Lake, the pedestrians limped into Shubenacadie, claiming a hard-fought 22-mile trek.

"The fierce winds nearly blew the eyes out of us," Burkman told the gathering of well-wishers at the station. "But walking has train travel trimmed a thousand ways, for it gives you an indication of the real good-heartedness of people."

Lewis Rice   DINING ROOM, STANLEY HOUSE   OFFICE, STANLEY HOUSE

The Stanley House Dining Room and Office, Truro, N.S. The Stanley House was the first of many hotels that didn't charge the hikers for a night's stay. Lewis Rice Photograph, NGC Archives

If Burkman and Carr still had any illusions that the cross-country walk would be a pleasure stroll, they vanished on the third day, Wednesday January 19, when the temperature dropped to −10°F and a fierce Atlantic nor'wester kept them sticking close to the rails. Forced to take a two-hour respite at Alton, their spirits were raised by a slap-up feed from the station master, Mr. Stewart.

Finally, after a second, shorter, warm-up stop in Hinton, the beleaguered pedestrians arrived at the hub city of Truro at 5.15 p.m.

"The only way to get at the real hospitality of Truro is to blow into the Hub in the first stages of a hike to Vancouver," said Burkman. "We breezed into the Stanley Hotel [The Stanley House], and were taken by storm. The manager says he won't take a cent for our board for the night. And this is only an instance of what we have been meeting with everywhere."

The pedestrians had admittedly grown lax in their toiletry on the trail, so, after eating an early dinner at the hotel, they took advantage of the special invitation for a shave and haircut extended to them by Spencer's Barber Shop. That

I.C.R. Station and Yards, Truro, N.S.

Intercolonial Railway Station and Yards, Truro, N.S. The *Herald* required railroad officials to sign the hikers' travel books to verify that they had indeed passed through.
NSRHS Postcard #77.109.10

evening the two well-fed, spruced and polished young men sold their 10-cent souvenir postcards as guests of the management at the Strand Theatre.

The next morning, Thursday January 20, Burkman and Carr got off to a late start to Londonderry after discovering that the generosity of Truro extended well beyond the Stanley when many local businesses showered them with presents. Significant among them was a pair of shoepacks—sturdy waterproof boots—for Burkman from Conner's Shoe Store. According to Carr, Burkman's new boots left him as tickled as a youngster with a Christmas toy. A visit to Stanfield's got both pedestrians a promise of winter underwear, to be picked up at the train station in Moncton, New Brunswick.

Burkman and Carr had agreed to the *Herald's* request that they have city dignitaries or credible railroad officials sign their travel book to verify that they had passed through cities, towns and train stations along the route, so that was another chore they had to see to before leaving town.

"The mayor being too sick to see us, we called on Chief of Police John Fraser, who gave us a letter of introduction to all the chiefs of police along the line," Carr explained to readers when he took his turn at writing the daily dispatch. "Town Clerk MacDougall put his John Henry in our book, thus guaranteeing that we had been to Truro and saving us turning back in case anybody didn't believe it."

Gathering signatures was a time-consuming enterprise, but it held the promise of commercial opportunity: "We sold a good number of postcards and added a fair number of dimes to the communal purse," Carr said.

Business done, Burkman and Carr finally set off for Londonderry, smack into a resurgent storm. The mild frostbite they had suffered on the walk from

Shubenacadie to Truro was further aggravated by the bitter cold and driving snow encountered during the last four miles of the day.

"We were walking blind and didn't know whether we were coming or going," Carr complained. Despite the ordeal, when they reached Londonderry around 5:30 p.m., they claimed to be 81 miles from li'l ol' Halifax and feeling better than they had ever felt in their lives.

"We were limbered up, stiffness gone," Burkman said.

"A mere 3,564 miles left to Vancouver," Carr scoffed.

"But not much when you say it quick," Burkman laughed.

Basking in the beneficial alliance they had forged with the *Halifax Herald*, the men spent the night as guests of the management of Peppard's Hotel, in Londonderry. "The people we meet seem to know all about us—we're sure everybody reads the *Herald*. It's really remarkable how they have followed up on our hike; they know just what we have done and what we intend to do."

On Friday January 21, the extreme weather that Burkman and Carr experienced during their walk from Londonderry to Westchester alternated between icy rain and driving snow, leaving only the hardiest Nova Scotians on high alert to encourage them on their way—such as the engineer on a passing train who threw them a greeting, wrapped in a copy of the *Herald*, which read simply: "Hullo, Hikers!"

In Folly, Station Master Fraser raised their flagging spirits with delicious beefsteak sandwiches, dill pickles and mugs of hot milk. And while they made quick work of the food, their eccentric host banged out a medley of old country tunes on the piano. Two hours later, warmed, refreshed and entertained, they struck out for Wentworth accompanied by Billie Walsh, a well-known New Glasgow hockey player, who said his goodbyes at the town limits.

The pair ducked out of the bad weather once more, to enjoy a steaming cup of cocoa with agent John Doyle at Wentworth station, and then continued on into the blinding snow to complete a 17-mile day to Westchester station. Despite the cold, miserable walking conditions, and the wind that breezed up and stung them straight in the face, the men were growing content as things settled into a predictable, albeit uncomfortable, routine.

That evening, after fine-tuning plans for a record-breaking 26-mile hike to Springhill the next day, the hikers ate a small supper in the village at their own expense. Afterward, the two innocents fell into an untroubled sleep, never dreaming that the dynamics of the great transcontinental hike were about to change.

The
Dartmouth Challenge

The exclusive coverage given to Burkman and Carr by the *Halifax Herald* acted like a magnet to John (Jack) and Clifford Behan of Dartmouth, who appeared at the *Herald* office on Friday January 21, 1921, with a letter written on their behalf by the mayor of the rival city across the harbour:

> *Gentlemen:—I have pleasure in introducing you to John Behan and son Clifford (both overseas men). They wish to confer with you regarding a trip on foot across the continent. These men expect to make the trip in six months or less.*
> *Yours truly,*
> ✒ MAYOR SIMPSON, DARTMOUTH, JANUARY 21

Barring accidents, the 44-year-old Behan informed the editorial staff, he and his 24-year-old son would not only hike across the continent in record time but would also pass Burkman and Carr before they reached Montreal. The well-known postman asked that the newspaper give him and his son treatment similar to that given Burkman and Carr. Quick to recognize the advantages of a competitive hike over a leisurely walk, the *Herald* agreed.

DARTMOUTH FATHER AND SON WILL HIKE TO THE PACIFIC

HALIFAX, January 21.—These pictures show John Behan, the well known Dartmouth postman, and his son Clifford, who will start out from The Herald and Mail building on Tuesday morning, on a hike to the Pacific... These papers have arranged for the exclusive story of the Behans...[to be told to] *The Herald* and *The Mail*'s great army of readers.

Jack Behan came with a certain reputation that lent credibility to his colourful swagger and boast. He was a Dartmouth letter carrier—thought to be the community's second—with a background in amateur athletics, who had served as vice-president of the North Star Rowing Club in 1904.

The mayor described Jack and Clifford as "overseas men," which meant they had taken part in the Great War. As a member of the 63rd Halifax Rifles, the elder Behan saw action in the front-line trenches and was returned home only after the signing of the armistice. Clifford had been attached to the Montreal Battalion, crossed to Europe in 1916 and was invalided back to Halifax after he was wounded at Vimy Ridge. It was this bloodbath on Easter Monday, April 9, 1917, in which almost 3,600 Canadians were killed and more than 7,000 (including 21-year-old Clifford) wounded, that allowed Canada to step out of Britain's shadow as an independent nation.

"Here's to a successful journey," shouted a local rowdy at the hastily organized Dartmouth Commercial Club luncheon on Monday evening, January 24.

"If anyone can do it, Jack can."

"You mean make a man out of the boy?" an ex-army civilian jeered, playing to the crowd.

The savage Great War had suited Jack's restless, outgoing nature, but the war adventure left his more sensitive son to deal with psychosomatic ailments like flashbacks, night sweats and general depression—a situation made worse by Clifford's inability to find employment in the plumbing trade for which he was qualified.

"We've been in training for the past two weeks," Jack said, brushing the comments aside, "to see if the boy was up to a 4,000-mile walk."

"And...so?"

"Truth is, we are more concerned about our financial resources than the hiking," Jack said. "Success, I'm afraid, will depend on the generosity of the home folk. We're ready to do our part, if the local sports are willing to do theirs."

Dartmouth declared that it was solidly behind "their boys," and the *Herald* published a list of items the two men needed for the trip: "2 maconan coats, size 40; 2 riding army britches, size 34; long boots, tan size 7 & 8; 2 pairs mitts or gloves; 2 army knapsacks; 2 pairs wool socks; 2 suits under wear, size 36; 2 sweaters, (light) normal neck; 2 water proof coats, size 40." Donations of money or in kind were equally acceptable.

Burkman and Carr already had a five-day head start, so if the Behans were to make good on their boast to arrive first in Montreal, they needed to get away as soon as possible. The *Herald* set the start for 9 a.m. on Tuesday January 25.

The paper sought no input from the pedestrians already in the field, even though Burkman was one of the initiators of the event. He and his walking companion didn't, in fact, learn of the challengers until Sunday January 23.

"We just found out when we reached here today that the two Behans of Dartmouth intend to start out and beat us to Montreal," Carr reported from Amherst. "Well you can tell the people who are backing them that nobody will overtake us to any place between here and Vancouver unless we break a leg... We are glad, however, that the Behans intend to try walking across the country, because it will be an incentive for us to walk faster."

"Let them know that we are just hitting our stride—and barring worse winter conditions, we'll continue to make even better time," Burkman said, adding his two bits' worth.

After greeting and selling postcards to the folks gathered at the Amherst CNR station, Burkman and Carr decided to enjoy a pleasant afternoon and signed in at the Terrace Hotel. They accepted a lunch invitation from Frank Cormier

I.C.R. Station, Amherst, N.S.

CNR Station, Amherst, N.S. Amherst treated Burkman and Carr like dignitaries. They were given a tour, free boots and a luncheon.
NSRHS Postcard #74.87.12

of the Amherst Independent hockey team. Afterward, Mr. Fraser, the assistant manager of the Canadian Car Foundry, introduced them to Mayor Ralston, who signed their book. Then Mr. Campbell, proprietor of the Terrace Hotel, took them for a motor tour, which Sid Carr described as "a pleasant relief from our usual mode of transportation."

They regarded the relaxing afternoon interlude as a just reward for completing 26 miles of arduous winter walking on Saturday—from Westchester via Oxford Junction to Springhill Junction—and an additional 17 miles on Sunday, to Amherst.

Burkman and Carr were the grateful recipients of a pair of boots apiece from the Amherst Boot and Shoe Company, and late Monday morning—just as they were about to leave town—the Amherst Commercial Club invited them to lunch. "They introduced us and we were asked for a speech," Burkman reported to the *Herald*. "This was something new to us. Carr didn't know anything, so I was the victim."

Later that day, in Sackville, Burkman and Carr took time to get the town clerk's signature, and at 2:40 p.m. they crossed the Nova Scotia–New Brunswick boundary. "Nova Scotia surely showed us a good time all the way," the pedestrians agreed.

Between Sackville and Dorchester, the famed jail town, they ran into the worst weather they had yet encountered. Of the two, Burkman was able to keep a healthy perspective. "After an exhausting 22 mile tramp, we are in Dorchester, but not in jail," he laughed. "Thru one province of Canada on our long coast-to-coast hike and into another. We are getting farther and farther away from the east coast and further and further north, so we expect awful weather and more snow—but we are going to stick to it until we bathe in the salt waters of the Pacific some fine day next summer."

Weather permitting, Burkman and Carr would leave Dorchester for Moncton the next day, and since Jack and Clifford Behan would be leaving Halifax for Enfield at about the same time, their threats would continue to be a mere echo across the winter landscape. Burkman and Carr intended to enjoy their eight-day advantage, certain that time was on their side.

DARTMOUTH HIKERS CHEERED AS THEY LEAVE HERALD BUILDING ON JAUNT TO PACIFIC OCEAN

The people of Dartmouth supported the Behans with gifts of warm clothing.
Halifax Herald,
January 26, 1921, p. 3

IT WAS BITTERLY cold as Jack and Clifford Behan prepared to leave Halifax, but the men were brimful of Nova Scotia stamina and grit and were warmed by the large, enthusiastic crowd of friends and well-wishers gathered for their send-off. Shouts of "Good Luck!" "God speed!" "Success in beating out Burkman and Carr!" rang in their ears.

"It speaks volumes for the quality of the stock that Jack Behan, especially—no longer young—should dare the three-thousand-mile journey on foot beginning... in mid-winter," the *Herald* reported. "For the first time in the history of Canada four men are engaged in a titanic struggle in a race across the continent, from Halifax to Vancouver. Interest in the progress which these men are making has reached a fever heat with the get-away of the Behans, father and son."

> Here are the starters and the starting place in the great continental "chase" from Halifax to Vancouver...Jack Behan, the father, and left Clifford Behan, son...They expect to overhaul Burkman and Carr...at Montreal.

From Moncton that evening, Sid Carr sent a surly challenge their way in his night letter: "If we had the Behans along with us today we would have shown them what hiking really is. This was one of our hardest days and, by the way, one of our best, for we stretched our legs over 27 miles of road."

"Was it cold in Moncton?" he continued. "We'll tell the world it was. Moncton is shivering in below zero weather tonight and we bucked thru it the entire day." Admittedly it had taken some of the sap out of them. "But it left our enthusiasm working on all cylinders," Carr insisted. He mentioned that his walking partner, in particular, should be praised. "Burkman is some sticker. I watched him closely today—a test in hiking—the boy played right with the game and is feeling fit for another stretch tomorrow."

Before leaving Moncton the next morning, the men enjoyed a leisurely cleanup at Joe Merry's barbershop, got their book signed by the town clerk and called in at Bellevieu's store for a gift of Stanfield's underwear. The biggest surprise of the day was a presentation of 500 Player's cigarettes from Harold Cole, proprietor of the Victor Tobacco Store. "If we keep on getting things like we have been, we will have enough stock to start a department store when we go back to Halifax," Burkman smiled.

The pedestrians arrived at Salisbury after a light day of hiking—"to give Behans a chance to catch up," Carr smirked.

For his part, Burkman assured readers that he was unconcerned the Behans had reached Enfield on their first night out. "It's a long way from Salisbury," he said. "Tomorrow, Carr and I intend to complete a thirty-three-mile hike to Sussex."

Jack and Clifford Behan were oblivious to the disparaging comments from Burkman and Carr and full of unabashed enthusiasm for the day's accomplishments. "Hiking is great fun! We didn't know we had so many friends," Jack wrote. In fact, Jack's only uncle, whom he hadn't seen for years, turned up at the hotel in Stewiacke to wish them well, joking that he was sorry Jack would be so long away. "So in addition to bringing the whole countryside out to see us, I'm bringing the family TOGETHER. It is worth walking to Vancouver to do that. And another thing," Jack admitted with some pride, "I had no idea of the kind of stuff that boy of mine was made of; he's sticking, that's what he's doing."

Between Enfield and Stewiacke on the 26th, CNR brakeman R. Redmand further raised their spirits by throwing a newspaper containing a note that said: "'Good luck, God speed...' and *something* that only brakemen talk about!" which was apparently not fit for ladies to read.

Jack Behan enjoyed the McRichie cartoon in the January 26 issure of the *Herald*. In a throw-away remark he said, "I hope those hikers due to hit the 'long trail 1 February,' do not start until we pass Montreal."

A mile from Stewiacke station, a crowd of well-wishers waited for the hikers, waving copies of the *Herald*. Jack reported overhearing the comment, "They sure look like their pictures, only they look so much alike we do not know t'other from which." Mayor Nelson was also at the station to greet them, and the hikers were tickled when his worship offered to sell 100 souvenir postcards for them.

In the next town, Alton, Station Master Stewart was so good to the hikers, insisting so nicely that they hang up for the night and make Truro on the morrow, that they couldn't resist the offer. It had been a long day, and the unseasoned pedestrians were exhausted.

THESE HIKERS START FEBRUARY 1

This McRitchie cartoon expressed the hope that crime, vice, bootleggers and boozers would follow the hikers out of Nova Scotia. *Halifax Herald,* January 26 ,1921, p. 3.

On Wednesday January 26 the *Herald* dropped yet another bombshell on the hikers in the field:

HUSBAND AND WIFE JOIN CHASE ACROSS CONTINENT

Pictures of F.C. and Mrs. Jenny Dill were featured above a second headline: "Hants County Man and Halifax County Woman to Hike To Vancouver." The article began: "This is in truth the Woman's DAY. In work, in politics, and in sport woman has found her place in the sun. Long-distance walking, like the measles, is catching."

Frank Dill, a "former and well known Windsor athlete," and "his athletic wife" Jenny, described as "a Halifax county girl who has a splendid reputation as an athletic, out-of-doors girl," expected to leave Halifax the following Tuesday, just one week after the Behans and fifteen days after Burkman and Carr. The Dills had taken a keen interest in the chase between Burkman and Carr and Jack and Clifford Behan, and they asked the *Herald* to give them the same publicity the other hikers were getting as they too had decided to make the trip to Vancouver.

The race took on new interest when Frank and Jenny Dill joined. The question on everyone's mind was "Could a woman do it?" *Halifax Herald*, January 27, 1921, p. 3

"Could a woman survive the hardships of a walking journey across a frontier country?" the *Herald*'s sports reporter wanted to know. The public wasn't sure.

When asked, the woman demurred: "I've been used to roughing it out of doors all my life and, if Mr. Behan, who is old enough to have a son to accompany him on the trip, can make it, I'll not fail."

The gauntlet was thrown. The newspaper acquiesced. A female in the mix would draw women readers. Besides, from the first time pretty little Jenny Dill appeared with her husband in the editorial room of the *Herald*, looking as natty as possible in her walking togs and jaunty warm cap and requesting equal support for their bid to walk across the nation, the editor was impressed with the manner in which she handled herself. He was convinced that an articulate woman like Mrs. Dill would make good copy. On that first visit she told the press:

> My husband happened to say on Sunday that if he had someone who could keep up with him, he believed he could catch up with the others who have gone ahead. "Come on out and have a little hike to keep me in practice," he challenged. So I said to him, "You're on!" And off we went… We walked a long time, and presently I urged him to try it a little faster. But by then, Frank was feeling a little tired, so I told him not to worry about the walk across the continent, because if he got tired, I'd pick him up and carry him.

"Then came a ripple of most pleasant, bright laughter; and indeed the editor found it contagious and laughed as well," the *Herald* reported. Captivated by the personable Mrs. Jenny Dill, the paper reported "that this Halifax county girl born and brought up at Petpeswick, Nova Scotia—who liked to skate, hunt, and fish—was…surprisingly feminine," with "not a single suggestion of the mannish in her personality. She [was] just as womanly as she can be, pretty withal, and her natural, simple way, her apparent unconsciousness that she was undertaking anything unusual or in any degree 'heroic,' her perfect naiveté, were just the very sort of thing to captivate the crowd."

THERE WAS NO acknowledgement from Jack and Clifford Behan that a third team was about to enter the transcontinental race. The mercury had registered –13°F when they left Alton for Truro, but an enthusiastic crowd braved the elements to catch a glimpse of the father and son in Brookfield, and that warmed their spirits. They had discarded their "long boots" for a gift of Larrigans at Enfield the previous day and were happy to have done so. In Truro they were met by an exuberant crowd of admirers who shouldered them to The Stanley House, where proprietor Arthur Stevens invited them to dinner. At the insistence of the gathered throng, they abandoned their plans to reach Debert and instead spent the afternoon walking around the city, selling postcards and visiting many returned men. John W. Fraser, chief of police, signed their book and gave them a letter of introduction to all the other police chiefs across the country. "Anything you can do for these men will be considered a favour by me," he wrote.

They called on Mayor Coffin and then on N.B. Stewart, chief of the fire department, who invited them to dine and have breakfast with him. At the YMCA the men were given a paper, signed by Donald McPhail, to pass on to other YMCA general secretaries across the country. John M. O'Brien presented them with a large number of cigars and the promise of a lunch for the road. He also gave them a calendar to be signed by the mayor of Vancouver, promising that he would make it interesting if they returned it to him after their journey was finished. They were promised new boots in Amherst, similar to what Burkman and Carr had received, and telegrams poured in from all over the continent wishing them luck. Arguably the most novel gift came from Frank Tattam, head of an Indian agency near McLeod, Alberta, who promised them a "powwow" and money from the proceedings.

It was a day of heady tributes, and Jack rose to the occasion: "We have been given such encouragement that we feel we can make the trip in much less time than we set out to do it in—barring accidents."

FATHER AND SON ON
TRANSCONTINENTAL
HIKE

HALIFAX *to* VANCOUVER

SOUVENIR PHOTOGRAPH of John Behan and his son Clifford both veterans of the Great War.

The Dartmouth men guarantee to beat out Burkman who left Halifax on January 17th for Vancouver

JOHN BEHAN   CLIFFORD BEHAN

The sale of these cards is our only income. Every one we sell helps us that much further on our long and difficult journey.

The official postcard of the Behans.
Postcard courtesy of Donnie Behan family

There was no dispatch at all from Burkman and Carr on Thursday January 27.

Readers were doubly puzzled the following day when they read a front-page interview with Jenny, who stated: "Many a woman has succeeded when men have failed. I know what we are up against, but we are prepared, and we are going to start, and FINISH." Mrs. Dill reiterated that she was accustomed to roughing it. Her father was a Halifax county fisherman, so she knew something about being out in rough weather. "To me and my husband our trip will be just a holiday," she said. "We have both worked very hard since we were married a year ago, and now are going out to see the world… You can leave it to us—we know what we are doing." Then she smiled at the reporter. "We are young. We have no home ties. Not a chick or a child. We'll just take our time, and we'll make it."

Still, the reporter emphasized the tremendous task that confronted her—a task "which has already caused one of the hikers to abandon the trip."

What was going on? Readers wanted to know.

3

The Lone Hiker

Charles Burkman headlined the *Herald's* sports page on Saturday January 29. He reported that Sidney Carr, his walking mate, had quit the race on Thursday, boarded a train and returned to Halifax.

BURKMAN SAYS HE IS RUNNING TRUE TO FORM AND WILL NOT QUIT HIKE
FIRST MAN TO SUGGEST WALK TO VANCOUVER AVERS HE WILL MAKE TRIP IF HUMANLY POSSIBLE.

By Charles Burkman

HAMPTON, N.B., Jan. 28.—I am alone, but I never felt better in my life. When Carr left me yesterday I felt blue, but I have made up my mind to walk to Vancouver and if I have my health, I will do it.

Burkman had known Carr for only a short time, but the young idealist believed him a suitable walking partner—a miscalculation that left him plugging along the tracks alone. His greatest concern was how it would be perceived by readers.

It didn't take long for him to find out. The reception given him at Depot House, Sussex, was one of the best he'd received. Proprietor R.A. McDonald went out of his way to be agreeable; he even got the town clerk to sign Burkman's book. At Apohaqui—a village with a queer name but a mighty warm heart—Burkman was treated to a hearty dinner; and at the Wayside Inn in Hampton, where he spent the night, the management couldn't do enough to please him. "Guess they think I am an orphan now, and the further I go the better they receive me," he said, adding, "Today the weather was great. I pushed along, singing to myself. I thought of Carr riding along in the train and looking out the windows. I would sooner be here. YOU BET."

The next day the lone hiker hoped to reach Saint John, where he had many friends, but he didn't intend to tarry. He had had enough of dilly-dallying. "I have no hindrance now and will push along."

"I am very much interested in the Behans," he admitted. "Carr said it was a race—I said the more the merrier. If we can show them we are REAL SPORTS the more the people at home will think of us. And when I heard that a man and his wife were after us, I was glad. Any woman who has the spunk to start out on a race of this kind has MY ADMIRATION. If I am beaten in this race I hope it is Mrs. Dill who beats me."

Speculation sold newspapers, and Carr's defection had papers flying off the stands. Had his concept of a leisurely stroll across the country been dashed by Jack Behan, who challenged the fundamental nature of the event? Or was it a whiff of female competition that changed his mind? To insure that the lone hiker didn't follow Carr's example and quit the race, the *Herald* leaned on a group of Halifax businessmen to put up a prize for the young man, conditional on his completing the walk to the west coast. The article ran in the January 31st issue.

$500.00 PRIZE FOR CHARLES BURKMAN

A Group of Halifax's sporting men with admiration for the pluck of Burkman, who has decided to make the long hike from the Atlantic to the Pacific alone, called The Herald office Saturday and stated that they would contribute $500.00 to Burkman if he completed the trip on foot within six months. It will be remembered that Burkman and Carr were the first hikers to start out and that Carr abandoned the task when he reached Salisbury, New Brunswick.

The Behans, meanwhile, got off to a late start from Truro, and Jack was full of excuses. "Had we known that we had so many friends here, we would have cut across the Board Landing Bridge and made Onslow direct," he said. "And when we got word about the Indian powwow in Alberta, we were wiped off our feet. I was never at a powwow and I am danged if I know how to act." Jack was chuffed to learn that they were to get the benefit of the powwow's proceeds. "I had visions of buying the Citadel in Halifax," he said.

He and his son spent the night at Folly, "a dandy little place near the lake, where all the Truro church folks hold their Sunday school picnics," Jack said. He anticipated an early start for River Philip the next morning. "That banquet awaiting us in Amherst is very attractive. I hate to miss the speeches." And in response to the Dills' entry into the race, he was grudgingly gracious. "Admittedly, we received our fair share of publicity yesterday," he wrote, "and will give over to the Dills today, with a warning, that when we reach Amherst, I want a column—even if I [have to pay for the space myself]."

While the Behans continued to enjoy the time of their lives, the *Herald* worked hard to elevate the charming, articulate Mrs. F.C. Dill to poster girl, introducing her in one story as "the woman hiker who became famous in a day—the day after it was announced in The Herald and The Mail that she would start with her husband, the well-known Windsor athlete, on a hike across the continent." The reporter added: "It's no use to tell Mrs. Dill that she is making an error in starting on this long 'jaunt.' She flashes her black eyes and snaps back: 'I AM PREPARED FOR THE WORST.' Mr. and Mrs. Dill…will not say where they expect to catch the Behans but they have an idea. Burkman has a good safe lead as he is nearing St. John."

Clifford Behan took up the pen for the family on Sunday January 30. "Dad's been writing all the stories since we left Halifax, but this one is too good for even him to tell," he said. "We had taken the old coach road from

Jenny Dill with her snowshoes. The papers all stressed her athleticism.
Halifax Herald, January 29, 1921, p. 3

Oxford Junction to Amherst and were plugging along at a good stretch when we heard a great snort. 'Great guns!' dad roared. I didn't say a word—too scared, I guess. Then came a second roar—louder than the first—followed by a rattling of bushes…and out charged a big bull moose. It was the biggest I ever saw. When it saw the HIKERS, you should have seen it 'hike.'"

The moose ran about a hundred yards along the middle of the road, stopped, looked back at the hikers, pawed its forefeet, ran another hundred yards, looked back a second time and finally bounded away into the woods.

The hikers had been well received since leaving Truro. At Debert, Mrs. Walsh did everything she could to make their stay comfortable, and John Doyle did the same at Westchester Station. "The receptions we are getting are more than making up for the sacrifices we are making at home, to take this long hike," Clifford assured readers.

The Behans were disappointed to find that all copies of the *Herald* in the towns along the route had been sold but were cheered by greetings written in a souvenir book that T.R. Bissett, travelling back to Halifax from Montreal, threw out the train window: "Good Luck, Jack, Keep It Up. We're All Pulling for You and The Lad."

The two stout-hearted men battled a fierce storm going through the Cobequid Mountains. "The mountains are very pretty in summer, but oh, the winds that do blow around them in winter time." Clifford said. "The scenery was great, though. It was wonderful to look down the Valley and over the tops of trees loaded with snow and ice."

At Oxford Junction, father and son were met by so many people that they thought a funeral must be going on. And at Amherst's Sterling Hotel that evening, Clifford wrote that they had been treated as "some big pumpkins." After a bang-up feed, a social evening began. "Social is right! First the music started and, the dancing began. You'd have died if you could have seen dad shaking a leg. He's been hiking for almost a week, but I bet he covered more distance dancing last night at the Sterling Hotel than we covered since we left home. As a matter of fact, I covered a bit of distance myself. Had one partner I could have danced to Vancouver with."

The Behans set off the next morning on a subdued note, which suggested a possible reprimand from the *Herald* regarding proper public decorum for their hikers. Jack's wife Catherine, at home in Dartmouth minding the family business, might also have had something to say about her husband's fun-loving behaviour.

"It is Sunday," Clifford wrote, "and Amherst is quiet on the Sabbath." It seemed that his father no longer had the need of a column, at his own expense, to disclose the adventures he'd hinted at when the Dills entered the race.

The hike's poster girl, Jenny Dill was again featured in the *Herald* of Monday January 31, talking about one of her most popular outdoor pastimes: skating. According to the paper's sports reporter, "Mrs. Dill is one of the best and fastest girl skaters in the Maritime Provinces." He concluded that "no event in sporting history in Eastern Canada has ... caused so much interest among so many people as this hike. Needless to say, the entry of Mrs. Dill is the most interesting, especially to women."

That evening, an exuberant Frank and Jenny bid farewell to the people of Halifax before an animated crowd at the Majestic Theatre. Their appearance on stage during a performance of George M. Cohan's musical comedy *The Little Millionaire* had been arranged by theatre manager, J.F. O'Connell. Jenny told the receptive audience that they "were very glad to have the opportunity to say good-bye in this way." And she promised, "When we return from our cross country adventure, we will tell you all about it."

"The brave little woman won the sympathy of the audience by her plucky manner," the newspaper declared. The couple also sold many souvenir postcards.

IN AN EVENING dispatch from Dorchester on the last day of January, Jack wrote: "We are in the big jail town and no two criminals have created so much commotion among the citizens." He went on to yarn about the raging blizzard they had battled while tramping the rails beside the Tantramar Marshes. As cold as it was, they were greeted by scores of farm folks along the way, wanting to know if there was anything they could do for the hikers. "'Can you stop for a bit to warm up?' they asked. I'll never forget the kindness as long as I live. And neither will the lad."

The *Herald* was "following the hikers in great style and certainly keeping the interest up," Jack said in his night letter. "Unfortunately there are no newspapers to be had in Dorchester, least ways none that anyone would part with."

On the road now for just a week, Jack and Clifford were 160 miles from home and had gained a day and a half on Burkman, leaving Jack to boast, "Burkman's a game kid, and deserves to be encouraged. We intend to give him a pat on the back when we pass him this side of Montreal." He signed off with a pensive, if somewhat disingenuous, look homeward: "We'd like to be in Halifax tomorrow to see the Dills get away. She's some plucky girl, that, and we wish her and her husband all kinds of good luck in their long hike. There'll be a great re-union of Halifax folks when we all meet at the Pacific."

While the Behans were relaxing at the Windsor Hotel, William Tait, proprietor, in Dorchester, Burkman was at the elegant Royal Hotel in Saint John, New Brunswick. "I am quite satisfied that St. John is not the unfriendly city to Halifax that folks in book lore claim she is. She loves Halifax as a sister should love a sister, and Halifax should not forget that."

At the registration desk he was met by W.J. McNulty, one of the red-hot sports critics of the Maritimes. "Many a roast I have received from McNulty. But I forgave him the minute I set eyes on him.

"'Burkman,' he said, 'I'm here on instructions from the chief at the Halifax [Herald] to see how you are behaving.'

"'I don't understand the newspaper game very well, but, go aboard me, and see what you can find.'"

McNulty just got through with him when along came Dutch Irving, another hard-hitting freelance sports reporter. "Of all things to go up against—McNulty and then Irving," Burkman laughed. "Anybody who can go thru their gruelling cross examination is worthy of a Victoria Cross." The interviews renewed Burkman's sense of purpose. "After receiving the promise of 'FIVE HUNDRED DOLLARS,' I made up my mind that the sooner I got out of St. John the better it would be for me," he joshed. "Furthermore, you can tell the Halifax business men who put up the money, that it is almost as good as won."

Burkman now resolved to walk 20 to 25 miles a day, regardless of the weather. And he intended to stick to the railroad tracks through to the coast, avoiding public roads, which were often longer and not fit for long-distance walking.

He left Saint John on January 31 and reached Welsford that evening, full of optimism and with a passport in his pocket. "The 24-mile walk was a breeze," he told the Herald. "I feel as if President Wilson and I have been pals all our lives. I wonder how far CARR WALKED TODAY?" He said that he expected to be in Montreal very soon. "It's a bad place for a hiker, but if it beats Lower Water Street, Halifax, it will have to go some."

On January 31, 1921, Carr was history, leaving Burkman alone but fixated on reaching Montreal first; the Behans were moving fast, ready to "take on" New Brunswick; the Dills were packed and eager to depart Halifax—and the great foot race across the country was about to get serious.

4

The Dill Factor

Shortly after ten o'clock on the first day of February, an estimated 2,000 people gathered in front of the Herald and Mail Building to wish the Dills bon voyage on their ambitious trek across Canada, and what Burkman and Carr originally intended as a casual walking tour officially became a spirited, three-way competition. The paper reported the Dills left "to a chorus before which the send-off to the Burkman and Carr combination and the Behans father and son pales into insignificance, and it cannot be questioned that the piquant figure of Mrs. Jenny Dill was at the centre of the interest and enthusiasm."

Cameras rolled and clicked once again, and crowds roared their approval. The Douglas Fullerton Iron Foundry, where Frank Dill was employed, "did the occasion proud and gave a holiday, so all the boys could come over and see the start. They were out in force each with a big horn on which he played gloriously, the music being of the kind that threw even the dogs in the neighbourhood into an ecstasy of enjoyment and made every horse on the block take notice." The cacophony filled the cold morning air, and the public love affair with the husband-and-wife team began.

The sustained shrieking of train whistles, the waving of hands and handkerchiefs, and the shouts of encouragement from passing train crews and passengers left Frank and Jenny Dill convinced that the hiking game was not without its recompense. They stuck to the main road as far as Bedford and then hit the ties, where they found the walking excellent but slippery. Jenny was full of questions and Frank full of advice:

"You never seem to slip back," Mrs. Jenny constantly charged her lord and master.

"You'll learn the trick if you follow me for a few days," was the lord and master's reply. "Hook your heels in good and hard, that's the way real hikers do it."

To the surprise of the enthusiastic groupies who boarded the Maritime Express in Halifax to follow the early progress of the Dills, the couple beat them to Windsor Junction. The followers piled off the train at the Junction to see if there was any word to be had of their whereabouts, only to discover the couple sitting in the station, toasting their shins at the pot-bellied stove. No one enjoyed the joke more than the Dills.

"The twenty-six-mile hike from Halifax to Windsor Junction left us feeling as fresh as daisies, but a little overwhelmed by all the questions and hospitality," Jenny wrote in her night letter to the *Herald*.

"Good Mrs. Ashe," who ministered to the wants of wayfarers at the Junction, provided Frank and Jenny with a hot meal, and the very mention of payment for the food and a night's lodgings nearly precipitated a small riot. Over cups of top-grade Blue Bird tea, the Dills chatted freely with their genial hosts, explaining their plans for traversing the huge country in somewhat biblical terms.

"It is going to be a case of eating into the distance by little laps day after day, week after week, and month after month," Jenny said.

"Four thousand and some miles across continent does seem a long stretch, but viewed in short hike days it is a case of sufficient unto the day is the HIKE thereof," Frank added stiffly. In the early days of the hike, he attempted to speak on behalf of the family, while his wife beamed approvingly at his every word.

The couple both extolled the virtues of the hike in terms of exercise. "Walking is the greatest medicine in the world," Frank counselled.

"And we would not turn back to Halifax for all the tea in China—not even for all the Blue Bird tea," Jenny laughed gaily. "If I thought they didn't use Blue Bird all along the line, I'd appropriate the balance of this package—then you could throw away that heart and nerve food of yours, Frank."

Sensing a serious change in tone between the couple, Mrs. Ashe discreetly changed the subject: "I think that we are all curious about what things you did find absolutely necessity [sic] to carry with you on the long journey."

Following an awkward cough, Mr. Dill replied, "A gold watch and fob given to me by my father." He extended the objects for inspection. "A Gordon Kinsley's first-aid kit packed in Halifax, and a business-like revolver—a gift from my pals at the Douglas Fullerton Plant."

"And yes," he added, "I do have a permit to carry."

The Dills acknowledged that they had entered the competition a week behind the Behans, and 15 days behind Burkman, but they were in excellent physical condition and quite confident of reaching the Pacific coast—possibly even winning the race.

THE BEHANS COVERED an impressive 27 miles in biting cold weather that same day, and Jack, in his dispatch from Moncton, reported they too were trailed by dozens of enthusiastic crowds. "Every farmer and his dog for miles around came out to see us on our way west," he said. "And our postcards went like hot cakes. We are sorry that we could not find time to deposit our funds in the bank, and so had to carry a very heavy load of dimes."

According to Jack, a friend battled the crowd at the Moncton station to retrieve a copy of the Herald so he and Clifford could stay current with the hiking news. He also suggested that, having taken some guff for shaking a leg in Truro, they were focusing on different activities now. "We were invited to a dance, which was arranged by the Moncton hockey team, but we declined the invitation. We are not out for jazzing, but to make a record across Canada in the interest of cheap sport. We have an agreement to go to bed each night at ten o'clock, and neither dancing nor nothing else will alter our plans."

A visit from T.H. Jackman—who in the company of John Hugh Gillis walked from Montreal to Vancouver in 1906—was a noteworthy event for the Behans. The famed Canadian hiker drafted a serious schedule for them, which included occasional jaunts of 35 miles a day. "We feel that after we have been on the road for a month that we will be hard as nails, and we can make it," Jack contended.

Burkman, the lone hiker, concluded a satisfactory 21-mile hike from Welsford through Gaspereaux to Fredericton Junction and spent the evening of February 1 as a guest of the American Hotel. With the Sid Carr crisis now behind him, Burkman was raring to demonstrate his individuality. "Tomorrow I intend to complete a record-breaking forty-mile hike to McAdam Junction," he said. "I can almost smell Montreal now, and after I skip thru Maine, it will not take me long to make the great Montreal metropolis where I have friends galore." His dispatch was short that night, "out of deference to the Dills' takeoff."

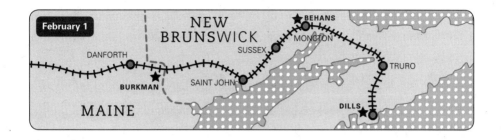

On day two of the Dill "takeoff," hundreds of country folks and enthusiastic schoolchildren lined the railroad ties between Windsor Junction and Milford to gawk and cheer. The sight of Mrs. Jenny Dill swinging along, setting the pace, "as tho being used to the heel and toe game," caused a frenzy of shouting at the station house. "Good luck and God speed you on your great hike to the Pacific," people shouted. "Good luck to Mr. and Mrs. Dill!" And "May all your troubles be little ones" was the message tucked into a newspaper chucked from a passing train.

All the attention showered on Frank and Jenny was flattering but unexpected, and a bit overwhelming. "We will make Vancouver in good time if we are not killed with kindness before we even leave Nova Scotia," Jenny said.

Their "regular go-as-you-please day," started with an old-fashioned breakfast provided by Mrs. Fitzpatrick at Windsor Junction. They had intended to stop at Milford for the night, but the ground was so good, the day so perfect and their spirits so high that they pressed right on to Shubenacadie and a delicious dinner augmented by flattering attention from the locals. "No sooner had we arrived in Shubenacadie, than we were taken in charge, bag and baggage by the members of the Ladies Aid of the Presbyterian Church in session at the home of Mrs. H. Stallard," Jenny said. Here the nomads were given a real Shubenacadie welcome. The ladies would not hear of their going to a hotel, and the honour of acting as hostess for the night went to Mrs. Charles Johnson.

In addition to the hospitality, the Dills received gifts. J.A. Kirkpatrick, merchant, gave Jenny a pair of ladies' stub rubber stockings and provided both of them with a number of oranges. A bottle of menthol liniment, courtesy of Gaskin's drugstore in Halifax, was shipped to them as well.

"The day's experiences were the experiences of yesterday raised to the tenth," sighed Mrs. Jenny that evening. And while Frank took time to thank the *Halifax Herald* and the *Mail* for their generous support, his wife continued to extol the sport of walking. "Walk and then walk a lot more; you will never cure what ails you hugging a radiator," she advised her host. "Besides, you have no idea what swarms of nice people you will meet. We had no idea there were so many big-hearted folks in the world."

"The popularity of the Dills was far surpassing that of other hikers," the *Herald* reported.

Comments about the Dills' popularity were of little concern to Burkman, since the affable hiker had already endeared himself to the public. He left Fredericton Junction at 8 a.m., and despite frosty weather conditions made good time that day. He was well received at New Brunswick House, where Mrs. Robinson laid out a great spread—one that not even his mother could have surpassed. Later, at Magaguadavic, he accepted the pleasant dinner invitation of the station agent before starting for McAdam Junction, where he spent the night at the CPR hotel and reported a record-breaking hike.

"I'm feeling pretty good all over tonight," Burkman said. "I am just about to turn in after doing the longest jaunt of the trip—made 40 miles today—and that is not so bad for a lone hiker. Tomorrow I shall become a Yankee, for I shall enter the state of Maine for a few days. But you better believe I shall not stay any longer than I have to."

The Dill factor was most disturbing to Jack Behan, who was not good at shar-ing the limelight—especially with a spirited woman like Jenny. Realizing that he would catch more flies with honey than with vinegar, however, he softened his tone. "Both [of us] were happy to discover—as had Burkman before [us]—that New Brunswick was a pretty good old province. We have received a wonderful reception ever since we crossed the provincial boundary line in Sackville. The same kindness, which we received in Nova Scotia, has been passed out to us in the sister province," Jack said.

A small gathering, which included the celebrated Jackman, was on hand at the Moncton station to say goodbye to the Behans on Wednesday morning. The hikers were flattered when A. Mosher, a traveller for Pyke Brothers, in Halifax, presented them with enough tobacco to keep them going for a while. "And you know that I myself am quite a smoker," Jack laughed.

Later in the day the ravenous pedestrians bolted down dinner at Foster's res-taurant in Salisbury. Foster was "some cook," and the Behans were "some hungry." They ate with relish and felt like kings afterward. "When we offered to pay, the proprietor said: 'Listen here, boys, I'm no piker. Give us one of your postcards. I think more of those cards than I do of all the money you have on you…' That is what the New Brunswick folk are like: kind and good. Always trying to do something for you and doing it to the best of their ability."

They were not entirely happy with their hiking score of 25 miles, Jack admitted, but "when we get a little more hardened, we will do better."

ON FEBRUARY 3, Frank and Jenny Dill set out for Truro. Determined not to be disadvantaged by the people swarming them en route, they travelled the less popular lower road from Shubenacadie to Stewiacke. They found the walk slippery, made difficult by a north wind that blew snow into their faces. Weather conditions did little to dampen the enthusiasm of their admirers, who somehow discovered their whereabouts and accompanied them.

At Stewiacke the couple hit the CN rails to Brookfield, but it was back to the roads at Alton—where they regretfully declined an invitation to dinner by the station agent, wishing to make up time. Several sleighs stopped along the route, with drivers offering them a lift—which they firmly turned down. Everyone, it seemed, wanted to help.

"We drank so much milk at various farmhouses that we felt no need for dinner," Jenny told readers. "Mrs. McCleave, who lives between Stewiacke and Alton, was one of those generous people, who also pressed us to stay for a beefsteak dinner as well."

Another lady in the neighbourhood gave the hikers sugar cookies, and Mrs. Langille, wife of the station agent at Brentwood, gave them milk and apples. At Brookfield, Mrs. Alex Brown, who lived about half a mile from the Post Road, waited for the milk-sated couple for half an hour with a pitcher of cream and two glasses.

So the day passed. Copies of the *Herald* were thrown off No. 5 train with "God speed" marked on one and "Good Luck, Dills!" on another. "All were highly prized," Jenny enthused.

Within two miles of Hilden, a mob of schoolchildren gave Frank and Jenny three cheers and begged the celebrities to stop awhile. Just out of Truro, 10-year-old Bertie Botts was waiting to shake their hands, exclaiming, while he pumped, "Some walkers!" A short time later, they were stormed by at least another 150 people.

"We couldn't make much time from there on in because of the density of the crowds," Mrs. Dill commented to the *Herald*. The local newspaper, swollen with pride over the town's support of the national competition, reported that "more than 1,200 folks gathered in front of the *Truro Citizen* office at 4:15 p.m.

where Mayor W.K. Murray officially welcomed them to Truro...The demonstration was the greatest welcome of its kind ever held in this part of the province." The fact that one of the hikers was a woman "created unusual interest among the ladies, a large number of whom were in the crowd that greeted the plucky travellers."

While photographers snapped and elbowed through the crowd for better opportunities, Mayor Murray acknowledged the magnitude of the commitment that the Dills had undertaken. But before he was half finished, the enthusiastic crowd cut him off with "three cheers and a tiger" for Frank and Jenny. Then hundreds of infatuated citizens escorted the hikers to The Stanley House, where the ever resourceful Mrs. Dill planted herself firmly in the front doorway and boldly sold picture postcards in large numbers.

"So dense was the crowd that all the light was shut out from the windows of the Stanley, and the outside lights had to be turned on," the local newspaper reported.

Like Burkman and the Behans, the Dills received many gifts from the generous merchants of Truro, including a suit each of unshrinkable Stanfield's underwear—made especially for them—to be picked up in Saint John; a large package of cough drops from W.B. Murphy, confectioner; and two seats reserved for them at the Princess Theatre, which they declined in favour of a good night's rest.

There was no doubt that Jenny Dill was the drawing card of the husband-and-wife duo, causing several astute observers to say that she made not only a charming poster girl but a competent walker as well.

Her husband agreed. "She's beating me all to pieces."

"He was behind me, and I had to wait for him," Jenny tattled.

"She is a better hiker than you?" someone asked.

"Yes. I'd say so."

FRIDAY FEBRUARY 4 was yet another day of adulation for Frank and Jenny Dill. Demanding crowds kept them at Colchester Hub until nearly noon. However, this worked to their benefit, the press said, as they left town loaded with dimes: "Twenty-two dollars (220 post cards), all in ten-cent pieces, is an awful lot of money, all of which goes to show the popularity of the pair, and particularly the game little woman who is playing the leading role in the coast-to-coast hiking drama. At Truro, their cards went like hot cakes, and long after they went to bed last night, the good people of the Stanley house were raking in the dimes for them."

At Onslow, on the way to their Londonderry destination, someone blew a bugle call to announce that Captain Bayne was extending an invitation to lunch, causing Jenny to remark: "It should have been a cookhouse call, but Frank swears it was 'dress for parade.' No matter what it was, it had the real spirit behind it." Mrs. Jenny reluctantly declined the invitation on behalf of the family. They wished to be farther on their way before taking a break; they did, however, accept some light refreshments before pushing on.

At Belmont they were treated to cheese and biscuits and two big bottles of grape juice, and between Belmont and Debert the station men held them up, insisting that they visit a spell. A host of kiddies greeted them like long-lost brothers and sisters. Photographs were taken and more postcards were sold. It was hard for them to refuse the generous offer of food and lodging that Mrs. Walsh offered, but they had their goal before them, so, after accepting a brace of eggnogs, the nomads took off again.

The reception at East Mines was equally generous. The station agent, Mr. McManaman, himself a runner who participated in the *Herald*-sponsored modified marathon in the early years of the century, when Boston Marathon winner Freddie Cameron was one of his competitors, was waiting for them with tea and cakes, cigars and chocolates. When they left he chased them down the tracks with other refreshments that, in his excitement, he'd forgotten to give them.

After arriving in Londonderry on Friday afternoon, they enjoyed a tour through the mines with Mr. Tatterie, whose son was a great friend of Frank's. According to Jenny, "Everyone had a great time exploring and enjoyed the variety of refreshments served by the hosts afterwards." Cigars and chocolates were presented all round before the guests were returned to Peppard's Hotel in Londonderry. Mrs. Dill reported that they had covered a meagre 18 miles and had endured dozens of kind-hearted locals with cameras, eager to immortalize them. If she expected sympathy from the *Herald*, she was disappointed. "Colchester County is simply papered with pictures of the Dills," it exclaimed. "No Parliamentary candidate ever received such widespread publicity; Mr. Frank and Mrs. Jenny have become famous overnight."

Eager to cash in on the growing success of the great coast-to-coast competition, the *Herald* ran its first major 4½ x 14 advertisement.

Coast to Coast Hikers
All Hit the Trail to Munnis

Here are our friends, Mr. and Mrs. Dill, just as they were ready for their cross Canada trudge. They bought their outfit from Munnis because, as Mr. Dill said, he had bought here before and the clothes wore well. Here is what we supplied:

—Shoe Packs.
—Heavy Golf Stockings.
—Combination Under- wear.
—Flannel Top Shirts.
—Mackinaw Coats.
—Riding Breeches.
—Shoulder Caps.

—Slicker Waterproof Coat.
—Slicker Waterproof Hat.
—Winter Peak Cap.
—Ties, Handkerchiefs, Braces.
—Mitts.

We also outfitted Burkman for his transcontinental trip. For it is well recognized that if you want it to wear you must buy it here.

Special Prices on Winter Wear

Mackinaw Coats, in handsome brown, tan and black plaids with all round belts. Sizes 28 to 44. $13.50 value **$10**	Coat Sweaters, $5 to $12; save $1 to $2.40 at the sale prices of ...... **$4 to $9.60**
Mackinaw Vests in brown corduroy, lined with sheepskin, button-ing to chin. Special at **$8.75**	Leather Mitts, with heavy wool lining **$1, $1.25, $1.50**
Mackinaw Pants, 13 ounce weight, made up ourselves from factory cloth **$9.50**	Heavy Golf Stock- ings ...... **$1.50 to $2**
	Heavy Ribbed Underwear. Special at, per garment **$1.00**
Grey and Navy Flan- nel Shirts **$2.50, $3**	Combinations ...... **$4 to $6**

W. S. Munnis Ltd.
563 BARRINGTON STREET.

The first advertisement that tried to cash in on the hikers and their notoriety.
Halifax Herald, February 3, 1921, p. 3

THE THOROUGHLY ROTTEN weather, the overwhelming attention showered on the Dills, and Burkman's unexpected record-making hikes caught the Behans unprepared and left them confounded. Even a 26-mile hike to Sussex on February 3 failed to impress Jack, although in night letters to Halifax he continued to insist that they were being well received. "Folks have been mighty kind to us all along the line," Jack asserted, "trying to outdo each other in matters of hospitality and accommodations." The *Herald* suspected that the other hikers' popularity was eating at him. So after receiving Jack's less-than-enthusiastic night letter, the paper set out to ensure the sociable hiker a memorable, if short, stopover in Saint John by attaching to him their special sports news correspondent W.J. McNulty, who secured front-page coverage for the Behans.

BEHANS COVER 44 MILES IN A SINGLE DAY FATHER AND SON REACH ST. JOHN LAST NIGHT AFTER HIKE FROM SUSSEX.

By W.J. McNulty

ST. JOHN, Feb. 4.—Jack Behan of Dartmouth took a long tramp from Sussex today. He brought the long tramp right into St. John. And the long tramp was no other than his tall son, Clifford Behan. The Behans covered 44 miles today on the ties. The last nine miles they walked in two hours arriving in St. John at 11 o'clock tonight. They covered the nine miles after partaking of Mrs. Kennedy's hospitality in a trifle over two hours, which proves they are fast walkers and also that they must have been supplied with liquid electricity in Rothesay along with the evening meal.

"The hikers attack the feed cushion three meals daily, and eat cornmeal, oatmeal, and Indian meal," McNulty teased in his column. "Truly, this is the pedestrian diet."

The reporter's attention and quirky humour were good therapy for Jack, and soon the garrulous Behan was drawn out, sharing even his most embarrassing stories with the invited guests at the St. John Hotel. He told how he and his son were royally received everywhere they went—except at Norton, N.B., where an angry station agent, James Gallagher, refused to affix his stamp to their book and harangued the crowd, inciting violence against the hikers. The disgruntled agent even accused the pedestrians of being tramps out looking for freebies. Later, Jack unearthed a sample of rolled hemp that had been presented to him in the lounge and proceeded to do an impersonation of the brilliant American trial lawyer William Jennings Bryan. This was a huge success.

There were few things in life that Jack enjoyed more than playing to an audience, and as the evening passed he grew increasingly loquacious, drawing out his hiking stats and making bold predictions for the outcome of the race. "We walked 250 miles from Halifax to Saint John over the CNR rails in 11 days, whereas Charles Burkman, the first of the hikers, covered the same distance in 13 days. Since starting from the Herald and Mail Building, we averaged 25 miles a day to Burkman's paltry 20. You could in fact, argue, that we've caught up 61 miles on the lad."

Basking in the warm glow of the hotel lounge, and caught up by the sound of his own voice, the balding, 44-year-old hiker told his captive audience that "if Burkman expected to reach Vancouver in six months—[he and Clifford] would accomplish it in five." Jack also insisted, "We started not merely to walk from coast to coast, but to make a record."

When McNulty asked the hikers early in the evening if they weren't exhausted after their 44-mile hike, Clifford admitted to being done in, but "his Pater uttered nary a chirp, appearing to be as chipper as a chorus girl in a

Broadway Girlie Show." The *Herald's* special reporter expressed surprise at seeing the two wandering along St. John's chief business streets, in search of more company, after the hotel lounge closed for the night.

BURKMAN'S NEXT NIGHT letter was written from Wyopitlock, Maine. "Wyopitlock!" he laughed. "Well, what do you think of this place for a name? It took me a long while to get my tongue around it, but it is sure some nice place and I got a splendid reception when I arrived."

At McAdam, Burkman was awed by the large CPR rooms and beds and by the Canadian immigration officers who signed his book. The walk from McAdam to Vanceboro, where he crossed into the United States, proved to be heavy going because snow was piled along the tracks, and gusting winds lashed at him without mercy. At Danforth, the first selectman to sign his book suggested: "You should get a monkey so you have someone to talk to."

Burkman arrived in Tomap at 6:30 p.m., but due to the darkness and the driving snow, he wasn't able to reach a telegraph depot to send a night wire. "After slogging through twenty miles of foul weather, I accepted the offer of a hot meal and a top bunk from Boss Kilpatrick at Camp Akerly pulpwood camp." He admitted that he "had a restless sleep. The Behans raced through my head all night long."

The *Herald* report told Burkman that his closest rivals were pushing hard, increasing their pace and gaining fast. During the final two hours into Saint John, they managed four and a half miles an hour and completed a record 44-mile hike. Burkman was continuing to maintain a good lead, but the bullying tactics used by the Behans made him uneasy.

5

Hell-Bent for Montreal

According to a staff correspondent who picked up the pen for a weekend report, Saturday was a repetition of the previous days. First the Dills found that they were hiking alone, and then, out of nowhere, crowds of admirers appeared, little affected by the severe winter conditions. At Folly Mountain Corner, the entire family of Dr. and Mrs. J.A. McLean and child awaited their arrival. The Dills declined the doctor's invitation to stay, saying that they had a long day of hiking before them. They made Folly at 11:30 a.m. and enjoyed being pampered by D.D. Fraser, the station agent, "who regaled them with music while they were partaking of the bumper meal."

Two o'clock found Frank and Jenny in Wentworth at a great reception hosted by the station agent, Mr. Sweet, and his wife. There they were plied with jars of good old-fashioned buttermilk.

"At East Wentworth, Mrs. W.L. Embree took us in hand," Jenny said, "and after making a pretty speech, she presented us with a box of food and drink along with the note: 'Wishing you every success and trusting some day next summer I may receive a letter from you mailed from Vancouver.'" The couple were very impressed.

The Dills stopped at Westchester only long enough to check their packs before pushing on to Thompson. Here the crowd gathered at the station gave them a hearty cheer when they finally hove into sight at 12 minutes to 7 p.m., after a 26-mile tramp. The crowd had been waiting to see them for almost two hours. That evening the couple were guests of E.M. Armour.

Foul weather on Sunday February 6 held the Dills up at Thompson later than they'd expected, but their spirits remained high, and after a dinner at the Sterling House in Oxford, they completed a 26-mile slosh through melting snow to Springhill.

"We arrived, fit and fine—but too late for church," Jenny mused.

Next day the walk was more of the same: bad weather, scores of curiosity seekers, countless drinks of milk and dozens of notes and trinkets (all of the good-luck variety). "Twelve copies of the *Herald* were thrown to us in rapid succession from the train," Jenny groaned. "And the newsy on Number 18 contributed a box of chocolates by the air line, and lots of apples and other stuff came to us by the same route. One apple had a couple of wishbones cut into it for luck. Even Frank was amused."

A member of the editorial staff of the *Herald* and the *Mail*, homeward bound to Halifax, wrote the Dills a regular letter, asking them whether they proposed to publish their adventures in serial form. Jenny said that she considered doing just that as soon as they arrived back home.

Despite the uplifting generosity shown the Dills along the route, the tramping was unpleasant during the entire weekend. The hikers wandered off track repeatedly, first into knee-deep, bone-chilling snowbanks and then into slush. Although the weather and the walking conditions and the crowds were a constant test of their prowess, Frank insisted that they had no intentions of quitting the race. "I want to say to the people who are so kindly interested in our progress that we are on this hike to see it to the end—and the only thing that can hang us up is sickness."

"Mrs. Dill," he further assured readers, "passed the Sunday test with flying colours—in fact, she didn't seem to mind it as much as I did. And rest assured, we will keep at it if we can only make two miles a day, and take ten years to finish it. Vancouver will be reached before we stop."

REGARDLESS OF THE challenges courageously overcome by the Dills, full honours for the weekend went to Charles Burkman.

"Hello, Halifax!" he crowed. "I'm halfway to Montreal, and am still six DAYS AHEAD of the Behans. And I believe the hardest part of the road to Montreal has been covered." Burkman's declaration was given front-page exposure in the *Herald* and solid coverage.

Burkman left Wyopitlock Saturday at 9 a.m., stopped briefly at Kingman and arrived at Mattawamkeag at 3:30 p.m., spending the night at the Mattawamkeag

Hotel. He left early the following morning, walking 17 miles to Chester, had dinner at Butterfield's Pulpwood Camp and then, since his friend the snowplough was out, followed it to Woodward, completing an 18-mile walk at 4:30.

"The road from St. John to Woodward was the hardest and most tedious I have thus far travelled," he reported, "but the reception at the end of the day was just compensation." There was, however, an even more serious downside to loneliness on the trail now. Burkman was entering bear country. "Hope the bruins are having a good sound sleep," he said.

ACCORDING TO THE account of the melodramatic W.J. McNulty, Jack and Clifford Behan enjoyed a recuperative day in Saint John after completing their record-breaking hike of 44 miles. They polished off their Saturday stay with several perfunctory visits around town, including meetings with Mayor E.A. Schofield and Chief of Police J.J. Smith, and were treated to a movie by R.H. Gale, where they had an opportunity to sell postcards.

"We received a letter from Lew Christie, manager of Stanfield's Ltd. in Truro, promising that two pairs of woolen underwear and two pairs of woolen socks would be waiting for us at Fredericton Junction," Jack told readers. The Behans also took time out of their busy day to obtain passports for the American leg of their journey.

Jack and Clifford were much flattered when a calendar-manufacturing concern promised them thousands of dollars for the right to use their likenesses in photographs and illustrations on calendars and advertising novelties—after they had completed the transcontinental race in record-breaking time. This sparked the usual boast from Jack regarding his five-month-deadline forecast.

The hikers were also flattered by several generous dinner offers but were unable to accept any of them owing to a commitment to dine with Dr. Peat, a physician and surgeon who had served in the same English hospital as Jack during the Great War. The men exchanged many war stories during the evening, the most popular concerning the ease with which alcohol was given by physicians for almost any illness or complaint during the war. Jack recalled "the propensity of one of the doctors at the same hospital where he/Jack [sic] was an attendant, for prescribing alcohol for practically every ailment from a bruise, abrasion or strain and most of the time without actually seeing the patient, relying on the attendant for the information as to what affliction a man had. It was the custom of some of the attendants and some of the soldiers to hoodwink in this wise."

"That old sob star Jupiter Pluvius shed a multitude of tears in St. John today in regret because Jack Behan and his son Cliff planned to shake the scent of the Bay of Funday fog from their physical scenery and resume their hike to Vancouver," McNulty wrote on Sunday February 6. "But the shower of moisture convinced the Behans that the old demon Jupiter Pluvius was in league with Charles Burkman and Mr. and Mrs. Frank Dill, and opposed to the Behans and despite the leaky sky, the father and son started from St. John this morning; it was their ambition to overtake Charles Burkman."

Father and son meandered north from the city on Canadian Pacific tracks, the first time they had used them since starting from Halifax. They intended to continue following the tracks to Vanceboro, a village at the border of New Brunswick and Maine; from there the Maine Central would lead them to Mattawamkeag Junction and the Canadian Pacific line to Montreal.

Even though they were following the railroad, the Behans managed only 16 miles. "Weather conditions were bloody awful," Jack grumbled.

It was also reported—if anyone was listening—that Jack and Clifford were still without raincoats.

The Behans had apparently not heard that Burkman was now only six days ahead of them instead of seven, but the salty McNulty questioned whether Burkman could stay focused without a companion on his long, lonely, coast-to-coast walk. If the answer was no, the Behans could get lucky, McNulty predicted.

POSITIONS OF HIKERS FEBRUARY 8

Dills—At Amherst, N.S.; out 7 days; did 18 miles yesterday

Behans—At Fredericton Junction, N.B.; out 14 days; did 28 miles yesterday

Burkman—At Brownville, Maine; out 22 days: did 30 miles yesterday

Halifax—0 miles; Montreal—760; Winnipeg—2,170; Vancouver—3,645

ON TUESDAY FEBRUARY 8, a tickertape box stretched across the front page of the *Herald*, summing up the transcontinental race in easy-to-read statistics. (Some readers continued to be confused because the information on the tape was published the day before the hikers' evening dispatches appeared—and the day after the actual hiking occurred.) The next dispatches from the hikers arrived on Wednesday, when Jenny reported from Sackville, and a special correspondent telephoned Burkman and the Behans and then wrote an update on their behalf "owing to a heavy storm raging in New Brunswick and Maine." Readers learned that Burkman had enjoyed another day of triumph, "whooping it up" over Mount Katahdin, Maine's highest peak, covering 33 miles from Woodward to Brownville in the process.

"Last night was a terrible night in these parts," he said. "Weather experts predicted that we were in for the biggest storm in years, so I had visions of staying here for weeks," which would have given the Behans an opportunity to catch him before Montreal. "But every cloud has a silver lining—even a snow cloud," he laughed. "The weather changed, and this morning I was up early, hell-bent for Montreal following in the wake of the snowplough."

Burkman left Woodward at 7:30 a.m., enjoyed a pleasant lunch with station agent Foster at Hardy Pond and was back on the road at 1:30, arriving at Brownville Junction at 6:30 p.m. after walking the last five miles in an hour and five minutes. He stopped at the Railway YMCA for the night and shared his adventures with the Herald: "It is no 'kid' when I say I feel great. I certainly do. I could make 30 more miles tonight, but I don't want to get arrested for exceeding the speed limit."

After the news of Burkman's successful hike over Mount Katahdin reached the Dills, no amount of cajoling by proprietor Mr. MacKenzie or his sister, Miss MacKenzie, could keep the hikers in Springhill. "The hospitality was memorable, but we heard the urgent voices of Amherst and Vancouver calling and said thank you and good bye."

The weather was much improved, and the Dills reached Athol Junction in good time. Unfortunately they had to turn down the dinner prepared for them by the station agent, Mr. Jyles. They reached Amherst Station late in the afternoon and were pleased to find that the boots promised them in Truro were ready and waiting in the hands of the craftsman, Mr. Gould, and his wife. "The footwear got a trial run at the Terrace Hotel that evening and it will get practical service on the trail to Dorchester tomorrow," Jenny promised.

The Herald headline that "Burkman was halfway to Montreal" jarred the Behans out of their need for social revelry, and they made a 28-mile jog to Fredericton Junction, resting up at the Canadian Hotel. "After eleven hours of heavy walking, we looked forward to stretching our legs on a mattress-sleeper instead of those under the rails of the CPR," Jack said. Father and son reported that they were feeling A-1, just tired enough to appreciate hospitable treatment at the hands of Mr. Patterson, proprietor. The men intended to start a 40-mile hike to McAdam the next morning—which would leave them only six miles from the Maine border.

"That is the kind of day that eats into the 4,000 miles from Halifax to Vancouver," Jack boasted. "Our ambition is to outstrip Burkman and the transcontinental hikers: Sagawa yesterday, Fredericton today, and McAdam tomorrow, that is the manner in which we will reach Vancouver." The elder Behan was obviously back in fighting form.

OWING TO THE heavy snowstorms raging in Maine and New Brunswick, it was impossible for Burkman and the Behans to get more than meagre stories over the wire. Both had made some progress and had managed to stay on schedule; Burkman pulled off 33 miles by trailing behind snowploughs as far as Greenville; and the Behans reached McAdam Junction after an arduous 40-mile hike.

Frank and Jenny Dill appeared to be more focused on social issues than on being hell-bent for Montreal. Jenny claimed that her Frank was "arrested by the beauty of the Mount Allison College girls," who swarmed down on them when they arrived in the college town of Sackville.

"Jenny, help me out," Frank pleaded, "I'm not used to this stuff—by Jove, they are pretty, ain't they?"

Jenny said that she had to keep an eye on her husband as she wrote up the day's events for the telegraph office.

The couple had been encouraged by two chefs on board a westbound train, who threw them a copy of the *Herald* along with a letter informing them that the men were greatly impressed with the hikers and would follow their progress clear to the Pacific. They also told the husband and wife that this was the first train that had taken returning soldiers home to Vancouver after the Great War, a trip made in eight days, so they were sure that Frank and Jenny could make the trip in seven months.

After covering only 10 miles and giving feeble excuses for doing so—"they had so many friends in Sackville who insisted on their staying the night to attend a theatre party; and felt that they couldn't ignore Mrs. R. Laurie, who had written a letter asking them to be her overnight guest; and besides, Frank didn't want to take any chances with the prison in Dorchester because hikers were now so numerous that officials might take them for tramps"—Jenny promised their fans it would be a swift trip through Dorchester for the Dills. "Tomorrow we will make up for the little loafing that we did today, and make some serious progress."

Perhaps she had read Jack Behan's reference to them as "transcontinental hikers," a slight that suggested the Dills were not serious competitors in the race.

IN EARLIER REPORTS the hikers had all cited injury and illness as the only possible reasons they would not complete the Great Trans-Canada Race, but the great Atlantic snowstorms assaulting the northeast now threatened to not only impede their progress but also blow them right out of the competition. The lone hiker found relative safety and made fair progress along the ties, which were kept open by snowploughs, but a blinding 30-mile-an-hour wind and driving snow obscured the vision of both Burkman and the Behans, and an unpredictable icy drizzle kept them soaked to the bone, making them question what madness had compelled them to participate in this perilous journey. Certainly it wasn't the money, for although some had been promised, none was yet secured.

Young Charlie Burkman managed to hike 26 miles to Tarratine, Maine, but Jack and Clifford were forced to eat crow—frozen, no doubt—slogging only 11 miles, their poorest showing to date. "Break it easy to our friends," Jack apologized from Lambert Lake. "Snow and more snow...is facing us now...And all I can say is that we will do much better."

The Atlantic storm was working its way north but had not yet hit the southwestern part of New Brunswick, and "poor, frail, little Mrs. Jenny" wired the news of their "dandy" 20-mile hike from Sackville to Memramcook, "which Frank had walked with her."

Mr. Tait, at the Windsor Hotel in Dorchester, complained that he had expected the hikers the previous day, and Jenny mused, "Yesterday is of the past, and we are already looking forward to the morrow." After a mild rebuke, the proprietor treated the errant hikers to a fine dinner.

"I guess they liked us pretty well, by the way they treated us," Jenny said. "And I do not think we would feel nearly as nervous to come to this town again; although Frank was kind of twitchy all the time we were in Dorchester, and the grim looking prison away up on the hill is sure a gruesome sight."

It was quite warm when the Dills reached College Bridge, clutching a copy of the *Herald* thrown to them by Ralph Pines from a passing train—"so mild that Frank wanted to go in for a swim." Jenny refused to allow it. "I was afraid he would get drowned. I don't want to be a lone hiker like Burkman." Jenny's teasing was probably initiated by Mother Dill's constant worrying about her son's health.

"Tomorrow we will at least go as far as Moncton, 20 miles away and perhaps if Frank CAN STAND IT, I'll take him further," Jenny confided. "He is doing pretty well, but he finds it hard to keep pace with his FRAIL little girlie companion."

That night Frank phoned home, as usual, assuring his mother that they were well and making good progress. The Dills had, in fact, beaten the Behans by nine miles.

6

Raging Storms

POSITIONS OF HIKERS FEBRUARY 13

Dills—At Moncton, N.B.; 185 miles; out 10 days; did 20 miles yesterday

Behans—At Danforth, Maine; 391 miles; out 17 days; did 20 miles yesterday

Burkman—At Jackman, Maine; 538 miles; out 25 days; did 12 miles yesterday

Halifax—0 miles; Montreal—760; Winnipeg—2,170; Vancouver—3,645

Burkman left Tarratine at 9:30 after putting away a great breakfast prepared for him by the telegraph operators. He stopped at Long Pond for lunch and arrived at Jackman at five o'clock, completing a 12-mile hike. He intended to hike the 44 miles to Megantic, Quebec, the next day. From Moose River House, where he stopped for the night, he was buoyant and optimistic: "I have already covered five-hundred and thirty-eight miles and intend to reach Montreal within the week."

Jack Behan and Clifford also reported a fairly good 20-mile walk to Danforth in spite of a heavy, three-day snowfall. "Danforth is a good town," Jack told the *Herald*. "We were gifted with a spiritual evening in church by a local clergyman friend and given the opportunity to whisper prayers to The Almighty for a safe, thirty-mile advance to Mattawamkeag tomorrow."

Frank and Jenny Dill found themselves engulfed in the predicted Atlantic storm and experienced their hardest seven-hour tramp since leaving Halifax. The hikers lost their bearings several times outside Amherst, but fortunately had the railway to guide them for the rest of the 20 miles to Moncton. The exhausted couple were grateful for the kindness they received at the stopping points along the way: "At A.D. LeBlanc's hotel, in Memramcook, we enjoyed the best night's sleep we'd had since leaving home, and at Fox Creek, Emile Bourgeois treated us to a small dinner."

Questions about Jenny's ability to complete the transcontinental ordeal continued to plague the Dills. "My wife will be with me at the end of the hike," Frank insisted. Jenny just laughed.

THE ATLANTIC STORM became a major blizzard, but it didn't succeed in sending any of the Halifax-to-Vancouver hikers to ground.

Burkman left Jackman at 8:30 a.m. and arrived in Lowelltown at 9 p.m. after 24 miles of walking in very heavy snow. Mrs. Watson, the camp cook of the Lowelltown Lumber Company, came in for high praise for showering him with kindness during his overnight stay. He set off again at first light the next morning for Megantic, Quebec. Two miles outside that city's limits, a couple of hardy townsmen braved the weather to walk him first to the Grand Union Hotel and then to a wrestling match between Maupas and Linfors of Montreal—which Maupas won.

"Sherbrooke loomed pleasantly on the horizon—only a mere two days and sixty-nine miles away," Burkman explained in his report.

The Dills no longer shied away from the bad weather. Frank wrote that they had left Moncton at 3:40 a.m., when it was still dark, arrived in Salisbury at 12:30 p.m. in a raging storm, fortified themselves with a big plate of ham and eggs at J.E. Foster's Quick Lunch, and then, with winter gales beating down on their backs, inched their way along the ties to Petitcodiac—with Jenny leading the 13-hour, 25-mile charge all the way. "Transcontinental Hikers," indeed!

"The weather didn't hold us back on Sunday, either," Frank declared. The intrepid couple slogged 22 miles to Sussex, but arrived too late to send a dispatch to the Herald. They were grateful for the hospitality provided by R.A. McDonald at Depot House. "I have never met anyone who tried harder to make us comfortable," Jenny wrote. "Possibly Mr. McDonald felt sorry for me—I don't know."

The somewhat disgruntled Behans spent Sunday night in Seboeis, Maine. They had battled for 31 miles along the Pulp Mill's long route the day before and had managed to complete 21 miles Sunday, but Jack admitted he was disappointed at their showing over the two days. With all the huffing and puffing they had done over the weekend, they had succeeded in gaining only three days on Burkman. Although the Behans were now only five days behind the lone hiker, catching him was proving to be more challenging than they had anticipated.

THE *HERALD* WAS happy to relate to readers on Tuesday February 15 that the big winter storm was abating and all the hikers had checked in. But in a letter to the editor, a Springhill miner expressed special concern for Burkman, who was passing through an area inhabited by timber wolves.

I am interested in that man because he is alone. I have been over that long, lonesome road myself but not on foot. There is 400 miles of nothing but rocks and scrubs and bushes. You go to bed at night, wake up in the morning, look out the car window, and you see the same thing all over again, nothing but rocks and bushes and the train thundering by.

If you are in touch with him, tell him to get a rifle as the timber wolves are thick. Perhaps he knows already, but it is better to tell him anyhow, as it is not safe to travel without a gun. That is all. I buy The Herald every day.

I wish all the hikers good luck. I hope to accompany the first fellow on his last mile to the Coast, as I expect to leave for Vancouver in the spring but, not on foot.

Tell Burkman to get a gun, is all I ask.

A SPRINGHILL MINER, SPRINGHILL, FEB. 14

Burkman reportedly made friends everywhere he went. In Megantic, the personable young man got the signature of Mayor Scott and bought a new pair of shoes. "There is a place for a shoe store here," he said.

Burkman left Megantic for Scotstown, and after a short respite continued on to Gould. "It was heavy walking because the tracks had been obliterated by snow," he said. "But I reached Bury in time for dinner at the View Hotel." The lone hiker left the village reluctantly at 8:15 p.m., walking the last nine miles to Cookshire behind a snowplough, guided by moonlight.

In a dispatch from the Behans that day, Jack finally admitted that although they were closing the gap on Burkman, they had given up hope of catching him before Montreal. "He is 'some hiker,'" Jack conceded, "and making a game fight of it." The Behans realistically refocused their attention on attaining the lead in the race by the time they were in Winnipeg. "Vancouver," they said, was "in the bag."

Father and son left Seboeis early after a good send-off; they enjoyed a royal reception at Lakeview and arrived at Brownville, completing 25 miles. According to Jack, "The scenery was magnificent—when the snow stopped long enough for us to see anything."

The hikers left Brownville Junction at eight o'clock the next morning and, in spite of the blustery conditions, reached Greenville Junction at eight o'clock that night, covering a stunning 33 miles. The hikers ate dinner at Onawa, intending to leave for Jackman early the next morning.

Frank and Jenny resumed the chase early Monday morning and reached Norton too early for dinner, so settled for an egg and milk at Campbell House before moving on to Bloomfield. After a lovely dinner there with Mrs. Theal, the Dills hiked the remainder of the 22 miles to Hampton, N.B., where they received a surprisingly frosty reception. "The station agent at Hampton was especially vociferous in showing his displeasure at the visit of the walkers," the *Herald* reported a few days later. "At the Wayside House where the Dills entered, the manager motioned to the price of admission at the top of the register. It spoke volumes, namely four dollars per day. They went out of the hotel and sought accommodations in a boarding house conducted by Mrs. McInnes."

They anticipated a pull into Saint John by early evening the next day. "The other hikers had a good long rest there, but we are undecided what we shall do," Jenny admitted. "Of course if St. John is nice to us we might be tempted to stay, but if there is a girl's college there like in Sackville, I'll drive Frank right thru."

Sensing that Frank and Jenny were dealing with more than underdog status in the race across the continent, George Jackson of Rockingham, Nova Scotia, wrote them a poem:

TO MR. AND MRS. DILL
By George Jackson
A message of cheer to Frank and Jenny Dill,
from a C.N.R. trainman near Rockingham:

We know the road is dreary,
That your goal is far away—
We know the hiking's heavy
When you're at it every day,
We know that you were game to try—
We want to see you thru,
So keep on going, Jenny,
Whatever else you do.

For if you "cash in" on this hike
Your sex will suffer then,
And the men will say you have no right
For to compete with them.
They'll guy you at your own expense,
And some of them will "boo,"
So keep on going, Jenny,
Whatever else you do.

If your feet get blistered
Or that corn it starts to pain
Put Blue Jay on that tender spot
And start right off again.
Bathe your feet in mustard—
Put foot ease in your shoe,
And keep on going, Jenny,
Whatever else you do.

And if your Frank gets weary
And talks of turning back,
Give him a dose of Nerveline
Or a bottle of Tanlac.
Paint his spine with iodine
Rub hemlock on him, too,
But keep on going, Jenny,
Whatever else you do.

As the doggerel suggests, there was no doubt in the public mind who the stronger member of the team was.

MONDAY WAS AN easy day for Burkman. He sauntered through the Quebec Mountains, seduced by the rugged scenery and savouring the memory of Jack Behan's boast of beating him to Montreal. In his dispatch to the *Herald* from Sherbrooke he said, "Already I can smell dear old Craig Street, and hear the feet of French girls tripping along St. Lawrence Main. No! Jack. No; I can't meet you in Montreal; but I'll be at the city hall in Vancouver for the civic welcome, when you arrive there."

Burkman had left Cookshire at 10:45 a.m. J.F. Pope, proprietor of Learner's Hotel, had treated him to a great time, and Mayor Larraber had signed his book. He passed through Johnville at 3 p.m., Lennoxville at 5:15 p.m., and reached Sherbrooke at 6 p.m., feeling as fresh as a daisy. There had been a few squalls throughout the day, but he had no trouble hiking almost 22 miles. That evening he was a "royal guest" at the Royal Hotel.

"The Behans are doing well, but it's the Dills who made the best time of all the hikers in reaching St. John," Burkman reminded readers cheerfully, though he ended his dispatch on a melancholy note: "Sherbrooke is sure a long way from Halifax—but it is a thousand times longer when you walk it alone."

The most impressive adventure story of the day was told by Jack and Clifford Behan. The good ol' Dartmouth boys might not be the first hikers to reach Montreal, but they sure knew how to deflect attention away from the front-runner. "We encountered three wild cats in the wilds of the Maine Mountains, and lived to tell about it," Jack told the newspaper. "But we're here and lucky to be alive. Thanks to the good old trusty revolver of mine, there are not two less hikers than there were yesterday."

The hikers were plodding along the railway track, minding their own business, Jack wrote, when suddenly he heard some yells worse than any he had ever heard at the Dartmouth ferry.

Down out of the mountains, pell mell, came three wildcats. They stopped when they reached the tracks, but showed every sign of fight and we prepared to battle for our lives. When the cats stopped, we stopped. Then the biggest of the trio started to crawl toward us. I fired at it but missed. At the discharge of my revolver, two of the cats turned tail and hiked off. The third fellow only blinked. I fired the second time and the big fellow rolled over, got up, and crawled toward us again. After a third shot, he stayed mighty still. When we came up to him he was pretty well all in. I gave him another bullet thru the head for good measure and he cashed in.

The Behans pitched the cougar from the tracks, since he was big enough to wreck the CPR express that passed them a few minutes later. "The body of the cat now lies beside the tracks where all doubting Thomases may view the remains," Jack concluded.

Meanwhile, Frank and Jenny were facing writers rather than wildcats. Having given the feature treatment to Burkman and the Behans, W.J. McNulty was ready to take on the Dills when they reached Saint John, February 15.

As the Adam and Eve of maritime walking neared St. John over the tracks of the CNR they were espied on the tracks by a vigilant policeman employed by the railway. He was about to arrest what he thought to be two men on the tracks. Then he perceived one of the supposed men was a woman. And he desisted.

McNulty was clever and quick to draw excuses from the Dills, which he reported at length: "It was the heavy snow storms of Friday night and Saturday morning that kept them from reaching St. John earlier, compelling them to stay in Petitcodiac...The storm also made walking difficult and they were unable to make the time they expected in the snow...Burkman and the Behans did not face the disheartening weather conditions that the Dills faced at the start of the race." McNulty was skeptical, summarizing their complaints as a suggestion that "it would have been more desirable had the men met with the stormy weather instead of the masculine-feminine couple."

Jenny told the seasoned reporter that she and Frank expected to make Vancouver in seven months but were not expecting to create a new record, unlike the ambition of Burkman and the Behans. "Between them there is a struggle that is attracting much attention," she said. McNulty explained:

The Dills do not expect or look forward with dread apprehension to forty-four mile walks such as do the Behans and Burkman. Twenty-two miles or perhaps at the most twenty-five miles per day is about enough for them. It must be remembered there is a member of the feminine gender in the outfit and too much must not be expected of them. All that will be hoped of the Dills is that they succeed in walking to the coast.

Most of the women in St. John are wondering if she will be able to make it...and Mrs. Dill will surprise many of her sisters if she succeeds in her ambition. It seems hard for the average woman to understand how a woman can walk nearly four thousand miles.

THOUSANDS OF CURIOUS Saint John women turned out to catch a glimpse of Mrs. Dill in her dapper togs during their stay, many of them expressing surprise at her seemingly fragile physique. Judging from the comments, some of the women expected to see a tall, buxom woman instead of the petite morsel of femininity that Mrs. Dill proved to be. "If I thought I could reduce to your weight I would be willing to try to walk to the coast, but I would last from St. John to McAdam Junction and it would take me a week to do it," confessed one woman in the crowd.

Mrs. Dill, it turned out, had little sympathy for members of the fair sex who would not take their lives in hand. "Walking has benefited my health wonderfully," she said. "The pure air and the exercise have worked wonders in me and removed the sluggishness. I am glad that I went with Frank... The woman of today should do more walking and less complaining."

Possibly Jenny's stand was determined by a rather unpleasant encounter, during their walkabouts around the city, when a woman questioned her status as a Canadian. "If being born in Halifax County is being a Canadian, I am that," she said.

"Owing to her brunette complexion, which is of the pronounced brunette variety, she has been mistaken for a woman of foreign extraction or birth," explained the insolent McNulty.

When asked what she thought of the Behans walking from Rothesay into Saint John, a distance of nine miles, in two and a half hours or less, Mrs. Dill told McNulty that she and her husband had walked eight miles in two hours the previous Sunday. Further questions inspired equally candid answers. Yes, she expected Charles Burkman to hold his own against the Behans in the walk to the coast. Yes, of course, she realized that Jack was a stellar walker—but he was being held back by his son, Clifford. When questioned for the umpteenth time how they were faring on the long journey to Vancouver, both Dills lost their temper.

"I am feeling great," said Frank.

"And I am feeling greater," said the increasingly testy Mrs. Dill.

Mr. and Mrs. F.C. Dill were relieved to exchange McNulty and Saint John for their first walk on Canadian Pacific Railway tracks.

ONLY SCANT REPORTS were received from Burkman and the Behans as they continued to battle fickle winter conditions. In a dispatch received at a very early hour, Burkman said that he had reached Magog, Quebec, but had only managed to make 18 miles. The *Herald* wondered at the brevity of his report.

The Behans made 21 miles. They had left Long Pond, Maine, at nine o'clock and walked the Chain Lakes before dinner at the Moose River House in Jackman. After a shave at Burton's shaving parlour, they started off again. Letters from Dartmouth were thrown to them from a passing train, and they were greatly encouraged to read that everyone at home was doing well. Invitations from trainmen to "have a ride" were ignored, after which they were called great sports and were told that the *Halifax Herald* was the greatest sports paper in Canada. They arrived at Holeb early in the evening and were guests at the McRitchie hotel, where they told other diners that they looked forward to walking over the 130-foot-long bridge outside Holeb—and yes, they knew that only a year earlier, a man had been blown off the same structure while making a crossing.

Although the Dills did not leave St. John until noon, the *Herald* reported that they covered more miles than the other hikers in the time they walked that day.

CHARLES BURKMAN REACHED St. John's, Quebec, on February 18 and was now 29 miles from Montreal. The *Herald* headlined its prediction:

BURKMAN WILL REACH MONTREAL LATE TONIGHT; DILLS TRAVEL 31 MILES

Charles Burkman, the first hiker who started from Halifax to tread the sod of Canada from Atlantic to Pacific, will be in Montreal tonight, barring accident. Last night he was in St. John [sic], Quebec, only 29 miles from the big Upper Canada metropolis.

The young hiker left West Sheffield yesterday morning, and arrived in Farnham early afternoon, where he received a warm welcome from train dispatcher, R.H. Santom. After crossing the mile and a half long bridge over the Richelieu River, Burkman reached St. John [sic], Quebec in time to see a hockey match between Les Canadiens of Montreal and the Singer team of St. Johns [sic]. The completion of this 29 mile hike sees Burkman well positioned for a triumphal march into Montreal by evening.

The Behans crossed the border into Quebec. "There was great excitement at Megantic when we arrived," Jack told the press. "Not even The Prince of Wales could have been better treated than we were at Springhill, Quebec." Some readers might have seen in Jack's hyperbole and penchant for attention an admission of frustration at not besting Burkman to Montreal. The hikers dined with a good old Scotsman, D.K. MacDonald, who cared for them like sons.

The Dills left Hoyt at 8:20 a.m. They ate dinner with Mrs. Walter Harris at Booth and arrived at Harvey at 5:30 p.m., where they stayed at the Brunswick House. Although a cold wind blew in their faces during the entire 31 miles, Jenny reported having a good day.

Her dispatch was short and cranky. After all, they were still in New Brunswick, while the Behans had already left Maine, and Burkman was within reach of Montreal. And after their uncomfortable sojourn in Saint John, their fleecing by McNulty, and an arrogant hiking status put-down by Jack Behan, it was enough to make a serious hiker question her game plan.

Vive Montreal!

POSITIONS OF HIKERS FEBRUARY 19

Dills—At Lambert Lake, Maine; 363 miles; out 19 days; did 20 miles yesterday

Behans—At Sherbrooke, Que.: 650 miles; out 26 days; did 23 miles yesterday

Burkman—At Montreal, Que.; 760 miles; out 34 days; did 30 miles yesterday

Halifax—0 miles; Montreal—760; Winnipeg—2,170; Vancouver—3,645

Charles Burkman reached Montreal on February 19 and was accorded a hero's welcome. After a press interview at the Windsor Hotel, a smitten *Montreal Star* journalist, Roy Carmichael, described Burkman as

looking every inch the matinee idol of the silver screen, such as the devil-ishly handsome Walter Reid; the brooding Conrad Nagel; perhaps even the smouldering Rudolph Valentino. Bronzed like an Indian and aglow with radiant health, Charles Burkman slim and boyish looking, strode into Montreal, Saturday afternoon. As with head thrown back and chest out, he marched through the crowded streets, his was a notable vigour. Youth and energy vibrated from him, and he must have been conscious of many admiring glances, some of them envious, for there is nothing the man who is "out of condition" envies more than the buoyancy of the trained athlete.

Charles Burkman's official hike postcard.
Postcard courtesy of Elinor Barr,
Swedes in Canada Project.

The young pedestrian spoke freely to Carmichael of his status as the lone hiker and his intentions for the hike: "I can now set any pace I like...I now intend to walk 21 to 23 miles a day for the duration, bringing me to Vancouver by 4 July...I mean to break the record set by Beresford Greatheed, twenty years ago, and I don't mean it to be broken by those who are following me." This was a reference to the great walker Beresford Greatheed, who around 1895 walked from Vancouver to Halifax in 12 months, averaging 22 miles per day.

Burkman said that he was grateful for the *Herald* coverage and for the kindness and hospitality showed him along the route, particularly by the trainmen. He was hard pressed to pick a favourite town. Sherbrooke was par excellence for hospitality, but in saying so, Burkman was reminded of his experience in Truro, and then in Amherst. In the end, the affable pedestrian found it difficult to praise one town over the others. "Unfortunately," he admitted, "I am unlikely to meet such hospitality in larger western centres."

When questioned about the effect of distance-walking on his feet, Burkman revealed what friends and family suspected but didn't want confirmed: he was suffering from "walker's curse."

"I find it difficult to get socks which do not trouble me," Burkman told reporters. "There is always a little knot somewhere on the foot where the sock is finished, and this sometimes works itself right up the top of my big toe, causing excruciating pain. It won't be ignored."

Burkman found the most effective treatment was to sit down frequently on the tracks, remove his boots and cut the knots off his woollen socks. Had he overcome the problem, a reporter wanted to know.

"No," he said. "I just keep cutting the knots off my socks and wait for the calluses to develop on my feet. So far I have suffered only a few blisters."

Burkman spent most of Sunday resting, not by any means an unwise decision, since the temperature outside was well below zero, and a damp wind rattled the corridors of the famed Windsor fortress. Besides, he was well ahead of his schedule and in no way concerned that his rivals might catch up to him.

The Behans, for their part, were spitting mad over one of Mrs. Dill's candid comments to McNulty in St. John. "The statement made by the Dills that I have been delaying my father on the hike is absolutely false," Clifford responded, "and if readers of the *Herald* watch the mileage they'll see there is nothing in it. We are feeling in great shape and going through the country in a whirlwind."

It was hiking strategy aimed at disorienting the Behans, but it didn't take the disgruntled father and son long to regain their focus on winning the next lap of the race. Now seasoned to the discomfort of below-zero temperatures and winter storms, they strutted along the rails to Cookshire, stopping briefly at the Grande View Hotel in Bury for a fine spread, and then, before it was properly digested, heading off into the drifting snow.

"Cold! You said it. It was two below when we started out and the snow came down like a real storm," said Jack. "We did two miles an hour, which was pretty good going considering the kind of weather it was. The North Pole has nothing on the district around here." The stalwarts recorded 22 miles under taxing conditions.

In the early light of the next morning, the hikers passed through some fine farming country in southern Quebec. After bolting down a small dinner at Lennoxville, they took off for Sherbrooke, putting up at the Royal Hotel, happy to have ripped off another 23 miles.

The Dills left Harvey at 8:30 a.m. and arrived at Magaudavic in time for "one of those regular meals that everyone dreams about," said Jenny. Their warm reception at the Fraser Lumber Company camp was outstanding. "We were treated to mountains of Boston beans simmered in molasses, dotted with chunks of smoked side-pork as big as your fist, accompanied by slabs of golden brown corn bread to soak up the sauces—all served on mounds of mashed potatoes." For dessert, the couple received generous wedges of apple pie slathered in cream and sprinkled with cinnamon.

Frank and Jenny reached McAdam at 3:30 p.m., recording a 20-mile hike in seven hours, and "received a 'not to be sneezed at lunch' of beefsteak and potatoes," served up by A. Lannan, who had patiently awaited their arrival. That evening

Mrs. Frank Dill took stock of her novel position as a woman in the epic hike across the continent, ending with what was fast becoming her optimistic saw:

Whether hiking to Vancouver from Halifax will ever become a popular hobby or not is very hard to say, but one thing is certain that it is the greatest fun in the world and neither of us would miss this for anything… We never knew that there were so many real people on this earth. Of course, the novelty of a woman and her husband setting out on a stunt of this kind has a lot to do with it, for this is the first time that anything like that has been tried… What Men Have Done, A Woman Can Do.

The well-sated couple left McAdam the next day, singing the praises of their countrymen. "McAdam," Jenny said, "is one of those towns where people push your money back and say, 'No, thanks!' The people here are simply lovely and can't do enough for us. The first thing they ask is if we have a place to sleep." Much of what she said appeared calculated to goad the Behans, who professed, on occasion, to sleeping on the boards.

After spending an hour and a half at Vanceboro with L.A. Cunningham, the U.S. Customs officer, the Dills set off into a fierce blizzard. "The kind you read about blowing around the Arctic Circle," Jenny off-handed. "However, that isn't much in a tramp to Vancouver."

The self-proclaimed superwoman continued to show her mettle as the Dills hiked through the infamous wildcat territory of Maine. "We've heard a lot about the wildcats that nearly ate up the Behans," she said. "And we were ready to tackle them on our way to Lambert Lake, but no such luck; so we haven't any exciting story for you this time. We are tonight with Mr. and Mrs. C. Gilferson and we don't feel as if we are nearly 400 miles from home. The people make us so comfortable that every place is home to us now."

CHARLES BURKMAN CHARMED the public non-stop on his weekend stay in Montreal, and an enthusiastic Roy Carmichael commented on his every move:

Charlie Burkman established himself as a popular favourite among the athletic boys of Montreal during his week-end rest and showed himself such an adept at terpsichorean art that he is being described as the man who is "dancing his way across continent." His popularity with the ladies at the dances he visited was almost embarrassing, his fair hair and tanned complexion attracted a great deal of notice... His slender, lithe figure showed to advantage in the activities of the dance and many were the inquiries as to who the handsome stranger might be. When it was explained that he was walking across the continent the interest became intense.

The popular, happy-go-lucky daredevil may have danced the night away, but he was up bright and early Monday morning, February 21. He made a brief visit to the office of *La Presse* to fulfill a promise made to his many French Canadian acquaintances who did not read English newspapers but who would look out for news of his adventures in the French press. While there he agreed to have his picture taken on the roof of the building, to hand out as souvenirs.

When Burkman left the city, walking along Ste. Catherine Street to Westmount, he was trailed by adoring fans. "His athletic bearing matching his outfit, and with an air of going somewhere to do something, caused heads to be turned as he strode along," wrote Carmichael.

Passing Westmount station, Burkman again took to the track and swung along two ties at a time, bringing an encouraging cheer from the workers he passed on his way out of town. The stations along the line are small, and as he passes the halfway to Ottawa mark, they are often placed at a distance of some miles from the villages they represent. However, there are farm houses scattered all along the route and many trains passing in both directions so the hiker will not be lonesome and his progress will be noted by an increasing number of railroad men.

The *Canadian Railroader*, a weekly newsletter circulated to railroaders as far away as the west coast, took an interest in young Burkman because he had chosen the railway in preference to the highway for his great hike. He was flattered that they intended to advise and support him as he moved westward.

From Saint-Polycarpe Junction that night, Burkman summed up "just another hiking day... went off my course at Vaudreuil without knowing it, and arrived at St. Lazare at twelve," Burkman said. "Had dinner with the station agent who suggested I go to Saint-Polycarpe Junction, and follow the Grand Trunk to Ottawa as it would only make the distance from Montreal a mile more. I left St. Lazare at two-thirty and got the mayor's signature at St. Clet. I arrived here, at seven, where I stopped at the Junction Hotel for the night."

Mrs. Frank C. Dill, who had assured McNulty in Saint John that the Dills had no intentions of getting caught up in the competition headaches plaguing Burkman and the Behans, casually admitted to walking a whopping 30 miles from Danforth to Mattawamkeag. The success story made its way to the front page of the *Herald*:

DILLS OUTPOINT OTHER HIKERS AND
MAKE 30 MILES IN SINGLE DAY
Husband And Wife Make Big Gain
On Other Contestants In Maine Tramp...

"You must confess," said giddy Jenny Dill, in an about-face, "that isn't too bad for a woman." The couple admitted to having one of the most pleasant days of the hike and were looking forward to another 30-mile walk the next day.

When she read in the paper that Burkman was making tracks to Ottawa, Jenny enthused, "Good Luck to him." He was her favourite of the front runners, and she made no bones about saying so—even though the admission about the handsome young hiker grated on Frank's nerves. After learning that Burkman had lost his way trying to take a shortcut to the capital, and that the Behans had gained on him and were now only four days behind, she knew he needed all the friends he could muster.

In a night letter, Clifford wrote that he and his father had hiked 26 miles from Foster to Farnham, Quebec, in −9°F temperatures, using a balancing pole, a device spanning the tracks and held on either end that was said to increase mileage. The freshly shaved father and son were in the pink when they attended a reception at the Temperance Hotel in Foster. And although everybody turned out to give them the glad hand, the hikers retired early—intending, they said, to complete a record-breaking 47-mile hike from Farnham to Montreal the next day.

THE BEHANS ARRIVED in Montreal but did not enjoy the rousing welcome they had anticipated. Unfamiliar with the intricate CPR routes, they walked from the north end of the city in the dark to Place Viger instead of leaving the track for the road at Mile End. Eventually the worn and weary hikers got rerouted and found their way to the St. James Hotel, happy to have completed the first leg of their trek to Vancouver. The Behans received only a tepid review in the press:

MONTREAL, Feb. 24.—Sergeant Behan and his son Clifford are in Montreal. They arrived here about 8 o'clock last night, and put up at the St. James Hotel. Today they set out to sell their post cards. They met several good friends and old acquaintances from overseas who gave them the glad hand.

Sergeant Behan was delighted to find that Henry Fortune, whom he had last seen in a military hospital in Halifax awaiting discharge, was now the night porter at the St. James Hotel.

Jack and Clifford were up bright and early the next morning and, after a good breakfast, called at the Knights of Columbus headquarters with a letter of introduction from J.D. O'Connor, the moving-picture censor at Halifax. Colonel Clarence Smith gave them a hearty greeting and, learning that their shoes were worn out, sent them off to the George E. Slater Shoe Store, where they were each supplied with a pair of the best walking boots in the shop.

When questioned by Roy Carmichael about the state of their feet, Jack Behan was quick to say that neither he nor Clifford was experiencing foot problems. But after hearing that Burkman was dealing with "the hiker's curse," Jack admitted that during the first day out—before exchanging their trench boots for Larrigans—they suffered a lot. After the Amherst Boot and Shoe Company gifted them with Scotia Curing boots, they had enjoyed 650 miles of pure comfort to Montreal. Those boots were now worn out—the uppers giving way before the soles—and needed replacing.

Ever mindful that they were in competition, Jack reminded Carmichael that although Burkman left Halifax eight days ahead of them, he left Montreal only two and a half days before their arrival in the city. Further, they had averaged more than 26 miles a day in the 29 days and 11 hours since leaving Halifax and were determined to increase that average to 30 miles a day.

The next morning the *Herald* reported that Burkman had again lost his way along the tracks to Ottawa while taking a "shortcut" to Glen Robertson. It ended up being the longest shortcut he had ever made. "There are too many railway tracks in Ontario to suit me," Burkman complained to the *Herald*. For the second time in four days, he was sidetracked between Montreal and Ottawa. He said that it was impossible to make Ottawa before the evening, and it would be late when he did arrive.

After that ill-fated start, Burkman did cover 30 miles to Chesterville, but he still had 25-plus miles left to reach Ottawa. The Behans were now only two and a half days behind him, but Burkman said that he expected to make better time after passing through Ottawa. Next day, while the Behans enjoyed meeting friends in Montreal, and Burkman was trying to point himself in the direction of Ottawa, the Dills reached Brownville, Maine, and Jenny continued to blow her own horn: "We often wonder what some of those people think now in Halifax, who said Mrs. Dill couldn't walk to Truro. Well she can tell them all she has not been tired yet and she has walked all day through snow up to her knees. Everybody says, 'You must be exhausted.' Some of the ladies say, 'How on earth can you do it?' Mrs. Dill laughs and says, 'Oh, it's only fun.'"

Most days, Mrs. Dill was content to be a transcontinental hiker, but seasoned now, and enjoying occasional bursts of speed, she found her attitude changing— although she still found time to taunt the Behans: "The Behans must have had fun shooting those wild cats. We hope they don't shoot them all before we get that far, for we would like to see some and try a few shots. Perhaps they think Mrs. F.C. Dill is frightened of wild cats, but, oh no. It will take more than wild cats to turn her on the hike to the Pacific."

Fêted and Lionized in the Capital

POSITIONS OF HIKERS FEBRUARY 25

Dills—At Onawa, Maine; 500 miles; out 25 days; did 20 miles yesterday
Behans—At Montreal, Que.; 760 miles; out 32 days; did 21 miles yesterday
Burkman—At Ottawa, Ont.; 876 miles; out 40 days; did 31 miles yesterday
Halifax—0 miles; Montreal—760; Winnipeg—2,170; Vancouver—3,645

On February 25, Charles Burkman reached Ottawa shortly after 7 p.m., completing 876 of the 3,645 miles from the Garrison City to Vancouver. He looked fine and felt as fit as a trapper. Even though the capital city of Canada was known for its athletic chic, the young hiker was instinctively accepted and immediately eulogized by the press: "Charles Burkman stands out from the lot, lithe and sinewy as a panther, tanned by wind and sun, springy of step and clear of eye. He doesn't belong on city streets. There is a touch of open spaces about him: A suggestion of the Open Road and the splendid distances that are Canada's."

This was young Burkman's first visit to Ottawa, but he wasn't much attracted to the idea of touring the city itself. Rather, he said he looked forward to a tramp around Parliament Hill. "The new parliament buildings are getting rave reviews down east," he told the press, "so they are a must do. The good fellows presently representing the people are also a must see."

Burkman was particularly interested in meeting Arthur Meighen, the prime minister, who had been born in Anderson, Ontario, near Thunder Bay, where Burkman himself grew up. Meighen, who represented the Manitoba riding of Portage la Prairie, was the son of a farmer and was widely considered the finest debater in the House of Commons.

After enduring a tour of the grand new buildings and introductions to the private members in the House, the cabinet ministers, the opposition members and their leader, the Right Honourable Mackenzie King, Burkman finally met the prime minister. Meighen was disappointingly cold, businesslike and without personal charm. "Could he survive the rumoured fall election with such personal failings?" Burkman wondered.

Most of the parliamentarians were impressed by Burkman's solemn, thoughtful attitude. "This boy is taking his long hike as seriously as he can take it," was how one of the politicians expressed their view. "With the eyes of Canada on him, he means to win through a schedule."

"He may not know about the fine shades of parliamentary debates," another member articulated to a strategically positioned reporter, "but he is possibly visualizing the day when he himself will stand in the great Canadian forum, placed there on his record as a transcontinental hiker."

The popular youth did not disclose to his hosts whether he was entertaining a future in politics, but he spent the day around the parliament buildings, fêted and lionized by the *Herald's* representatives in the press gallery. "There is nothing too good for Burkman," they said. "Possibly the only reason he stayed at the Russell Hotel is that the Chateau Laurier was filled."

Guests at the parliamentary luncheon held in Burkman's honour had an insatiable appetite for his hiking anecdotes, "weather stories" being among their favourites.

"Of course, I expect to experience more brutish storms before the winter is over," he told a spellbound audience, "but none likely to compare with the bitter cold weather in the New Brunswick marshes between Dorchester and Moncton—the harshest day imaginable."

When asked by one of the honourable members if he really believed he would make Vancouver on time, he answered truthfully, "I can only do the best I can." Which was interpreted as meaning: "You bet your sweet life I will."

"I haven't yet hit my stride," Burkman argued, "[I] have been testing myself as I go. I can cover 50 miles any day I choose, and when I strike the North Ontario country, where people won't constantly be stopping me to talk, I will be able to get along faster." He clarified: "Of course I do not mean I can do 50 miles every day, but I can do it once in a while—I'm sure of that."

The brief sojourn in Ottawa amused and flattered Burkman, but he was aware that his rivals were now only 50 miles behind him, and barbed comments by parliamentarians were not well received. So, he had his fill of the city, had his boots repaired in Ottawa and then set out at 6 a.m. the next morning for Arnprior, following the Grand Trunk and later switching over to the CPR tracks for the rest of the journey across Canada.

THINGS MAY HAVE gotten off to a slow start for the Behans in Montreal, but they picked up when Jack's friend Colonel Webb met with Sergeant Behan and his son and took them along to the Windsor Hotel. After official letters were presented, the hikers were told that the place was theirs.

Next morning, Jack sent an effusive dispatch to the *Herald*. "The Windsor Hotel in Montreal is the snappiest place in this city," he gushed. "And last night, the whole works were thrown open to us. We couldn't carry the Windsor away with us, but we did our best. The Hotel orchestra entertained us, especially, and we did a roaring trade with our cards." The Behans were well satisfied and generally appeased.

When the hikers returned from the revelry arranged for them by the Colonel to their rooms at the St. James Hotel, they discovered that their host, Mr. Ferguson —"a rip-snorting, good fellow"—had organized an enjoyable hour-long concert party for them. The grateful hikers retired at 11 p.m., agreeing that "continental hiking is simply IT."

The Behans left the city at noon and set off for Ste. Anne de Bellevue. The 21-mile walk left them "feeling just right."

While Burkman was leaving Ottawa, and with the Behans off to the capital, the *Herald* reported a not-too-shabby hike completed by the Dills. "According to a dispatch received early this morning, the Dills have reached Onawa, Maine, twenty miles from Brownville Junction, where they spent Thursday night. The next stopping place is expected to be Somerset, thirty-one miles from Onawa."

It was necessary for the newspaper to emphasize to the public, on occasion, that this was indeed a three-party transcontinental race, but what people, including the reporters, did not yet realize was that the farther Frank and Jenny hiked, the better they felt, and the more encouragement they received, the more confident they became.

Frank and Jenny didn't send a wire to Halifax over the weekend, causing friends and family some consternation. When the couple re-emerged on Monday February 28, they denied being lost—uncommunicative maybe, but certainly not lost.

"The woods of Maine are thick, impenetrable and fraught with potential hazards," Jenny said, "so we kept to the safely traversed routes and arrived at Jackman, Maine, on Sunday evening." Their next jump would bring them into Quebec, close on the heels of both the Behans and Burkman.

It had been an interesting weekend, with a slow start for the hikers. They stayed with Mr. Brown at the section house of the Columbus Mountain Lumber camp on Friday evening; left early Saturday morning for Greenville, arriving at the YMCA in time for dinner; and finally reached Somerset at 5 p.m., thus completing a satisfactory 27-mile day.

Things picked up on the Sabbath for the increasingly competitive Dills, who set out early, bucked stiff winds and drifting snow for 25 gruelling miles to Jackman, and ended the day by chalking up the best hiking average of the entire weekend.

In contrast, the Behans, in Ste. Anne de Bellevue on February 26, took time out to visit Ste. Anne's hospital to sell postcards. The infirmary was home to more than 600 patients, including many Nova Scotians. Dr. McMursich, the superintendent, accompanied the hikers around the wards, and later some of the sisters treated them to an institutional lunch. The Behans also toured MacDonald College in Ste. Anne de Bellevue and were honoured to sign the same leaf in the guest book as had His Royal Highness the Prince of Wales. They took tea at Hudson and arrived in Rigaud at 8:35 p.m. The walking had been bad, but they felt fine, and they'd sold a few postcards.

On Sunday, Jack and Clifford tried to make up the day lost at Ste. Anne de Bellevue by trudging 23 miles to St. Telesphore, Quebec, where they bedded down for the night.

ON FEBRUARY 28, after the final dispatches of the day had been received from the hikers, the *Herald* issued a statement: "The Behans are close on the heels of Burkman, and the Dills are making better time than Burkman. Father and Son were expected to reach Ottawa by noon, March 1, and looked forward to a two-day visit with parliamentary friends before leaving the Capital early Wednesday morning. They related their frustrating experience with the Sunday weather, complaining that rainstorms had forced them to 'hang up' for a while at the Union Hotel in Rigaud."

But the proprietor was a dandy good sport who showed them a dandy good time.

And afterward the relaxed and fortified hikers walked 35 miles to Plantagenet.

"We know we are closing up the gap on Burkman and can almost hear him pant as he leads the race," Jack-the-adversary snarled, having put in his most difficult day so far.

Caught up in the hiking drama, and no longer satisfied to just tag along behind the others, the Dills resorted to eating as they walked. The determined couple covered 25 miles from Somerset to Jackman on Sunday and walked an additional 25 miles on Monday, bringing them as far as Lowelltown, Maine.

"The weather was splendid," said the upbeat Mrs. Dill. "We are in excellent condition."

The snow was deep in places, but they had made good time and looked forward to reaching Montreal, where an enthusiastic welcome was assured them.

Poor Burkman had the worst showing of all the hikers over the weekend. He managed only 17 miles in a heavy downpour with no rain gear, which forced him to seek shelter early in the day. If the weather co-operated, the frustrated hiker expected to complete a 53-mile walk from Renfrew to Pembroke the next day— or bust. If successful, it would become a hiking milestone.

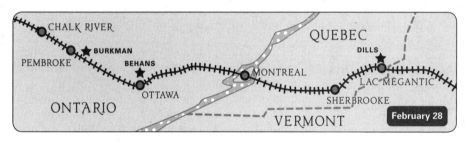

MARCH 1 SAW the Dills in Megantic, within six days of Montreal. After the challenging 19.5-mile hike they had just completed, Jenny admitted to being tired. She hoped that walking through the Eastern Townships would be easier.

"We see that the Behans had a lovely time in Montreal," she added. "They seem to be pulling up on Charlie."

A disappointed young Charlie sent a night wire from Haley, Ontario. The weather was bad, and he had completed only 27 miles.

"I left Renfrew at 6:30 this morning and had to walk five miles to Sandpoint to get breakfast as the hotels and restaurants in this burg don't open until 9 o'clock," he said. Burkman got as far as Hampton by 12.15 p.m., found the town clerk, who signed his book, and then headed for Haley. He spent the night with a friend, John Rose.

As anticipated, the Behans arrived in Ottawa shortly after midnight, to little fanfare, but the *Herald* suggested one more time that "Nova Scotia members and other official dignitaries will have something ready for them in the morning. A watchful eye will be kept in the Capital for the Behans and it may be anticipated that the reception accorded Burkman will be hospitality duplicated."

And under the paternal wing of P.F. Martin, the MP for Halifax, their brief stay in the city even overshadowed the attention given Charles Burkman. The newspaper claimed that only dignitaries of other nations received the quality of attention lavished on this pair of continental pedestrians, and Prime Minister Meighen, cabinet ministers and senators went out of their way to honour the returned men, exploiting a little healthy publicity in anticipation of the rumoured fall election.

The "royal tour" included an excursion through the new parliament buildings, from cellar to attic. The sanctums of cabinet ministers were thrown open to the Behans, as was the fine new parliamentary restaurant. They were "fêted and shook hands with half the Senators and the House of Commons" and then spent some time "in the vast Parliamentary Reading Room, pouring [sic] over their own exploits as chronicled in the newspapers. When the attendants there found out who they were, they simply said, 'Read every paper here—and come again.'"

Later, Jack Behan bragged that if they were to read all the words that had been printed about them in the presses around the continent since they started out from Halifax, they would have to add another six months to their walk. He was keen to share hiking statistics and anecdotes with reporters and parliamentarians alike, as had Burkman before him.

"We beat Burkman's time by five days less a few hours," he pointed out first. "[We] averaged 26 miles a day to Montreal, and 23 miles per day to Ottawa—while Burkman averaged only 21.5 miles a day for the full distance.

"The weather between Dorchester and Moncton was miserable," he continued, "and the temperature was 13 below between Stewiacke and Alton, but it was in Maine that we nearly froze our balls off." The audience laughed at his plain talk, which was all the encouragement Jack needed. "The snow storms were so wicked that at one point we had to crawl across the railway trestles for fear of being blown away by the bloody gale—worst of it was, I had blisters on my feet—not that they deterred me.

"Burkman is mainly handicapped by being alone," he concluded. "If he had a partner with him, he could walk the rails with a bar stick," a reference to the balance stick that he and Clifford were using to help steady themselves as they walked atop the rails. He also suggested that if he and Clifford had raincoats, permitting them to walk in the wet weather, they would have exchanged cards with Burkman in Ottawa.

Clifford spoke to the press about the good health and well-being of the pair, revealing that he had lost seven pounds since leaving Halifax, and Jack, four. "Father says he feels as good today as he did 25 years ago—and that is saying something for a man with a 24 year old son as a hiking partner."

WHILE JACK AND Clifford basked in the parliamentary favours garnered for them by the press, Mrs. F.C. Dill entertained the public with her thoughts on the competition advertisement that T.J. Wallace, Optometrist and Manufacturing Optician, had placed in the *Herald*, offering round-trip rail tickets for a distance as far as the hikers walked.

More merchants got into the act once the hikers became national celebrities.
Advertisement, *Halifax Herald*, March 3, 1921, p. 3

No Wonder Folks Stare at Mrs. Dill

Jenny Dill.
Halifax Herald, March 3, 1921, p. 3

"Gee, I was glad when I saw that ad of Wallace the optician," Jenny punned. "It's just a dandy idea; and anyone can SEE that it is good…I just want to know who is going to pick the Dills. Who ever they are, they will see the whole stretch of the country from Halifax to Vancouver, and though they will see the country by train, they won't have any more fun than we are having."

She was tickled to reach Scotstown, Quebec, after another hard-fought 25-mile tramp. "It rained cats and dogs most of the way and we feel that we can accomplish anything after that."

The *Herald* continued to emphasize Mrs. Dill's poster-girl status with the release of yet another photo. "No Wonder Folks Stare at Mrs. Dill," the headline read. "Her pants are attracting an awful lot of attention."

In contrast, readers had to feel sorry for Burkman, struggling to gain his former advantage over the Behans. Citing continued bad weather and no raincoat, he managed only a 22-mile walk, from Haley to Eganville, before calling it a day. "If only the weather man would co-operate, I'd soon spread the gap between myself and those Behans," he said vehemently.

THE NEXT DAY began for the Behans with an early morning breakfast at the expense of the Hon. F.B. McCurdy, member from Colchester, Nova Scotia, and minister of public works—against whom Jack had played hockey in the old Halifax Commercial League.

"McCurdy owned the first pneumatic-tired bicycle in the Garrison City," Jack told the press. "But being a public man, he did not sympathetically claim that glory against the possible claim of some other one-time cyclist."

After a pleasant meal, the honourable member escorted the Behans to Prime Minister Meighen's offices, where, to the first minister's surprise, Jack demanded his autograph—and got it—along with something for the "exchequer" in return for their postcards. From there the trio called on the Hon. J.A. Calder, minister of immigration and colonization. "Here the autograph book was enriched by the signature of another minister of the crown and the exchequer was still further replenished by card money...From Mr. Calder's office, the pair accompanied Mr. McCurdy on a still further tour of Parliament Hill, meeting all sorts of celebrities and even getting a peep into that sanctum from which orders-in-council emanate."

The generosity and kindness of McCurdy, P.F. Martin, Senator Stanfield and scores of other members left Jack and Clifford Behan convinced that the people on Parliament Hill were a pretty warm-hearted class of men. The special correspondent appointed to cover the Behans' Ottawa visit assured the hikers that the sentiments were mutual: "Ottawa is not easily taken off its feet. It meets dignitaries and characters with considerable sang froid—to watch their comings and goings is all in a day's work: But not so with Burkman and the Behans. They brought something invigorating—a suggestion of the big outdoors and the atmosphere of magnificent space."

Government publicist Raymond Peck preserved the Behans' second visit to Parliament Hill in motion pictures shortly before they left the city that morning.

"Burkman and the Behans have come and gone," wrote the *Ottawa Sentinel* correspondent. "Next will come the Dills, and for a full day it is hoped that the courageous little lady herself will be the centre of attraction in the federal capitol [sic]."

Shifting Gears

A s the Behans made their exit from Ottawa, Burkman walked 32 miles from Egansville to Chalk River and marked the thousand-mile point in his journey. He had shifted gears and was no longer above tooting his own horn. "Chalk River papers are publishing reports that the Behans are on my heels. Are they really? If they are, my heels are much longer than their heels," he mocked. "If you only knew the country I am passing through you would not wonder that my speed has been reduced a little. But it is the same country the Behans have to pass through, so just watch the time they will make."

Burkman ate dinner at Cobden—the first community in Canada to build a memorial hall to honour the fallen heroes of the Great War—then took a break at Nelson's in Meath to get out of the rain. He arrived in Chalk River around 8 p.m. and put up for the night at MacDonald's boarding house.

Haligonians were serious about the transcontinental race, and since it was now public knowledge that Burkman was quietly experiencing foot problems, his cranky behaviour and uneven hiking scores led one Halifax sport to bet "thousands of dollars" that the Behans would catch the lone hiker by March 12.

The Dills, meanwhile, were marching toward Cookshire, Quebec. After a long, hard, 23-mile grind through harsh winds and bottomless drifts, they arrived there in good condition and spent the night at the Hotel Bury.

AFTER SWEEPING OTTAWA off its feet and adding shekels to their treasury, Jack and Clifford Behan hit the Grand Trunk rails shortly after noon on Friday March 4. The Knights of Columbus at Arnprior had planned a reception for them the previous evening, which they had spent in Ottawa. "Further arrangements are being made at Pembroke instead," Jack said in his night letter. "And we hope to be on hand for those festivities."

Clifford expressed his relief at leaving the capital and resuming the chase after Burkman: "We are in Renfrew and believe me I was glad to get away from Ottawa. While listening to the debate in the Federal House, dad wanted to get in on the argument. He thought that an election would be called before he got back, and it was with great persuasion that I managed to get him started on the road again."

En route, Jack and Clifford stopped briefly at Carp, where they were treated to a real Irish stew served up by a genuine English lady.

Real Irish Stew with Lamb and Beer

Yields 6 generous servings

❧ INGREDIENTS ❦

1 bunch fresh parsley/dried
1 bunch fresh rosemary/dried
1 bunch fresh thyme/dried
3 pounds lamb shoulder with little fat, cubed
½ cup flour
2 large onions, roughly chopped
3 to 4 cloves garlic, finely chopped
3 large carrots, peeled and chopped
6 stalks celery, peeled and chopped into ½-inch pieces
12 ounces Guinness stout
3 large russet potatoes, peeled and chopped
1 cup pearl barley
2 quarts lamb or beef stock as needed
2 teaspoons cornstarch
Salt and pepper to taste

⟶

continued on page 90

❧ DIRECTIONS ❧

Cut off some of the parsley leaves and chop enough to make 2 tablespoons; reserve. Cut off some parsley stems, and tie them into a bundle with a few sprigs of rosemary and thyme; reserve.

Season the meat with salt and brown the meat in a little lard. Remove and reserve, and sprinkle with flour, shaking off excess.

Add the onions, garlic, carrots and celery to the pan and sauté, tossing to coat with fat. Add the Guinness and deglaze, scraping up any caramelized meat juices. Add the potatoes; return the meat and the barley to the pot. Add enough stock to barely cover, cook at the back of the stove until just boiling, then simmer for 40 minutes, until meat is tender.

Check seasonings; add salt and pepper to taste, then remove from the heat, stir in the parsley and the cornstarch, which has been mixed into 4 teaspoons of water, and stir. Cook over low heat for another few minutes to thicken. Serve with plenty of Irish brown or white soda bread, tea and more Guinness if you like. ⏣

"It sure hit the spot after the long 32 mile journey," Clifford told the editor. The young man wasn't too exhausted by the hike to insult the Dills: "Cobble stones are numerous on the tracks, and we are trying to arrange with the manager of The Grand Trunk to have them raked off so Jenny and Frank won't hurt their tootsies."

Swapping insults was becoming something of a sport between Jenny and the Behans. Calling down the Behans was her only active option as the aggressive father and son threatened to overtake her favoured hiker, Burkman, while she and her husband trailed them both by several hundred miles.

Burkman arrived at Mackey, Ontario, with dukes up, ready to spar. "It makes me laugh to read the stories of the Behans and the Dills catching me before I reach Winnipeg," he said, "because the more I walk, the better I feel. I am only starting off on my real gait now, and if my rivals hope to catch sight of me this side of British Columbia, they will have to travel some."

But readers were beginning to doubt that he still had the stuff to win the race. His rhetoric sounded as tired and sore as his feet, and in a March 5 headline the *Herald* asked: "Will he?"

AFTER COMPLETING AN arduous 33-mile trek from Stonecliffe to Eau Claire, even Burkman finally admitted that he was in for a "hot" chase from the Behans. He still believed he could hold his own until Vancouver and still insisted he would join in welcoming them to the city, but given the muscle and determination fuelling the athletic Behans, it was not going to be easy. He knew that more than luck and healthy feet would be necessary for him to stay ahead of the iron resolve behind the Behan machine.

Jack Behan described their typical weekend:

We left Renfrew Saturday at 10 a.m. We got to Cobden, 3:02 met at the train station, by M.J. Kane and we went to McCoy Hotel; went to bed. Rained all day. Wet clothes dried by proprietor... Arrived at Pembroke 3:30. Met at Pembroke station by Mayor Jones... After lunch the mayor and several other men accompanied us out of town... Proceeded toward Petawawa, ten miles further. Pembroke is the best lit town we have yet seen. A thousand candle power every fifty feet, all over town. Arrived at Petawa at nine p.m. Travelled sixteen miles Saturday; twenty nine today.

There was no doubt that the hard-living Behans were focused and on the move, but even though all the hikers did well during the first weekend of March, and the standings didn't change, the Dills were now posting daily averages equal to those of Burkman and the Behans.

The Dills reached Montreal early Monday morning, and Roy Carmichael wrote a glowing special on their visit to the French city.

Putting up at the Windsor Hotel they attracted a great deal of attention, and the charming little lady in riding breeches, in particular, was the cynosure of all eyes... They spent the early evening seeing the city and were rather unfortunate in not being able to get in touch with the manager of the English and Scotch Woolen Company, from whom they had hoped to get new riding breeches. It was necessary for Mrs. Dill to buy new boots here and the $11 they cost ran away with a lot of post-card money.

The Dills were happy to share their repertoire of hiking anecdotes with Carmichael, who was especially interested in the reception they were receiving in Quebec, since few French-Canadians in small communities spoke English.

"We didn't experience the kind of hospitality we received elsewhere," Jenny said, parsing her words. "And of course we felt the strain on our joint purse."

"Fosters was the exception," Frank was quick to interrupt.

"It was," Jenny confirmed. "We reached the village on Saturday night—our second anniversary—and were taken around town by A.M. Hunter, manager of the Picture Theatre, and enjoyed a big sale of our postcards, then stayed the night with Mrs. M. Hollingsworth, who was very kind to us."

The absolute worst experience, they said, was at the station in St. Philippe.

"We took only a brief lunch stop at Farnham, but it was dark when we arrived in the village."

"Exhausted and famished with a 35 mile walk under our belts," Frank said. "So it was no wonder we were disappointed to find a gruff agent locking up."

"He refused to send a telegram to the *Herald* for us—"

"Said he was finished for the day."

"When Frank tried to explain that we were walking to the Pacific and needed some place to stay for the night, he demanded: 'Can you please speak French?'"

"No, we said together."

"'Well then, you had better keep on walking.'"

"And he slammed the door and scowled at us from the station window."

The Dills, exhausted and worn, were now angry but determined. They wandered through the little village until they found a kindly store keeper who spoke some English, and he took them to a boarding house, where they were made quite comfortable.

Jenny went on to show Carmichael three congratulatory telegrams she had received from important folks back home in Halifax. It was a proud moment for the Dills, especially Jenny. The first message was from Premier Murray:

Mrs. Jenny Dill:—
    Congratulations on your achievement. The feat you have accomplished shows the stuff of which Nova Scotians are made. The people of your native province look forward to your successful completion of the trans-Canada trip.
    G.H. MURRAY

The second, from W.H. Dennis of the *Herald*, was very cheering but brief:

Hearty congratulations on your great achievement in reaching Montreal. The people of Halifax are proud of you.

✦ W.H. DENNIS

Mayor Parker of Halifax sent the longest and windiest message of all:

Congratulations on your achievement in arriving in Montreal. You have covered the hardest part of your journey. Our one wish is for your success and safe arrival at the coast. THE WOMEN OF NOVA SCOTIA congratulate you upon your courage, daring and pluck in attempting such a difficult trip, and will follow you with just as much interest, if not more, from Montreal to the Coast, as they have since you left Halifax. They are proud to know a Nova Scotian woman has the honor to accomplish a walking feat of such magnitude and are as one in wishing you the greatest success.

✦ JOHN S. PARKER

As the couple marched victoriously through the streets of the great Canadian metropolis to the Windsor Hotel, Burkman dispatched an admission to the public, hoping for a little empathy. He had arrived in Mattawa at 9:15 that morning, ate dinner with the section hands at Olric—generous fellows—then managed to hobble as far as Rutherglen in the dark.

"My feet are so painful that I holed up for the night, hoping against all odds, to reach North Bay the next day," he said. "From the Bay, I planned to strike out for northern Ontario—a country scarcely populated—and if all goes well, I hope to celebrate Easter Sunday in Port Arthur with my family. It may not mean much to readers, but I still hold a 100 mile lead over my rivals."

Jack and Clifford didn't intend to slow down to accommodate any hiker, blistered feet or no. "We are entering the wilds of northern Ontario, a wondrous land of 60,000 square miles of boreal forest and hundreds of lakes," Jack wrote. "The locals say that it is a landscape with few rivals in North America."

At dusk the rising howl of wolves added a chill to the air. The hungry yellow eyes pierced the darkness, and the hikers clutched their firearms "just in case." The intrepid Behans were not easily frightened, but they were forced to spend the night in a barn a few yards off the road. They managed some shut-eye—with one eye open. And someone had to get up several times to keep a fire lit.

"After sending our message last night, we prowled around for two hours in the dark," Jack wrote later. "But as nearly all the inhabitants of the village are Germans, they did not take kindly to us, so we wandered by without giving them a call."

The walking had been splendid, and unless they encountered trouble with *Canis lupus*, the determined Behans intended to continue increasing their speed. "We are proceeding along the track and have seen many wolves at a distance," Jack wrote. "The hunters we meet tell us that there is a bounty of $40 on each wolf, so we will take a shot at any stray on our path."

THE HIKERS RECEIVED a spectacular page 3 spread on Wednesday March 9 that included reports from the Dills and Burkman—but nothing from the Behans.

In a strenuous effort to hold on to first place, Burkman travelled 25 miles through spectacular rain and lightning storms as far as North Bay, arriving in the early evening wet and shaken but still intact. He had left Rutherglen at 7:15 a.m.; arrived two hours later in Bonfield, where he ate breakfast; then changed into his oilskins before setting off on the final leg of his journey. "Believe me, the thunder was fierce and sent thrills through my body," he said.

He stayed at the Bay the next day to have his boots repaired and his gun oiled in preparation for his northern Ontario adventure.

"At three o'clock this morning no word had been received from the Behans," reported the *Herald*. Skeptics were inclined to believe that the absence of a dispatch was a ruse to confuse Burkman, but friends of the family argued that this was uncharacteristic behaviour, suggesting that something more serious had happened.

CURIOUS TO SEE the courageous little woman who had set a new record in feminine athletics, noted society writer Miss M.J. Dewar called at the Windsor Hotel on March 9 and reported: "I was surprised to find her so slight and girlish; her vivacious, frank personality greatly attracted me. I thought I had seldom seen a more winning smile. Rouge or powder would have been wasted on Mrs. Dill's healthy, tanned complexion. She radiated life and vigour, and impressed me as being full of 'pep.'"

Mrs. Dill was clad in a hiking costume, Miss Dewar said, and looked very athletic in her riding breeches, which Jenny told her were ideal for walking.

She could not possibly have undertaken the trip in skirts, she claimed. The couple travelled light; their baggage was checked and sent ahead to the next stopping place.

"Her merry laughter rang out as she disclosed some of the more entertaining experiences of the trip," said the enthusiastic reporter. "For instance, at one point along the train tracks, a light engine overtook them, and the driver invited them to jump on. When they declined, he sped away—. They noted that a hobo walking the ties some distance ahead of them was not offered a ride by the same engine driver."

"He was evidently just trying us out," Jenny offered, "seeing if we were on the square."

On another occasion, just outside of Sherbrooke when they left the track for a short time, an automobile overtook them.

"'Jump in boys,' invited the driver," Frank said. "That really tickled Jenny. And when the invitation was refused, the motorist drove off with his friends raising his cap."

The Dills were touched and inspired by the interest and curiosity shown by the passengers and crew of the Halifax–Montreal train, who looked out for them and then entertained them with an impressive show. "The engine driver tooted the horn to give them warning, then passengers, chefs, and waiters in their white clothes lined up at windows, in doorways, and at the rear of the train, yelling congratulations and cheering them on."

"At McAdam," Jenny said, "we were actually treated too well by Mr. and Mrs. McLennan who made us feel ashamed for taking things from them."

Asked if she had seen any bobcats, such as the Behans described, Mrs. Dill showed great amusement, but she did admit to being nervous about passing through mountainous and wooded country in case a bobcat or lynx did appear. "The largest animal we have seen was a deer and the smallest a field mouse—nothing more ferocious," she said.

Only once had they experienced real danger and that occurred when rounding a curve on a downgrade of the railroad, each holding a balancing pole. "We had just rounded the curve when we felt a vibration. Looking around we had only time to skip aside, for a locomotive was within ten yards of us," Jenny explained. "A curve made it impossible for the engine driver to see us, and as they had shut off steam for the descent, we didn't hear the engine approach."

Mrs. Dill imparted one very interesting confidence to Miss Dewar: the couple had been married only two years, and this trip was their honeymoon.

"So you are 'honeymoon hikers,'" Miss Dewar mused.

"Yes," Jenny agreed, "or you could call us the 'hiking honeymooners.'"

Mrs. Dill was delighted with her congratulatory messages from Halifax, especially the assurance given by Mayor Parker that the women of Nova Scotia were taking an interest in her achievement.

"We'll get to Vancouver," Jenny said, with new conviction. "There is no doubt about it."

And Miss M.J. Dewar had no doubt that they would.

MRS. FRANK DILL ADMITS
THAT HIKE TO COAST IS THEIR "HONEYMOON" TRIP
Noted Montreal Woman Writer
Gets "Startling" Confession From Mrs. Jenny.
Written Especially For The Halifax Herald
The Evening Mail
By Miss M.J. Dewar

To the relief of everyone, the Behans popped up alive and well at Eau Claire on March 9. They had hiked an impressive 70 miles in two days. On the way they were greeted by the 96-year-old Big Chief, Richard Ferris—the oldest living Indian of the Kegnecaig tribe—who had tramped 40 miles and canoed 12 miles in one day to meet them.

"Ferris was a pilot on the Ottawa River for 80 years," Jack said in awe. "He said he took the first load of sheep ever transported down the river, but they [the sheep] were attacked and killed by Indians before they reached their destination."

Jack and Clifford were flattered by the chief's attention, fascinated by his stories and only wished they had more time to listen.

"We need to stay on Burkman's heels," Jack told the old man.

Neither Burkman nor the Dills sent dispatches to Halifax the next day. It was believed that Burkman was still in North Bay, while the Dills were spotted leaving Montreal at 7:15 a.m. during a downpour.

THOUSAND DOLLARS ARE WAGERED BEHANS
WILL BE WITH BURKMAN SATURDAY

FATHER AND SON HIKERS DRAWING CLOSE
ON RIVAL, WHO LOSES WHOLE DAY.

Interest in the progress of the hikers is unflagging. On the contrary, with the Behans rapidly overhauling Burkman, sporting men in the city are beginning to develop an enthusiasm which finds expression in wagers... Last night, two-well known citizens put up the coin and wrote out cheques for a cool thousand, the bet being that the Behans would catch up to Burkman by Saturday.

The Behans had shifted gears, and were fast becoming the favourites to win the great transcontinental hike, but it was hard not to feel pity for Burkman, whose feet had given out on him. "The walking is rough," he complained. "The rock ballasts make it impossible to keep to the inside of the rails."

In a telegram from North Bay, Jack Behan sounded sympathetic: "Thirty-four miles today is our little bit and if I am not mistaken, we'll overtake Burkman by the weekend. According to what we could gather in North Bay, Charlie didn't get very far yesterday. He's having trouble with his feet and we can sympathize. The tramping is pretty bad around these parts."

Father and son had followed the Ottawa River for six days, bid it adieu at Eau Claire, and headed for Bonfield. They stopped for salmon trout at the Ottawa Hotel and left at 12:30 p.m. Three miles later, it began to snow. "The wind was pretty tough too, blowing right in our faces," Jack said.

He and Clifford reached North Bay at 6:30 p.m. and put up at the Queen's Hotel. "The highlight of the day was a letter from John Egan of Solos, South America, wishing us 'Good Luck!'"

The Dills bobbed up at St. Polycarpe Junction after covering a paltry 35 miles in two days. "Friends tried to keep us in Montreal," Jenny said in her night letter. "But we were focused on Ottawa and couldn't be dissuaded."

Decked out in raincoats, they persevered against fierce winds and blinding rain from Point Fortune through to St. Polycarpe. From there they intended to follow the Grand Trunk line to Ottawa. At the end of the day, they conceded that the extreme weather conditions impeded their progress, and their gains were less than hoped for, yet Jenny remained optimistic about catching their rivals. "The winter is practically ended and we hope to shortly greet the Behans and Burkman with a slap on the back," she reported gamely.

The Real Race Begins

POSITIONS OF HIKERS MARCH 12

Dills—At Greenfield, Quebec; 821 miles; out 39 days; did 26 miles yesterday

Behans—At Verner, Ont.; 1,170 miles; out 46 days; did 34 miles yesterday

Burkman—At ???, Ont.; ??? miles; out 54 days; ??? miles yesterday

Halifax—0 miles; Ottawa—871; Port Arthur—1,748; Winnipeg—2,170;
Vancouver—3,645

"Accordingto a telegram received from Behans last night, it looks as though the father and son hikers are cutting across country to head off Burkman without actually passing him on the road," the *Herald* informed readers on March 12.

Apparently Jack and Clifford had learned that Burkman never reported passing through Verner, Ontario. They had just travelled a daunting 34 miles and said that unless Burkman was able to put out an extra spurt, they would cut ahead of him somewhere in the Ontario woods the next day.

Charlie's friends claimed that Burkman was letting his rivals catch up with him and would then step out and lead them to Port Arthur, his hometown. The *Herald* acknowledged this was a possibility, but it was cautious. "Burkman stated yesterday that he would try and make 44 miles during the day, and the result of his efforts will be watched with interest," was the editor's strongest comment. "There is much wagered on the race which is now becoming close."

The Behans did not divulge their route or disclose how near they might be to Burkman. They did say that they were having an interesting time with the Indian chief at Beauche; they were much amused by his pioneer tales, which took place before the railroad was built.

Jack took time out to say how pleased he was to read in the Ontario papers that the Dills had reached Montreal. It was a gentlemanly gesture, since he had made his feelings about the couple quite public—but it also suggested that he didn't regard them as serious competition.

"The hiking honeymooners" made 26 miles after getting off to a bad start. "We wandered along the track, not noticing anything in particular, when we suddenly found to our horror that we had taken a route entirely different to the one leading to Vancouver, where we hope to greet Charlie Burkman, John Behan and his son Clifford," Jenny said.

After correcting their mistake, they made excellent time. At West Polycarpe, Mr. Hardy, the station agent, gave them such a grand welcome that they were sorry to leave; and Harry Collins, a great chap who was also at Hardy's, did much to make the hikers forget that they had taken the wrong route. They made very good time after leaving Hardy's and finished at Greenfield, where Jenny fell asleep plotting the couple's next moves. "The other hikers cannot be very far ahead, as we have been making great time," she yawned. "So it's dollars to doughnuts that we will overtake them before Winnipeg is reached... The Behans are close on Burkman's heels, and before long the Dills will be patting the Dartmouth men on the back, and then we will go after the lone hiker who has held the lead for many weeks." Her snoring did not awaken Frank.

THE BEHANS FAILED to overtake Burkman over the weekend. In fact, father and son hiked only 21 miles on Saturday, while Burkman bragged about covering 70 miles in two days—some accomplishment for a boy with sore feet and hiking alone.

"The great race between the Behans and Burkman has turned into a gallop," reported the *Herald*.

"The Behans may now be leading the lone hiker, but they have not let their friends in Halifax know it. If they are leading Burkman, they must be travelling some," Burkman's loyal friends jeered.

Burkman was now in a desolate part of the province, with few villages and people, which hampered the sale of postcards. There was little time for sales any-way, and in a Saturday night telegraph, the besieged hiker wrote: "Left Warren at eight-forty. Had a call for five, because I wanted to get to Sudbury in time to see a hockey match, but the hotel proprietor slept in, and I woke myself. Ate dinner at Markstay hotel, and when it turned cold in the afternoon and started to rain, I added a layer of oilskins. Reached Sudbury at ten, walked the rail most of the way; I have devised a roller skate conveyance to enable me to balance myself on the rails."

The next day, Burkman called on old friends in the city and didn't get away until 1:30 p.m. "Ate lunch with Mayor Lalhege and Mr. Andersen, the chief engineer of British American Metal Company of Murray. Cartier tonight; thirty-four miles from Sudbury," Burkman reported in conversation with the *Herald*. "Thirty-six miles yesterday."

The dispatch from the Behans, in Markstay on Saturday, was terse: "Left CPR Hotel Verner and had breakfast. Good soul proprietor—let off light, four dollars: bed, breakfast, big hearted. Tough walking today: rained, frost covered rails with ice. Saw a dog hit by a train and killed. Had dinner at Warren. Wilk, Attorney, Sheriff, and Barber gave us shave and signed Cliff's book… 21 miles."

By the time they reached Bailey, the Behans were so exhausted they didn't even know where they were—but they did know they were sleeping nine miles closer to Burkman.

BEHANS CATCH BURKMAN AND HIKERS
NOW RACE NECK AND NECK ON DOUBLE CPR TRACKS.

"The battle is on!" declared the *Halifax Herald* on March 14. Canada's greatest hiking contest was now at a neck-and-neck crisis. John Behan and his son Clifford, father and son hikers, and Charles Burkman had met, shook hands and played pool together. "But is it ALL OVER? The friendship was fine, but the men are out FOR HONORS," the editors assured readers.

The Behans set out from Halifax with avowed determination to catch the young hiker at Montreal. They failed. Burkman, in the meantime, ploughed along, alone. Day by day he lost his lead to the faster Behans. But they had company. The great out-of-doors was Burkman's ONLY COMPANION. Mile after mile he travelled without seeing A HUMAN BEING, without anyone to talk to… All this time he knew Jack Behan, an experienced hiker, was drawing up with him, and coaching his son, Clifford, in the hike to Vancouver.

And so, the chase has ended—AND NOW THE RACE BEGINS!

The hikers' interpretations of events were printed in the March 15 newspaper.

Jack Behan's Version

CARTIER, March 14.—We met heavy snow at Cartier, where we are even with Burkman…He took his medicine right and smiled. "High Balls" came from train officials who delivered the news to the people, and excitement ran high when we arrived at the station. We hit a clip of four miles an hour for five hours, but Burkman, with his patience, stuck like glue, and beat us two yards at the finish…Big race tomorrow. We are still confident of beating the Ontario man.

Burkman's Version

CARTIER, March 14.—Last night the operator at Chelmsford wired Azilda for me and received information that Behans were stopping for the night there, but evidently they had fooled the operator there to give me the wrong information, so this morning about two o'clock, the proprietor of Algoma Hotel woke me up and told me the Behans were in the next room. So this morning I thought I would start early and steal the march on them, but they started only a few minutes after me, and it was so dark, I could not see them, but when I reached Larchwood great was my surprise to see Behans on my heels. So I stopped and we congratulated each other and talked for a few minutes and started to hike on the rails, the Behans on one track and me on the other, keeping pretty even all the way. I found my side-car a great help and the Behans sure envied my idea, but I only wish the people of Halifax could have seen us, neck-and-neck racing along. The people at Windy Lake saw us and wondered what was coming, and they laughed when we explained that we were racing from coast to coast…We arrived in Cartier neck-and-neck and the people sure laughed when they saw us coming along the track.

"Jack and I played pool while Clifford 'manicured' and shaved," Burkman added. "The hike from here to Metagama is thirty-six miles, and being too far to go to today with no stopovers between, so will go there tomorrow."

While the *Herald* was sorting through the different versions and moving the story along, the Dills were the centre of attention in Ottawa. They had arrived on Saturday March 12, looking the very picture of health and good spirits.

"She looks five years younger than when we left Halifax in February," Frank told reporters. Like his wife, he too was "browned like an Indian and as keen as steel." It was obvious to all that the couple were thriving on the adventure.

The staff correspondent had nothing but admiration for Mrs. Dill:

When Mrs. Jenny comes swinging along with the Atlantic at her back and her feet set in the path to the Pacific, the women of Ottawa do not throw up their hands in holy horror. They recognize that Jenny Dill is playing like a true sports woman, one of the finest games in the world. Like the women of the Old Land, the women of this country, thousands of them realize that walking is nature's own cure for half the ills to which street-bred flesh is heir, from the Capital of Halifax to the Capital of Canada, on foot is a grand accomplishment for any woman.

Parliament Hill was pretty well deserted on Sunday, and after church the MPs and members of their families did the visiting that was denied them during the week. But on Monday the busy bustle began again, as it did for the Dills. Parliamentarians and their wives were in competition to show the lively couple the time of their lives. While the men folk entertained "hubby," the ladies would "show Ottawa to Jenny in all its parliamentary and social capitalism." According to Miss Alice Higgins, Ottawa society writer, there was a reception and all sorts of good times planned. The itinerary included a spread at the parliamentary restaurant. J.C. Douglas, MP for Cape Breton, had put in long ago for the post of host at this spread, and it was expected that many down-east members would be out in full force.

"Mrs. Jenny, of course, came in for the lion's share of attention," said the newspaper. "Ottawa has been for her from the start of this great transcontinental race. Everybody wants to see this little woman keep RIGHT ON HIKING and land at the other coast with a record set."

Mrs. Dill, with her pluck and daring, drew cheers and admiration from all corners of the city, and it was said that not since the great fire on Parliament Hill in 1916 had anyone been given such total acceptance and unencumbered entrance to the hallowed new halls and the multitude departments of state: "Even the old pukka sergeant-majors, guardians of the doors, whose frowns strike awe to ordinary hearts, thaw out when Jenny approaches them, and become her willing slave.

It was reported that one MP declared that an old, war-tried soldier here, smiled today for the first time since sixty-seven."

The athletic attire of Canada's premier pedestrienne was also worthy of commentary. "Ladies in breeches are not usually found in the house of parliament," Miss Higgins wrote. "Not that Members of Parliament object—they could hardly—when the lady looks as attractive as Mrs. Dill in her corduroys and mackinaw."

In the forenoon the Dills spent time getting acquainted, and by afternoon they felt almost competent enough to lead the house. There was a Nova Scotia reunion just before lunch, following which the whole party adjourned to the parliamentary restaurant as guests of Alex McGregor of Pictou and Mr. Douglas of Cape Breton. Frank and Jenny lost considerable of their meal time becoming familiar with the forms and faces of outstanding figures in Canadian public life, and then, after a round of picture-taking, A.L. Davidson, the member for Digby and Annapolis, acted as guide on a tour of the city's sights. Of particular interest to them were the Mint and Archives.

"We saw dimes made a great deal faster than any two pedestrians could pass out postcards," Jenny said.

Their tour also included a trip to the National Art Gallery and the Victorian museum, which had been destroyed by the parliamentary fire in 1916.

The couple received a hearty welcome and a generous donation from A.R. Moscher, Grand President of the Brotherhood of Railroad Employees, an organization of which Frank Dill was a former member.

The hikers had earlier been invited to the home of the Honourable F.B. McCurdy, one of Nova Scotia's MPs, for Tuesday afternoon, but it happened to be Mrs. McCurdy's reception day, and the Dills were not eager to make a formal call and risk encountering all the ladies of government circles with their card cases and white gloves. Jenny's reluctance to appear in her out-of-doors clothes was rivalled only by her husband's horror of experiencing a "receiving day," so they accepted Mr. McCurdy's offer of a second city tour instead, and his car was waiting for them when they returned to Parliament Hill.

After spending a corking good afternoon, which included a visit to Rideau Hall, home of the Governor General, the Dills were entertained at a second spread in the parliamentary restaurant. Mr. Davidson; Colonel H.B. Tremain, member for Hants County; the *Herald* representative; and other distinguished persons clustered at nearby tables. Alice Higgins hosted the evening soiree.

"We do punish the food," Mrs. Dill admitted to the guests, looking down at the menu card. Later, when the fish arrived, she admitted candidly what all easterners say when they eat fish inland: "But this isn't fish—you have to come down home to get fish."

Following dinner, the couple chose to have more entertainment on Parliament Hill over a visit to the theatre.

"The best day yet" is how Jenny described it later in her night letter, insisting that they would not forget Ottawa and all the fine people who put everything aside for a time and contributed so generously to their entertainment and their finances.

When asked about their progress, the Dills said they had lost four clear days through storms and other handicaps. They were out 41 days from Halifax when they landed in Ottawa, having averaged over 23 miles a day on actual hiking time. The hikers had set their mark at 20 miles per day when they left Halifax, but from now on intended to average 25. Both made statements to the press insisting that they were not the same couple who left Halifax on the first of February. "It is a simple fact they do not mind a twenty-five mile hike any more than they would have minded one of a mile a couple of months ago," reporters wrote. "They take it as a good joke when people doubt their ability to go through to the Pacific on time. It is all in a day's work with them now."

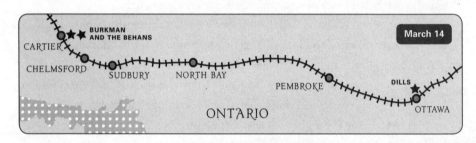

AS THE DILLS quit Ottawa on March 15, Alice Higgins offered up her final comments to the public. She was especially interested in Jenny, she said, and held her under close scrutiny as the female participant in the race, noting that Mrs. Dill was too keen on the outdoor life to want to stay around the city very long, and no theatres or comfortable society affairs could tempt her.

"'Are we downhearted?'" Higgins asked. "Mrs. Frank Dill's answer to the old war-cry is as strong as the soldiers used to sing it—and that after treading all the countless ties that separate Ottawa from Halifax. Railroad ties they are."

"Of course there are days when I'm tired," Jenny admitted, "because walking is like anything else. Some days it feels more like work." But equal work for men and women was never more accurately illustrated than it was in the Dills' work days. "Of necessity their mileage is the same but, as a matter of fact, Mrs. Dill keeps ahead of her husband. His step is longer, and when he gets ahead, she finds it more trying to keep up. The thought of the step and a half she must take to cover one step of his hasn't a good mental effect, she found. So, just to be on the safe side, she keeps in the lead, and the very striving to keep the lead makes the time go faster."

The March 16 *Herald* reported that no clear winner in the neck-and-neck race between the Behans and Burkman had emerged over the weekend. This was confirmed by the hikers in dispatches from Pogma. Hiking conditions in Northern Ontario continued to be brutal.

"I left Cartier at nine and had dinner at Benny, at the Puly Wood Camps," Burkman wrote. "It was the best meal I have had since leaving Truro. Villages are pretty scarce here, with stations few and far between. I was up at five this morning but could not start on account of the storm. The Behans arrived here tonight soon after I did. They are determined to stick with me, tho' I am trying my best to shake them off."

The Behans too had suffered through the long walk from Cartier to Pogma. "Big storm has been raging all day and we have not made more than 23 miles," Jack reported with disappointment. "Reached Pogma soon after Burkman…It snowed all night and the snow was six inches deep when we left Cartier this morning, so the walking was very hard…Although the race with Burkman is a great human test, we are confident of wearing him down before next week. And if it is fine tomorrow, we will show him our heels."

TUMULTUOUS STORMS THROUGHOUT Ontario the next day made it impossible for the *Herald* to track down Burkman or the Behans. Where they spent the night was anybody's guess. The Dills, however, sent a cheerful dispatch from Glasgow, Ontario. They had left Carp at 7:30 that morning on the tail end of a sleet storm.

"A beautiful sight when the sun came up," Jenny enthused. "We were met at Kinburn by very nice people who treated us to ice cream and chocolate cake, ate dinner at Arnprior, and arrived at Glasgow at four-thirty to celebrate a twenty-six mile tramp."

Without a copy of the *Herald* to keep them informed, it was not easy to stay current. That night Jenny fell asleep wondering where the boys were.

FRIENDS OF THE Behans and Burkman were relieved to see their adventures back in print the next day. The hikers admitted that they were just trying to get the advantage; so far, no one had succeeded.

Charles Burkman sent a telegram from Biscotasing, Ontario, describing the great hospitality they continued to receive. The agent at Pogamasing wouldn't let them pass until they had something to eat, and as soon as the hikers arrived at Wye, the station agent, Mr. Kingston, started to fix up a place in the trapper's cabin for them.

In his dispatch from Biscotasing, Jack claimed that he had never slept better in his life. In the morning, their big-hearted host had a wonderful breakfast waiting for them—as well as sandwiches for the road. The walking was bad, though they ate a memorable dinner of bacon and beans at the Metagama Lumber Camp. "It is the one meal I will always remember," Jack said, "as it only cost a dollar!"

"Mr. Bates at the lumber camp is Canada's great Airedale dog raiser and he took us around his kennels," Jack told readers. "He is a Nova Scotian, and belongs to Louisburg, and if we stayed until he finished talking dog, we would have been there yet—even if he knew what he was talking about. He sure had some great dogs. I had lost a glove about two miles down the track, so he gave the dog the other glove to smell, and away the dog went. And it wasn't long before the critter returned with the glove."

The Behans arrived at Eureka at 6 p.m. The section men, mostly French boys, urged Jack and Clifford to stay for supper and spend the night. "We didn't pass up the offer of hospitality, because in this lonely country you never know what is in store for you," Jack admitted.

The Behans left Eureka for Roberts the next morning at 8:30, unable to get a wire back to Halifax. They had dinner with the boss of Shannon Lumber Co., the largest fur dealer in Ontario, who showed them more beaver skins than they'd ever seen in their lives. "Canada is the best beaver country in the world," they were told.

Mrs. Shannon overheard Jack lament that it was St. Patrick's Day and he couldn't find a shamrock anywhere. "On the way to the station, the good old lady ran after us," he said. "She presented me with a box of cigars tied nicely with green ribbon and a bunch of shamrocks. It made me feel like a millionaire; afterwards, I walked a little better. Mailed the box home, and set off singing."

Jack told readers that Burkman was quite a vocalist: "He's short on wind, but with training could improve."

In a revenge remark, Burkman boasted that Halifax girls had nothing on Ontario girls.

A hobo they met at the station walked nine miles with them and had them laughing so hard they nearly fell off the rails. The hikers' camaraderie made it hard for them to break away from one another.

Jack noted that the station houses were five to nine miles apart and operated by weary-looking agents. They were now in "no man's land: Burkman country," he teased. Jack signed off their joint dispatch crowing that he had lost another four pounds since meeting Burkman and was feeling better than he had 20 years ago.

Meanwhile, the spirited Dills tramped 26 miles from Glasgow to Cobden, making significant gains on their rivals. At Haley, when they went into a store to buy a drink, a kind Miss Crozier presented them each with a hot cup of tea. Their spirits were further lifted by a gentleman in Cobden, where they spent the night, who said he was betting on Jenny to win the hike—and when Frank gave out, she was to send for him. Jenny was sorry to learn that the Behans had overtaken Burkman.

11

Cat-and-Mouse

During the third week of March, heavy storms in northern Ontario had Burkman and the Behans working hard for every mile they gained. In the cold, still air of the lumber camps that they passed, smoke spilled from the chimneys and hovered above small kitchen windows lit with kerosene lamps, illuminating people starting the day.

For three long days the hikers struggled, playing cat-and-mouse, with neither team able to gain a definitive advantage, but then on March 18, Burkman finally gave the Behans the slip at Woman River and the race was wide open once again.

Burkman had stopped at Woman River to swallow a quick bowl of hot buck-wheat laced with dried cranberries and thin milk. When he was informed by telephone that the Behans were entering the town, he set off again.

Jack had naively believed that Burkman would wait for them there. "We were confused, and we didn't know whether to stay the night or push on after him—especially since the lad had already covered 26 miles." The next sleeping place was 10 miles farther along, and if they didn't reach it, they would have to spend the night in the woods. "Not something we would relish doing."

Frank and Jenny Dill, 350 miles behind the front-runners, faced a quandary of their own: could they actually win the race? When they left Nova Scotia on February 1, they were quite comfortable walking 22 to 25 miles a day. Jenny even told McNulty, back in St. John, that they had a dread of walking 44 miles a day, as their rivals were doing. Yet here they were, toughened up and quite capable of going farther, and encouraged by people to believe that they could win the big race. The steady gains the couple were making on the other hikers lent credibility to the idea.

At Petawawa, where they stopped to eat lunch with Mr. Price, the local roadmaster of the CPR, Mrs. Dill faced the situation with candour: "I guess some of the home folk awakened to the fact that we *are* in this race across the continent. They seemed to think that we would be left far in the distance. While we were a little doubtful ourselves at first as to whether we could compete with the other hikers' speed, I think we have demonstrated so far that we can do it even better.

"Province by province, day after day, we are tramping across the mighty nation," Jenny told readers. "Soon we will be in Winnipeg, and with continued good luck, we could see the heels of the Behans and Burkman."

As the Dills crunched along the railroad ties, heads butted against the icy winds, woollen-mitted hands jammed deep into the pockets of their sheepskin-lined winter coats, the tantalizing possibility was shaping a dream: "I want all the people to know that our enthusiasm in this hike has increased, because we have so much to look back on and know what we can do."

THE *HERALD* RECEIVED no word from the Behans over the weekend. It was a pretty safe bet that they had not caught up with Burkman, because if they had done so, many words would have been written, and much posturing would have followed.

Burkman appeared to be regaining his advantage. He checked in with the press from Chapleau on Sunday. "Heavy rain kept me from getting a good start on Saturday, but I travelled as far as Tohet before hanging up for the night with an Italian section gang. It was still raining the next morning when I set out, and by the time I reached Nemegos, I was soaked to the bone." The great spread he got from the station agent's wife was a boost to his dampened spirits.

The next morning Burkman forgot his gun when he left, but the agent at Nemegos shipped it ahead to Chapleau, and he was grateful to receive it. Over supper that evening at the YWCA, Burkman enjoyed the company of infamous world travellers:

I was excited to meet a man and his wife who are trotting around the world, Mr. and Mrs. Arthur Thibaudeau, who have nineteen thousand miles yet to go for the world's championship; when they will actually have covered fifty-nine thousand nine hundred and sixty-five by train and boat. He is the only one left of 327 competitors who left Vancouver on May 1st 1912. Time expires May 1st, 1925. We had supper together, and some very interesting stories were told... Forgot to mention that the Thibaudeaus are accompanied by a son, sixteen months old.

While Burkman was exchanging hiking adventures with the world travellers, the Dills were toiling through a freak winter storm. "We travelled thru an electrical storm from Petawawa that nearly broke my nerves," Jenny wrote. "We reached Moore Lake at 5:15 tonight, shattered and worn. (27 miles for us today)."

The thunderstorm had started a few miles out of the military camp founded in 1905 and named after the Petawawa River. "For a few miles, I wanted to turn back, but Frank wouldn't hear of it, so we kept right on with rain assaulting us at every step...Now we know why they call this Thunder Bay," Jenny said.

A fine dinner was served the Dills at Chalk River, but they couldn't stop long to enjoy it. They were now seriously committed to catching their rivals before Winnipeg. Jenny was glad to learn that Charlie had given the Dartmouth men the slip. "That chap seems bent on reaching the coast before the Behans and we give him credit for his nerve as the tramp must certainly be a lonesome one without a partner," she said. Congratulations where they were due seemed a good motto to espouse.

Relaxed and safe from the storm, Jenny was again in good spirits. "We hope to make at least 25 miles tomorrow. Weather permitting, we might even cut off thirty."

THREE DAYS PASSED without any word from the Behans. Not even Burkman could shed light on their whereabouts. In a terse dispatch from Nicholson, Burkman admitted to being as anxious as anyone about their disappearance. According to the *Herald*, "The silence from the Behans is exciting hiking fans more than ever and numerous phone calls are received at The Herald office enquiring if there is any word. Expectation runs high awaiting the message that shall tell whether they have been able to get the lead on the doughty lone hiker or whether they must admit that Burkman outdid them."

The editor continued to downplay the situation, assuring the public that the hikers were now in remote areas: "Instead of the hotels of Moncton, St. John, Montreal and Ottawa, and the scores of places they have passed thru in Nova Scotia, New Brunswick, Quebec and Ontario, they now must depend often upon the hospitality of section men and the lone cabins of outpost settlers. It should be no surprise, therefore, if a few days passed without hearing from them."

Reporting from Klock, Ontario, Jenny claimed that she and Frank had been informed of the intensity of the race between Burkman and the Behans during a brief hiatus at Deux Rivieres before resuming their chase.

"The road conditions are improved over yesterday," she said. "All the same, we battled through slush and mud for 24 miles. How we long for spring!"

The Dills left Moore Lake at 8:40 a.m. and travelled several miles before taking a lunch break. "The walk was a dreary one as we tramped for 23 miles without ever seeing a post office or house. At Deux Rivieres, we had dinner, which was prepared so tastily that we were able to cover the last miles of the journey in good spirits."

WHEN THE BEHANS and Burkman failed to send a dispatch to the *Herald* the next day, even the newspaper became anxious, revealing that "all the operators along the Canadian Pacific Railway Lines in Ontario failed up to three o'clock this morning to get any word from the three men. The Herald has kept the wires hot for three days for news from the Behans." However, a rumour circulated that the Behans tried to slip past Burkman by taking a trail through the woods—a ruse to beat Burkman to Port Arthur, his home town—but had got lost.

The silence of both parties caused one worried citizen to write to the *Herald*, expressing hope "that Burkman, who is alone, will not be lost as it takes days and sometimes weeks for lost parties to find their way out of Ontario woods which skirt along Lake Superior."

Only the Dills sent in a night wire that evening. It packed a wallop and provided a welcome distraction from concern for the other hikers.

"We were attacked by a wolf!" Jenny said. "When we telegraphed yesterday, we stated that we would make 25 miles today, but we were feeling so good over an adventure that we had en route, that we decided to make 30 miles… Walking peacefully along the track, our attention was suddenly attracted by the baying of an animal a hundred yards or so behind us, and before we could say Jack

Robinson, a big timber wolf sprang at Frank. I drew a revolver from my belt and fired. The bullet stopped the wolf, and Frank killed it seconds later with his .35 calibre pistol." The Dills buried the animal in a snowbank before carrying on to their evening destination.

Jenny was very grateful to the boys of Dartmouth for giving her a gun as a departure gift. "We will have our guns oiled up before leaving Rutherglen, as we now expect to again battle a few wolves.

"This is the best day we've had since leaving Halifax," she added. "And I cannot get the idea out of my head that this is some kind of omen, and we were meant to reach Vancouver first."

THE BEHANS FINALLY surfaced at Nicholson on Thursday March 24. They had followed a false tip given to them by an Indian guide. "Lost 50 miles trying to gain 100 on Burkman," Jack admitted.

Father and son left the CPR tracks shortly after passing Woman River. They were told that a branch line used by lumber operations would cut 100 miles off their trip. "After travelling for a day we came to a lumber camp and were told that the tracks ended there and the only way we could get back on the main line of the CPR was to retrace our steps. This we did—peeved but wiser—determined to never again put faith in Indian guides."

A bleak financial situation was adding to the Behans' woes: "Weather conditions are unfavourable and we have to make certain distances daily to make connections for each night. Weather is not fit to camp out in, in such a wild and dreary country. We have found it very difficult to sell cards, but are able to pay our way so far, and will pull thru I hope. This will be the worst part of our journey. When we get to Port Arthur, we will then come to habitation, where we will get along better financially."

At Esher, the Behans met a generous Nova Scotian operator, Mr. McIsaac, who arranged dinner for them six miles down the track, where Mr. Freeborne prepared a tasty boiled cabbage and potatoes dinner. In appreciation, Jack and Clifford gave him one of their cards before leaving for Nicholson, where L.A. Goodwin, an agent formerly from Yarmouth, Nova Scotia, arranged a bountiful supper and a night's rest.

It had been an emotional week for the Behans, and after reading a back issue of the *Herald*, Jack was overcome: "It was better to us than a day's rations, to once more see our paper."

Refuelled and refocused, the Behans spent a good night and awakened the next morning raring to take on the lone hiker—if they could find him.

While the lost were being sought after by the many, few appeared to be paying serious attention to the Dills. "We completed a 26 mile hike to North Bay in bright sunny weather, and enjoyed every minute of it," Jenny chirped.

At Rutherglen, Mrs. J. Campbell packed them a lunch, which they ate on a pile of railway ties, watching rabbits dance around them. "The weather was very warm and the rabbits did not have the colour of fur one sees in the winter time when the animals are on sale at the Halifax meat markets. I guess they too were on a hike, as after getting a bit of our grub, they scampered off along the railroad track."

The Dills had been well received at North Bay, and many people had extended personal invitations to spend the night. "It was not easy to choose, but we accepted an invitation from CPR engineer Robert Davidson, a mile from Bonfield. He threw us a note from his cab inviting us home." Mrs. Davidson treated them splendidly, even providing a big basket of delicious fruit and sandwiches for the road next day.

After reading about the latest Burkman/Behan cat-and-mouse games, Jenny reaffirmed her solemn prediction: "There will be another team in that race within the next six weeks…as we now feel positioned to go after a record."

THE NEXT DAY, Mrs. Dill announced what appeared to readers to be an about-face: "We are hoping Charlie wins and only wish we had as many friends along the route as this boy has. Everywhere we go the people speak in glowing terms of Burkman and say that they hope that he beats out the Behans. If I were back in Halifax, I would have some startling stories to tell the readers. Just know that the Dills are with Burkman to win." So were the Dills out to win or not? Her night letter was puzzling.

The Dills had hiked 23 miles, from North Bay to Sturgeon Falls, and were satisfied with their progress, since they had been obliged to hold up and have their boots repaired.

"How can we complain when people are so good to us," Jenny said. "The railroad men along the line provided us with no end of pampering."

The couple even enjoyed receiving the back issues of the paper sent by Frank's attentive mother. "The old red headlines and the great make-up of the paper certainly look good to us," Jenny said.

Burkman didn't make an appearance on Good Friday as nervous friends had predicted. The attitude of the always pragmatic *Herald* was that Burkman had a gun, and if he was able to find food, he should be fine.

The no-show of Burkman left the Behans shadowboxing: they carried on at their own speed, but in a vacuum. "It was a real day for us," Jack smiled, ruefully. "We cooked dinner on the side of the road, made tea and sat around like real pioneers." After a one-hour break, he and his son hiked into Franz, where they put up for the night. "It has been a fine day and we are feeling 'Jake,'" Jack said.

ANXIETY ABOUT BURKMAN increased the next day, as the lone hiker had not broken his silence for three days, and worried friends were told that he was probably still plugging along through the vast wilderness of northern Ontario.

Since the Behans didn't mention their rival by name in their dispatch, readers assumed they continued to trail Burkman and didn't know his whereabouts. The father and son team had intended to reach Amyot on Friday "but we ran into a railway man's shack three miles this side of the village," Jack chortled, "and were treated so hospitably that we decided to remain for the night."

The Dills may have felt concern for Burkman's welfare, but it certainly was not affecting their pace. "We reached Hagar after doing 26 miles and were put up in great style," said Jenny. Her message, as usual, was brief and cheerful.

THE LONE HIKER was overtaken by his Dartmouth rivals on March 26 at White River, Ontario—a place traditionally thought to be the coldest spot in Canada.

"No doubt there will be some anxiety among my friends in Halifax and throughout Nova Scotia, owing to my failure to send in reports during the past few days," he said. "The fact is that the telegraph operators along the line were tipping me off as to the progress of the Behans, and I was able to keep ahead of them. On Friday, however, Jack got wise to what was going on and they made a determined effort to catch up, because today they overtook me at White River and so, the three of us are together again." But after a two-day visit in his hometown of Port Arthur, young Charlie intended to show the Dartmouthians his heels. "I will beat them on the stretch between Port Arthur and Winnipeg," he vowed.

Jack announced to readers that he, Clifford and Charles were "star artists" in a White River "Y" lecture that day. On reaching the town, the three hikers discovered that they were all expected to lecture at the YMCA. "Mr. Bamforth, the railway superintendent, met us at the station after our twenty-one mile hike, and invited us to tea. This is the first for the 'Y' I can tell you." On reaching the building, the hikers found all the citizens of the community—men, women and children—waiting to hear their hiking stories. "Rev. Mr. Simpson was present and took the chair, of course."

Jack Behan was first to recount some of his favourite hike anecdotes. Burkman was next and amused the crowd with stories about the operators who gave him daily postings of the Behans' whereabouts for almost a week, before they smelled a rat. Clifford, the last to speak, brought the house down in laughter when he told the congregation what poor cooks Jack and Charles were, always upsetting the tea or burning the bacon.

"Rev. Mr. Simpson concluded the entertainment with kind words and prayed that we would be spared any real hardships on our tramp to the west coast," Jack said. "Then after several songs were sung by the ladies, we finally got to sell our post cards."

The Dills were unaware of Burkman's situation when they woke up in Warren, Ontario, on Saturday morning. After wolfing down a glass of milk and a plate of toast, the couple set off for Wanapitel, soon encountering a rainstorm. "After experiencing a thousand miles of hiking, weather conditions mean little to us," Jenny said dismissively. "We took a short respite from the rain, at Markstay, and then plodded on to Wanapitel for dinner. See if you can pronounce it," Jenny challenged readers in her evening telegraph.

It had been a day full of variety and pleasant incidents. "A kindly intentioned passenger on a train, wishing perhaps to stand the treat for us, threw us a sum of money," Jenny said. "And Mr. and Mrs. Arthur Thibaudeau—the globe-trotting family mentioned earlier by Charlie—passed us on an eastbound train en route to St. John. We tossed them one of our post cards and asked for one of theirs in return."

BURKMAN AND THE Behans continued to put up with each other's company for a few days after the White River revival meeting.

It was Burkman who wired from King the next day: "White River was the best town yet! The people could not do enough and especially the YMCA. They never charged a cent. We left at three-twenty, as it rained all night and kept up until late in the afternoon. We had lunch at the Tie camp...arrived at King, ten-fifteen and had a great supper, cooked up by the operators." Burkman noted that many people were asking him where Jenny Dill was and seemed to be interested in her progress.

While the *Herald* was reporting a "love-in" between Burkman and the Behans at King, trouble was brewing in the Dill camp at Cartier.

"It is not often that I sigh, but when we reached this little town tonight, I was tired and I sighed, good and plenty," Jenny said. "It was the hardest day yet, but we made 26 miles." Jenny noted that they had faced into a cold, raw wind from eight o'clock in the morning to five in the afternoon, with only a break for dinner at Larchwood.

Then she came over all girlie, adding: "Here is a little family squabble I must let you in on. The other day, I got a letter from Charlie Burkman and then again today, I got another. Now that is not so much, but we were told at the telegraph office that Burkman had again allowed the Behans to catch him. Now Frank has it that he intends to wait for us. I told him he was silly, but he said it looked 'fishy' to him."

BURKMAN SLIPPED AWAY from the Behans early Wednesday morning, headed for Heron Bay, but managed only 10 miles before his rivals caught up with him. "Not only did I have to stay with the Behans yesterday, but I had to sleep with them," Burkman complained to the newspaper. "I guess they do not intend that I should put anything over on them. Of course I would not, you know, but my bunk was hard, and I couldn't sleep very much. I got up early to stretch myself. When I saw Jack and Cliff snoring away, I thought I would start out on a little stroll. I had only gone about ten miles when I heard the hello of Jack Behan."

The truth is, it was 11 below zero and Burkman was happy enough to have company. The hikers walked 33 miles to Heron Bay. Jack and Clifford smoked to provide some warmth, while Burkman sang from behind a layer of scarves covering his face, leaving only his eyes exposed to the frigid cold.

On the way to the bay, the hikers took a break and visited J. Campbell's black fox ranch at Mobert, where they saw 20 registered foxes. "And we ate a dinner of ham, eggs, and everything nice at Helmo with J.R. Le Cours, the CPR operator," Jack said. "Le Cours served with me overseas. This makes seven of the old boys I've met who are operators."

The Dills did not fare as well as the other hikers. They covered only 20 miles to Fogamasing, Ontario, where Jenny noted: "Everybody is laughing at the way Burkman had given the slip to the Behans and how the Behans were sleeping like dogs do—with one eye open—and it on Burkman."

ON THURSDAY MARCH 31, it was the Behans who gave Burkman the slip as they became the first of the trans-Canada hikers to see the frozen expanse of Lake Superior. "The wind was very strong and the waves were running mountain high," Jack said. "A beautiful sight, one we will never forget."

The rail line impressed the men as well—"curving around and through cuts of rock hundreds of feet high on either side, demonstrating the great engineering carried out in building the line." The victorious hikers rested briefly at Peninsula after hearing from the locals that Governor General Victor Cavendish, the 9th Duke of Devonshire, was arriving in 10 minutes.

"When the train pulled in to the station to take on water, a burly policeman jumped off, so I approached him, requesting to see the Governor General and have him sign our book," Jack reported.

"The policeman stuck out his chest and said frankly, 'NO. IMPOSSIBLE.'"

But Jack boldly asked to see the Governor General's secretary. "Moments later a fine pleasant little man alighted from the train, and we presented our cards. He asked in a nice way if we would like to see the Duke. When we said, yes, he immediately boarded the car and in five minutes His Excellency was with us, asking us questions of our trip...Then the Duchess appeared and passed a tray of fruit."

The Governor General signed the Behans' hiking book, told them they had a beastly trip ahead of them and offered them a ride. They refused, of course, but "in a Royal way."

As the train was pulling out, the duke realized that he was still holding the Behans' book, so he ordered the train stopped. After the book was returned, the duke and duchess stood waving from the observation car, and the crowd cheered and waved until the train was out of sight.

After passing through the famous Middleton tunnels, the exhausted hikers made for the station house, arriving at 10:30 p.m. "For the first time in our hike, we have taken the lead," Jack exulted. "A friend of ours wired that Burkman had put up for the night and had retired."

While the gregarious Behans hobnobbed with near royalty, and Burkman continued to make the best of things, the Dills, with much to prove, pushed hard. They did battle with a wind that almost bored through them on their 20-mile hike to Biscotasing. "At times, I felt like finding a place to nap," Jenny said. "But I didn't." There was no time to dawdle if they wanted to finish first, and she knew it.

HIKING WAS A treacherous experience for the Behans on the last day of the month. They ran into a blizzard and made only 16 miles. "Snow, more snow and still snowing" was the best description Jack could find to describe the weather. "One h— of a day, the worst kind of day I was ever out in. Our position in the trail at the top of the page tomorrow will look sick, for we only did 16 miles today."

The station agent at Middleton had warned them not to leave that morning. He said storm signals had been sent all along Lake Superior, but they refused to listen to him. Two miles from the station, they were sorry they hadn't taken his advice. "How she snowed, how she blowed, and how the snow whirled," Jack said, waxing eloquent.

At times the hikers could walk only two miles an hour, and on one occasion they were forced to crawl over a 150-foot-long trestle bridge that was 60 feet high. Clifford had been very nervous. "With snow blinding my eyes, I crept ahead of the lad and told him to take his time and follow me. We kept to the middle of the track, so we wouldn't be blown into the gorge. Thank God we got over to the other side safely to Jackfish."

The station agent at Jackfish told the Behans that the telegraphers along the line had been trying to locate Burkman throughout the day, with no success. "Wire us at once if you've heard from Burkman," Jack told the editor of the *Herald* when they reported in. Then, too exhausted to hike any farther, the Behans hunkered down for the night to wait out the storm.

While the Behans were inching their way through the blinding snow, the Dills experienced an exhilarating 32-mile tramp in sunny, springlike weather. "62 miles in two days," Jenny announced. "And we increased our gain on the Behans and Burkman."

Before sitting down to an agreeable meal set out by their host at the telegraph station in Woman River, Mrs. Dill sent off a chatty night-letter brag, describing their overnight stay at a sawmill in Biscotasing. "Some people are under the impression that the beds in a lumber camp are not nice, but the bed we had last night was one of the finest we have ever used. And talk about real eats, why one could hardly want better food then that which we ate last night." The cook's wife, a good old soul, packed up a fine basket—which they hadn't asked for—and it had disappeared by the time they reached the next town.

The Dills were also pleased to receive a copy of the *Herald* from Mr. Kingston, the sawmill manager. "It certainly was a treat to get hold of Eastern Canada's leading journal again and find out what the folks back home are doing. It was almost as good as meeting someone from home."

Jenny recounted an adventure from the previous day, when a small animal darted out of the woods a few feet in front of them, nearly frightening them to death. "At first I thought it was another wolf and pulled my gun, but the animal proved to be only a rabbit, and neither Frank nor I wanted a shot." More importantly, the Dills knew that the woods were dense along the northern route, and it was not unusual for a lumberjack to make a sudden appearance: "Best to think first than to be sorry later!"

The hikers were amused to come across lumbermen dressed in outfits similar to their own, and they laughed when asked what camp they were working at. "When we informed them that we were hiking to Vancouver, they shrugged and proceeded to warn of possible dangers. When we told them that we had started at Halifax, they became interested and offered us advice on the short-cuts through here and told us to beware of prairie wolves after we pass Fort William." One of the lumbermen offered Frank a big plug of chewing tobacco, but as he was not a chewer, he refused the offer.

"We received a big ovation by the crew of a passing train last night and one of the passengers shouted: 'Good

A Perfect Day
(a.k.a. The End of a Perfect Day)

Words and Music by
Carrie Jacobs-Bond (1862–1946)

When you come to the end of
a perfect day,
And you sit alone with
your thoughts,
While the chimes ring out
with a carol gay,
For the joy that the day
has brought,
Do you think what the end of
a perfect day
Can mean to a tired heart ...
Well, this is the end of
a perfect day,
Near the end of a journey, too,
But it leaves a thought that
is big and strong,
With a wish that is kind
and true.
For mem'ry has painted
this perfect day
With colors that never fade,
And we find at the end of
a perfect day,
The soul of a friend
we've made. 1

Luck, Dilly and wife, go to it and beat the others.' They must have read in the *Herald* that we were part of the cross country race." Jenny was pleased by the gesture and sentiment offered by the crew and the passenger.

Nothing was heard from Burkman on March 31. The mouse appeared to be at an impasse with the cats.

12

The End of a Perfect Day

POSITIONS OF HIKERS APRIL 1
Dills—At Nemegos, Ont.; 1,345 miles; out 60 days; did 35 miles yesterday
Burkman—At ???, Ont.; ??? miles; out 75 days; did ??? miles yesterday
Behans—At Schreiber, Ont.; 1,615 miles; out 67 days; did 19 miles yesterday
Halifax—0 miles; *Port Arthur*—1,748; *Winnipeg*—2,170; *Vancouver*—3,645

Friday April 1, the Dills tripped lightly down the tracks and into the village of Nemegos, singing "The End of a Perfect Day." It was, too, according to Jenny. And no April fool's joke! The sky was blue, the air was crisp and the day was cold, but folks living close to the train tracks ventured out of their hastily thrown-together clapboard constructions to cheer the couple on.

"Strangers we passed on the route did a lot for us and it would take chapters to write of their kindness," Jenny said. "Everyone seemed interested in us and asked all about the trip to the coast. They told us that Burkman and the Behans are not making as fast a time as we are, and we should overtake them before reaching Vancouver."

Mr. Bryne, a gentleman they met on the platform at a small train station the previous night, had bought them each a box of the loveliest chocolates; two young girls offered them 50 cents to buy a present as well; and everyone wanted their postcards. Best of all, the hikers racked up another 35 miles from Woman River to Nemegos—establishing a personal best daily mileage. Something to sing about, indeed!

"We had planned to go only 25 miles, but I urged Frank to add another ten miles to the day's trip, he consented, and we arrived in this town feeling in the best of spirits. When one goes 35 miles in one day, it certainly keeps up the spirits."

Burkman travelled 39 miles Saturday and caught up to the Behans at Cavers, Ontario. "They were at the Post Office, picking up their mail, when I slipped in through the front door and smacked them on the back. They were some surprised!"

Burkman was peeved that his strategy to overcome his hiking rivals was being misinterpreted by friends and family. "I do wish my Nova Scotia friends would stop worrying about me," he said. "When I arrived here tonight, I had at least 20 telegrams which have been following me for three days. They all said: 'Boy where are you?'

"You must not think that the timber wolves have eaten me if you do not hear from me every day," he pleaded. "I am playing my own game... And I have found that sometimes telegraph wires leak." Burkman knew that the Behans were chummy with some of the telegraph operators along the way who kept them informed of his whereabouts, enabling the wily pair to steal a march on him. But he was back now, claiming to be in good shape and confident that he could remain even with the Dartmouth men until they reached Port Arthur—where he intended, "come hell or high water," to spend two whole days with his family, as promised.

Burkman had no illusions about the Behans, and he had a trick or two up his sleeve to deal with their cunning ways. "I expect the Behans will push along from Port Arthur and thus get a two-day jump on me," he admitted. "However, I know the country from Port Arthur to Winnipeg, and I want to tell you right here that the CPR is not the most direct route to the big prairie city. I know some highways that will cut off more than 100 miles to Winnipeg, and I guess that will make up for the two days' jump the Behans will get on me while I visit my folks... The Behans mean well, but you can take it from me, they are not planning to WAIT FOR ME."

He revealed that blizzard conditions had forced him to put up at a lumber camp in Schreiber the previous night. The howling wind and blowing snow blinded and disoriented him. Never had he been at the mercy of such weather. "At one stretch today around the lake, I walked 29 miles only to find myself exactly opposite where I was when I started out in the morning," he said. "That is enough to discourage anyone."

At Selim, Burkman was happy to share a simple meal of boiled bacon slabs and canned beans, washed down with well water, courtesy of the station operator. "He told me how the good sports in the camp *squealed* on Jack and Clifford, and how the sly Behans rose early every morning in order to give me the slip."

In a telegram to the *Herald*, the Behans got their story out to the public. "We were talking to a couple of boys from back home, Roy Smith and J.L. Connolly, when Burkman walked in on us," was Jack's unenthusiastic comment. He had thought they were well rid of the young upstart and was annoyed at the prospect of starting a new round of cat-and-mouse.

Terrific gales blowing down from the Canadian Shield kept the Dills at Chapleau for the night, grateful guests of the YMCA. "Even Frank complained about the walking, and agreed to stop," Jenny said.

THE NEXT DAY, Burkman and the Behans encountered a pack of angry wolves at a lumber camp outside Nipigon. "For once in my life I am glad not to be ahead of Jack and Clifford," Burkman said. "If I had been...I am certain there would have been one dead hiker."

Burkman had experienced many lonely nights since leaving Halifax, but never had he felt so vulnerable. "The Behans were just as frightened as I was," Burkman maintained. "And as soon as we saw [the wolves] running toward us, heard their snapping teeth, and witnessed their glowing eyes, we sensed we were in danger."

People disagree about whether timber wolves will attack humans, but the terrified hikers were not interested in confronting the feral creatures in order to find out. "With night coming on, we decided to make a run for a shack that Jack knew about four miles off the main trail and take refuge," Burkman said. For almost an hour the pack sniffed at their heels but was kept at bay by the weak beams from their flashlights. "The incensed creatures menaced us right to the shed. After we were inside, Jack slammed the door, and I leaned an old chair under the flimsy handle for safe measure."

The wolves took shelter nearby and continued to unnerve the hikers with a cacophony of wailing throughout the night. Burkman found it impossible to fall sleep. "And I don't think that the Behans got any more shut-eye than I did," he said. At daybreak the howling ceased and the beasts slunk into the shadows of the woods, leaving the hikers to ease themselves cautiously back to the railway tracks. Late morning found three tense hikers crossing the longest CPR bridge west of Maine, reaching the outskirts of Nipigon and safety. "We ate breakfast at the Commercial Hotel, happy to be alive," Burkman reported.

William McKirdy, the oldest resident in the village, laughed at them. And, after a good feed, the hikers felt up to exchanging a few anecdotes with the old-timer. They learned that McKirdy's son Jack had paddled the Prince of Wales down the Nipigon River during the prince's 1919 visit to Canada.

Port Arthur was still 65 miles distant, and Burkman told the *Herald* not to expect another dispatch from him until he reached the Port City. "The Behans," he said, "would probably go on a little further to Fort William."

The Dills did not experience such a thrilling day. "We managed to tramp the 24 miles to Nicholson despite the strong, cold winds, happy of an excuse to exchange the miseries of the weather for a dinner invitation," Jenny wrote. "We whiled away a few pleasant hours with some 'Down Easters' at dinner—among them, several folks from Halifax and Dartmouth—who said they'd been waiting for weeks to greet us.

"Before leaving...this morning, we were toured through the town and met many prominent residents, anxious to buy our postcards." Self-promotion was not a talent confined to the likes of Jack Behan.

A VIOLENT STORM kept Burkman and the Behans from reaching Port Arthur on April 5 as planned. "How the thunder did roar across Old Superior. How the flashes of electricity did glimmer over the waves, and how the torrents of rain did splash upon old mother earth," Jack wrote.

During the bad weather, the hikers took shelter with a Russian family and were fed a meagre meal of piroshki and what Jack suspected was shredded cabbage and ground bear meat. Several toasts of raw potato vodka followed before the hikers left for the village of Pearl down the line, where the station agent, Mr. Barr, and his wife, expats from Nova Scotia, welcomed them for a good visit and a proper midnight supper. The hikers were informed by their hosts that the Nipigon area was fast becoming a popular sporting destination for hunters and fishermen and was being laid out in building lots to sell to summer visitors.

Pleasant though it was to wait out the storm in good company, the men became overtly impatient to get on with the journey. "We are determined to reach Thunder Bay by dawn, leave Burkman to visit his parents, and carry on to Fort William," Jack told their genial hosts.

Lest he sound too ungrateful, Jack explained to the Barrs that "Burkman will have a big advantage over us from Port Arthur to Winnipeg, for he knows every inch of the roads. There are many shortcuts which will cut off anywhere from one to two hundred miles by leaving the tracks, so we will need the two days he is resting at home to get a good start." Having already been sidetracked once too often, the Behans were not looking for shortcuts. "Once bitten, twice shy," Jack said.

The storm subsided at first light, and the hikers struck out for Port Arthur (now Thunder Bay). Mr. McKay, a native of Londonderry, Ontario, walked three miles down the tracks to meet them, and hundreds of people were at the station to greet Burkman when he arrived. After a short goodbye, Jack and Clifford strode off toward Fort William, happy to leave the lad behind with friends and family.

The Dills lopped off another 36 miles from their long jaunt to the coast and spent the night at Missanabie, professing renewed enthusiasm for their "hop" to Vancouver. "We also ran into bad weather after leaving Nicholson," Jenny volunteered. The lightning was so fierce that it almost scared her to death. "But after going a few miles, I decided to take a chance, and be brave like Frank, who did not seem to mind the dangers of the storm." Shortly before entering Missanabie, the couple were shocked to come across the body of a dead cow ... evidently killed by lightning. "The rain was so heavy; we stopped at Missanabie for the night. Our clothes are soaked thru and we will perhaps need repairs to our boots, since the muddy roads are playing havoc with the soles. We have been advised by local Indians to use adhesive plaster on our feet, to prevent blistering."

Rumours that the Behans and Burkman had passed through Missanabie the previous week raised their spirits and fed their optimism. "We are on their trail, which should end shortly if all goes well," Jenny said.

Port Arthur Station, Ont. Violent storms around Port Arthur made for hard going for all the hikers.
Thunder Bay Public Library P1878

WHEN JACK AND Clifford reached Fort William, Mr. McFarlane, the CPR station operator, shared his copy of the *Herald* with them. "And you can be sure we gave it a thorough read through," Jack said. "We had a marvellous day. And will be on the journey again at nine tomorrow morning." After a brief hesitation he added: "Hope Charlie is having a pleasant time at his home."

Nineteen cards and letters from all over eastern Canada—as well as a letter from Thos. Godfrey, proprietor of the Royal Hotel, Strand, England—awaited the Behans at the post office at Fort William. Mr. Trembley, manager of the Royal Theatre in the city, phoned them for an account of their trip and extended an invitation to tell their adventures to the Wednesday-night theatre audience, after which they were treated to dinner and an entertainment by Alderman Firth, an excellent ragtime aficionado. "So good that we didn't hit the quilts until around 1:30 a.m.," Jack laughed.

Frank and Jenny enjoyed the day as well. After a pleasant walk from Missanabie to Franz, the couple were enchanted by a dazzling display of butterflies. "They led us in a merry dance right to the heart of the village," Jenny sighed. "The butterflies are so thick that we believe we will be favoured with warm weather from now on out."

Eager to improve on their daily distances, the Dills enjoyed a day of extremes. They left Missanabie so early, they were forced to carry lamps to light their way for the first six miles; then, close to noon, the weather became so hot that they had to carry their heavy coats. "When we reached Franz, men were going around in their shirt sleeves as they would during a regular mid summer day," Jenny told the *Herald*.

That evening over dinner, Mrs. F.C. exchanged pleasantries with their hosts—although her mind never strayed far from the facts of the race. "I'm sure that the storm which held up Burkman and the Behans at the Bay has given us a chance to make a big gain," she said. "We can't be more than 200 miles behind them now."

THE WEATHER CONTINUED to be unseasonably warm throughout Ontario, and the Behans went shopping to replace their winter caps with lighter gear before they left Fort William.

They stopped briefly at city hall on their way out of town to have their books signed by Mayor Dennis and the city clerk, and a *Journal-Times* reporter collared them and took them to his office. After he "loosened them up," Jack's tongue began to flap at both ends, and hiking secrets were disclosed. "Burkman told us that he planned to stay at home for two days, but promised he'd soon catch up with us," the elder Behan laughed. "Young Charlie is way off in his predictions. He will probably read in the papers—miles behind us—of our entry into Vancouver."

In their dispatch, the Dills were bursting with compliments for all the fine people of northern Ontario. Manager McDougell of the Franz Hotel had been such a glorious host during their stay, and the wonderful people of Amyot had treated them so well, that Dill money had been considered "counterfeit" at the hotel. Mr. McDougell would not even let them buy their own lunch for the road.

Hundreds of schoolchildren were out picking mayflowers on the hills and in the hollows between Franz and Amyot as they passed by, and Jenny remarked how wonderful it was to see little children dressed for summer romping in the fields, which only a few days earlier had been covered with snow.

Temperatures continued to soar throughout the day, forcing the couple to slacken their gait so they could "keep the hot, hot sun from burning Frank's face," already tender from a sunburn received over the previous days. At Gasset, 23 miles later, Mrs. Davis had a delicious meal of stuffed game birds waiting for them. "You should have seen Frank assault the mashed potatoes," Jenny exclaimed, "and we both devoured two servings of rice pudding."

The Dills were jubilant to have covered 28 miles in just eight hours—their fastest average yet, Jenny said. They spent the night at the Amyot train station.

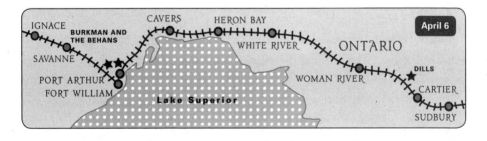

13

Hungry for "Beans"

POSITIONS OF HIKERS APRIL 9

Dills—At Peninsula, Ont.; 1,566 miles; out 68 days; did 24 miles yesterday

Burkman—At Kaministiquia, Ont.; 1,775 miles; out 83 days; did 27 miles yesterday

Behans—Savanne, Ont.; 1,851 miles; out 75 days; did 31 miles yesterday

Halifax—0 miles; *Kenora*—2,050; *Winnipeg*—2,170; *Vancouver*—3,645

Burkman was back in competition on Monday April 9. "Well I'm away again," he wrote from Kaministiquia, Ontario. After spending two days at home, he told friends that he was raring to go and hungry for "Beans" (Behans). It took courage to start out again from his home, with the prospect of going the full half distance to Vancouver alone, "but I have given my word and intend to honour it," he said.

Charlie was well aware of the jokes Jack and Clifford were telling about him and was happy to return the favour. Noticing that the Behans were just 200 miles off the shortest route to Winnipeg, he remarked, "At that rate, and with good luck, I am already two days ahead of them."

"That is the first joke I have cracked on the hikers," he said, "although I know there have been many going around since I left Halifax."

Burkman was equally candid about his letters to Jenny Dill: "Dill accused me of waiting for Mrs. Dill to catch up with me. He need have no fear about that! It's true that I did write twice to encourage her along, because I think she is the pluckiest woman in Canada to start out on such a trip. However, I am not waiting for any woman; I intend to reach Vancouver ahead of all the other hikers."

Burkman spent only a few hours at Fort William before setting off, stopping to spend the night with A. Johnson at Kaministiquia, where, it turned out, he had spent the entire winter of 1917, prowling the wilds of northern Ontario.

The Behans made no mention of Burkman in their dispatch. They had spent one evening at Raith, entertained by Dan Connors, formerly of New Glasgow and now the hosteller of the Canadian National Hotel, who put them up for the night. Connors was in the 85th Battalion and was one of Jack's war buddies "who sure knew how to party." The next morning Connors could be seen howling drunkenly after the Behans as they strode out of town: "Go to it you herring chokers."

"It was a great day for travelling," Clifford wrote—making an unusual appearance in print. "We saw partridges all along the line, and if there hadn't been a fifty dollar fine against poachers in place, I might have popped a few with my trusty rifle."

At Savanne, Jack and Clifford declared that they were now officially halfway to Vancouver. They celebrated the occasion with section foreman Mr. Olson. "1,851 miles—and the rest of the distance down hill until the Rockies!" Clifford larked.

The Dills announced on Saturday that they had only managed to cover 64 miles in two days—40 miles on Friday and 24 on Saturday.

"We didn't find sleeping accommodations the previous night, so we left the tracks in favour of a rutted road, slipping and sliding in thick mud in the dark, through a number of small villages where people slept peacefully, not knowing that two coast-to-coast hikers were passing their doors." The couple finally reached Peninsula, where two telegraph operators, Fleishman and LeCours, greeted them warmly, offering hospitality. "Although the station was small, the food was good and the company delightful," Jenny said.

The weather had improved by the next morning, but Jenny's boots were as hard as rocks. She had put them by the stove to dry, but the mud had become like plaster. "They caused me such agony along the tracks whenever I hit a small rock that I wanted to scream out with pain." After a few miles, the Dills were forced to stop long enough to buy goose grease and give the boots a brisk rubdown. It had not been their best day.

THE TELEGRAMS FROM all the hikers were short and to the point the next night. The Dills put in a punishing day, rounding Lake Superior between Peninsula and Jackfish, and hiking through the tunnels. The station agent at Jackfish treated them to a big supper of salted white fish, boiled potatoes and freshly baked flatbread.

Jack Behan signed in from Ignace. Father and son had enjoyed the scenery along the route and benefited from a fresh catch of rainbow trout taken by their host in an ice-fishing adventure. "If only some of the Halifax anglers were here they would enjoy a real fish," he said. Enthusiasts greeted the hikers outside the telegraph office at Ignace and insisted on showing them the town, which "was quite a task," Jack complained, "after walking 36 miles during the day." However, the men padded around town until the crowd was through with them. "Then we were taken in hand by Engineer Doan who paid for our supper and breakfast the next morning. The YMCA offered to bed us for the night," Jack added. "The secretary refused to accept any money, so we were able to bank some of the hard earned cash from the sale of our post cards, and we didn't have to draw on the treasury."

Burkman left Kaministiquia at 10; had dinner at Stewart's Mill in Sunshine, where he enjoyed the company of several old friends; ate a baloney and fried egg sandwich and downed a glass of milk at Buda, before tackling a harrowing walk through a long tunnel; and continued to walk as far as Raith. He was pleased to cover the final four miles in 48 minutes and 30 seconds. "That should have the Behans sweating!" he thought.

ALTHOUGH JACK AND Clifford didn't retire until midnight in Ignace, they were up early the next morning. After a second forced trip around town and a meal of garlic sausage, stale bread and pickles with an Italian section man, they finally pushed off to Tache, where they were mobbed at the train station.

"The farther we go, the more people seem to know about us," Jack told the newspaper. "We are sure popular as hikers go, and we are going some."

Jack was having the time of his life, and he couldn't thank the paper enough for their excellent exposure. "This hiking puts new life into one. Here we are, Cliff and I, feeling like two Jack rabbits, and to tell the truth, we will be sorry when the hike is over."

The cross-Canada competition filled a void in the returned men's lives. Family life and unemployment could hardly be expected to compete with a hard day's walking and the fellowship of former comrades over a whiskey or two, or more, at night.

While the Behans were being overwhelmed by the good people of Ignace and Tache, Jenny spent an annoying two hours at a cobbler's shop getting her boots back in shape. "All things considered, twenty-two miles were a fair tramp under difficult circumstances," she said.

The couple had left Jackfish at 9 a.m. with a box of beef sandwiches supplied by a Mrs. Nicoll, who offered them clothing as well—because they called themselves tramps.

"We continued to meet with more than the usual kindnesses along the way," Jenny said. "I suspect it's because I'm a woman." A kind old farmer had even offered them a ride; however, they didn't intend to violate the rules of the hike and were determined to cover the entire distance on foot.

At Schreiber, Jenny took time to applaud Burkman for not dropping out of the race. "He is a game fellow to pull away from his home town, when all he had to do to get out of the race was feign sickness."

The *Herald* received no night letter from Burkman and issued a stern reminder to all the hikers—intended especially for Burkman—that they must get their books signed every day as proof that they were sticking to the rules.

AFTER BREAKFASTING WITH a Norwegian station agent in Tache, the Behans hit the trail. "The heat wave continues to give us discomfort," Jack told the press. "It's time to think of changing into summer duds."

At noon they stopped at a section house and were given a real dinner: "Meal fried with pancakes, topped with syrup, and lots of coffee to wash it down. Hiking rewards we really appreciated," Jack laughed.

While passing through the area surrounding Wabigoon Lake in the late afternoon, Jack and Clifford were impressed by the beauty of the countryside with its many islands and picturesque summer places. "Many boats and canoes are already on the lake, and some locals said that summer residents were arriving daily, even though the ice had not yet completely disappeared."

That evening, father and son disregarded the tip they received from telegraphers in Dryden, who said that Burkman had taken a shortcut through the woods west of Lake Superior and would beat them to Winnipeg. It was an old saw, and Jack wasn't buying it. "I hope he has better luck with short-cuts than we had when we lost 100 miles by trying to be smart," he said. "We pulled into this town tonight after doing 35 miles. If Burkman does as well on his shortcut, he will be doing something worth while. But we expect to be in Winnipeg in lots of time to tell our friends that Burkman is 'on his way.'"

Frank and Jenny Dill left Schreiber at 8:30 a.m. and reached Cavers with the intention of continuing on, but changed their minds after receiving an urgent plea to stay the night from a lady in the town. "The visions of a party in our honour, and bribes of nice eats, were too hard to refuse," Jenny said. But feeling full and sassy, Mrs. F.C. Dill did promise the press that after they had passed through Port Arthur, they would start at a faster clip in pursuit of their rivals.

"Frank was fit," Jenny said, and thought that they should try for 40 miles the next day. "Should the weather be fine, the mark will be our aim."

FRANK AND JENNY were as good as their word and travelled 34 miles the next day. The *Herald* noted it was twice the distance covered by the Behans—and remarked that they were rapidly overcoming the lead father and son had established since breaking away from Burkman.

"We are proud of the day's work, and now more certain than ever that we will reach the coast inside of three months—if people don't kill us with kindness."

They were still being pursued by mobs of well-wishers wherever they went. In some cases, whole towns came out to see and cheer them on. At least it was not hard to get free meals or to rest their weary heads, since someone almost always extended their hospitality. "Everybody wished us luck as we strode through the villages and I am as happy as a little school girl and Frank is also all smiles," Jenny said. "With this wonderful encouragement, our journey will be much easier. If we are not in Vancouver before August, we will be awfully disappointed."

That morning, Mrs. Valiquette and Mrs. Needs, wives of the operators in Cavers, drove 11 miles to Gurney to cook the Dills a delicious dinner, then sent them off with a large basket of food for the road. "Mr. Easton, the Gurney operator, also kindly hunted down other necessary supplies for us," Jenny noted, without elaborating. "It has been another remarkable day, and if our luck holds, we will experience many more like it before reaching Vancouver. We are certainly not sorry that we decided to enter the race across Canada."

The Behans were no longer enjoying the adulation they had experienced in Ignace and Tache. Worse, it was now Jack's turn to suffer from a case of raw feet. "My feet gave me a lot of trouble today—blisters all over them," Jack complained. "So will lay off here and get patched up for tomorrow."

He and Clifford did take time out to tour the thriving pulp mill town of Dryden, where they were successful in selling some of their postcards. After one last stop to do some shopping, the hikers left for Eagle River.

The upside of the day for the Behans was provided by a trainman from No. 1 west, who tossed them two pounds of real maple sugar wrapped up in a copy of the *Ottawa Journal*. "What a treat on a mere seventeen mile day," Jack said. "We sat down and ate one pound."

The Behans were happy to leave "no man's land" and delighted to see more habitation each day. It wouldn't be long before they reached the Manitoba border and Winnipeg—sore feet and Jenny Dill be damned!

Charles Burkman's column did not appear in the *Herald* of April 15, disappointing readers once again. Easterners had become used to the adventure serial, and the newspaper did not enjoy disappointing them: "It makes their day passable! They wash it down with a cup of coffee in the morning and for a short time, they can forget about unemployment and the floundering economy."

Sore Feet on Prairie Soil

POSITIONS OF HIKERS APRIL 16

Dills—At Port Arthur, Ont.; 1,784 miles; out 74 days; did 32 miles yesterday

Burkman—At ???, Ont.; ??? miles; out 89 days; did ??? miles yesterday

Behans—At Kenora, Ont.; 2,050 miles; out 81 days; did 30 miles yesterday

Halifax—0 miles; *Kenora*—2,050; *Winnipeg*—2,170; *Vancouver*—3,645

On April 16, the hiking community was shocked to read in the *Herald* that Burkman had been injured while attempting a shortcut to head off the Behans. "The lone hiker appears to have seriously injured his back in a fall, attempting to scale a precipice," the reporter explained, and the newspaper stated that it was attempting to locate the young hiker "to ascertain how serious his injuries were; and whether in fact this hiker, who had demonstrated such great sportsmanship and gained so many admirers since leaving Halifax, could continue on in the race."

Although some regarded this new rumour as a ruse—a story circulated to gain sympathy for Burkman, now so outdistanced by the Behans that there was little hope he could beat them to Winnipeg—most readers were sincerely worried about Charlie's safety. It was particularly distressing news to Burkman's many friends, who thought that with Jack Behan now suffering from "bad feet," Burkman had an opportunity to regain some lost ground.

The accident was good news for the intrepid Behans, now 50 miles from the Manitoba border and more than halfway to Vancouver, having passed through four provinces and one state. Yet Jack was worried. Diminishing cash and the Dills were not his only concerns. "My feet, which have been giving me a great deal of trouble, being covered with blisters, are better tonight. They were in such a condition before starting out today that I used my last top shirts for bandages," he said. "This, coupled with the fact that the Dills are increasing their daily average, is causing us some worry. We did thirty miles today, out of the Dills' reach."

The hikers left Eagle River at 10 o'clock that morning, had dinner at Vermillion Bay, where the Duke of Connaught had enjoyed his last fishing trip while in Canada and where he had bestowed his name on one of the offshore islands. "There used to be a thriving gold mine in the area and a fella told us that a horse drowned in Vermillion Lake when it broke through the ice while transporting provisions across to the camp," Jack reported.

In the meantime, the Dills reached Port Arthur and were making better time than either of their rivals. Oblivious to the trials presently being faced by the other hikers, the couple completed their 32-mile hike to Charlie's hometown with ease. "When we entered Port Arthur at 7:05 p.m. scores of people, notified by telegraph of our coming, were on the street to greet us, and many kind invitations were tendered," Jenny wrote in a cheery dispatch that extolled the virtue of the port's fresh air, which she thought might explain the wellness exhibited by many westerners.

"We stopped at the residence of one of the prominent citizens," she added. "Port Arthur looked a long way off when we passed thru Barrington Street on the first leg of the journey many weeks ago—. But now Winnipeg does not seem to be more than a stone's throw from here."

The Dills had their book signed at the Port Arthur town hall and received other credentials "which we intend carrying to Vancouver—if we don't lose them," Jenny laughed.

After a good night's sleep, and a short stop for an interview with a local journalist, the Dills intended to leave Port Arthur "on the trail that leads to the Behans and Burkman."

To the delight of the *Halifax Herald*, small-town newspapers across the country were beginning to cover the Great Trans-Canada Race, although it was left for the hikers to set up interviews with local journalists.

By CANADIAN PRESS

PORT ARTHUR, April 15.—Mr. and Mrs. Dill, pedestrians crossing the continent from Halifax, have passed through Nipigon. They made the distance in two days better time than the male hikers, preceding them by a few days.

ON APRIL 18 the *Herald* reported that Burkman intended to continue the hike despite sustaining a sprained hip in a fall from a precipice in the Ontario woods while checking out a shortcut that would have put him ahead of the Behans. The newspaper also revealed that no announcement about the Trans-Canada hikers had aroused as much interest and regret as the account of Charles Burkman's unfortunate accident.

In a catch-up article from Ignace, Burkman explained that, yes, he had sprained his hip "slightly" after leaving Raith when he fell off a greasy rail, but the whole story had been blown out of all proportion. He had still managed to walk 18 miles between Raith and Savanne, where he spent the night. The next day he had overextended himself in a 25-mile tramp to Niblock, for which he'd suffered the consequences the next day when he managed only 28 miles to Martin. Later, stiff and sore but determined, he ended his "silent march" with an additional 28-mile hike to Ignace. He was sorry, he told the *Herald*, not to get the stories dispatched earlier.

And just when it seemed that all the hikers were back on track and accounted for, both the Behans and the Dills failed to send in dispatches.

Up to a late hour last night no word had been received from the Behans or the Dills as to what progress they made in the hike Friday and Saturday. The last news received was Friday night when the Behans reported they were at Kenora, which is the last town until they reach Manitoba, which province they should have entered yesterday—and the Dills reported they were at Port Arthur and in Ignace, only 150 miles behind where Burkman reported from on Saturday. The hikers are now going through the district, which is very lightly populated, and with telegraph offices few and far between.

The *Herald* update brought little comfort to the public rooting for accident-prone Burkman or footsore Jack Behan; they shook their heads and worried as the Dills inched their way forward toward the finish line.

"THE CHANCES OF the Dills catching up with us are very poor," Jack told the *Herald* in a night dispatch from Rennie, Manitoba.

He and Clifford had taken a good look around Kenora, "where they'd spent the night, and seen some very nice buildings." Jack singled out the YMCA as a fine structure of grey granite, with good beds, good tables and fair prices. The men took time to have their boots repaired and answered a backlog of correspondence. On leaving Kenora at 1 p.m., they stopped to take pictures of some bridges. "We'll send along copies after they're developed," Jack promised.

Three miles out, the Behans came to Lake of the Woods Milling Company, where 6,500 barrels of Five Roses flour were shipped across the country each year. The superintendent met them at the station and toured them through the mill, and they were grateful for the "rare privilege." Three hours later, the men were happy to meet with a reporter from Keewatin. "We were taken over to the big hotel, where all the rich class from Winnipeg spend the weekend," Jack said. "They have moving stairs from the boat to the hotel: Some classy place!" Clearly, he was flattered.

Leaving the mill behind, Jack noted that Lake Kenora was full of islands that stayed in view as they walked throughout the entire afternoon. The hikers ate supper with a "Rumanian" at the station house. "Bear meat is good stuff, dark and stringy, but tender," Jack reported. "By the time we reach Vancouver we will be wild eating this meat."

After supper, Jack and Clifford walked to Lowther to share a cup of coffee with the section foreman, P. Wells—a Swede—before continuing west along the line. They arrived in Rennie at 11:30 a.m. the next day, exhausted, but too excited to rest. "So close to the Manitoba border, thoughts of Winnipeg raced thru our heads, and instead of trying to sleep, we enjoyed a good read thru of the newspapers we'd received in Kenora," Jack said.

"Mrs. Dill seems to be quite interested in us," Jack observed. "They have as good a chance of catching us as Burkman—and his chances are very poor—. Those Dills can consider themselves lucky if they are at the Great Divide when we reach Vancouver. Tell them that we made thirty-three miles today!" The day, with its special privileges, had agreed with Jack, and he was again ready to take on all comers.

The Dills, the subjects of the Behan rancour, wrote from Raith, Ontario, about the big time they had in Port Arthur and Fort William with friends. "We left Port Arthur at eight-thirty Sunday morning and came as far as Sunshine, covering thirty-two miles. No station there. We intended to leave

Bear Stew

Yields 8 generous servings

❧ INGREDIENTS ❧

¼ cup flour

1 teaspoon dried oregano

1 teaspoon salt

1 teaspoon ground black pepper

4 pounds bear meat

2 teaspoons oil

4 teaspoons butter or
lard renderings

1 onion, chopped

1 cup beef broth or water

4 bay leaves

2 pounds white/red potatoes,
peeled and chopped

5 carrots, peeled and chopped

2 medium turnips,
peeled and chopped

⟶

Port Arthur, Saturday, but were kept busy all day seeing Frank's old school chums, two Hilcup brothers, William Lecain and Harry Ward, boys from Windsor, N.S., and my cousin who invited us all to his home at Fort William, where the boys took us to the movies and sold our cards."

Mrs. Brooking from Halifax was in town as well, so the Dills called to see her and enjoyed a good visit.

At Buda the next day, the couple took turns churning cream so they could have fresh buttermilk for supper, while their hostess prepared the meal. "After she took fifteen pounds of butter off the top," Jenny explained, "she gave us a large jar full of buttermilk to carry with us for our tea." They hiked as far as Raith, completing a 25-mile journey.

JACK BEHAN'S SORE feet hit prairie soil the next day. He and his son had left Rennie late in the morning after a lengthy breakfast with agent Jack Fawcett, another of Jack's wartime pals. Since they weren't making good time in the heat with Jack's bad feet, they decided to rest up and try a night hike to Winnipeg. "We had dinner at the first farm house in Manitoba, and it was quite a treat to get away from the hills and rocks and drop into prairie farming country."

With a bellyful of grub, and in a province where a track ran so straight you could see a town five miles away, Jack felt reborn. At 6 p.m., father and son crossed the swollen Whitemouth River. And because there were no more operating stations outside Winnipeg, they made a mental note to report to the *Herald* from the city after they arrived, then settled down for a night of shut-eye under the stars.

They were the only hikers to send a dispatch to Halifax that evening.

Winnipeg Triumph

POSITIONS OF HIKERS APRIL 20

Dills—At Savanne, Ont.; 1,851 miles; out 79 days; did 21 miles yesterday

Burkman—At ??? ; ??? miles; out 94 days; did ??? miles yesterday

Behans—At Winnipeg; 2,170 miles; out 86 days; did 37 miles yesterday

Halifax—o miles; *Kenora*—2,050; *Winnipeg*—2,170; *Vancouver*—3,645

On Wednesday April 20, Jack and Clifford Behan completed a triumphant 37-mile lap and became the first of the transcontinental hikers to enter Winnipeg, Manitoba.

The men left Molson at noon and strode purposefully toward the Manitoba capital, noting prairie farmers at work planting their spring crops as they went. "At last we sat down on the banks of the Red River, took off our shoes and socks and bathed our feet for half an hour," Jack said. "The water was cold but the day was perfect."

Refreshed and renewed, Frank and Clifford walked to Hazel Ridge, had supper at Scott's Hotel and tried to relax until morning, but at 5 a.m., too excited to catch any serious shut-eye, they struck out for Winnipeg and arrived six hours later. The victorious hikers went straight to the YMCA, where two suits of summer underwear from Stanfield's were waiting for them at the front desk. "We take great pleasure in thanking Stanfield's for keeping us from catching cold," Jack said. "Without this underwear we would have frozen coming around Lake Superior."

Scores of letters, from old friends at home and new friends in Ontario, awaited their arrival at the Y. "Both [of us] are well; and never has a thirty-seven mile hiking day felt so good," Jack wrote in reply.

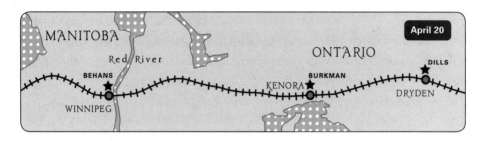

CHARLES BURKMAN BOUNDED back into the news on April 20. In a combative dispatch from the Commercial Hotel in Kenora, written two days earlier, he said he had completed a 45-mile hike—his longest jaunt since leaving Halifax. "Few people believed I would ever get as far as Port Arthur when I left the Herald office in early winter," he wrote. "But I'm not a quitter, and I think I've demonstrated that. The Behans still have a few days on me, but they won't hold the lead for long if my health holds out."

Burkman intended to reach Winnipeg in three days, bringing him closer to where the Behans were resting. "Hear rumours of Jack's sore feet," he said gleefully. "The Dartmouth hikers seem to have shot their bolt."

After their 30-mile hike to English River on April 21, Jenny Dill was not too tired to send the *Herald* a chatty update: "We do not know what kind of weather you people are having down in good old Nova Scotia, but up here it is glorious. A few miles from here, we picked large bunches of May flowers in full bloom. The sun is so bright that it nearly burned our eyes out and we are now certain that summer has arrived at last."

The Dills had taken to walking on the roads because they were in good shape and made walking a pleasure. "We travelled many miles without reaching a railway station and feared that we had lost our way. It was a relief when we finally reached English River station. The operator provided us with dinner and a very nice lunch for the road tomorrow morning."

It wasn't until the Dills arrived at English River that they learned Charlie had met with an accident. "Tell him that we wish him well," Jenny wrote the *Herald*, "and hope that he will continue in the race and leave the Behans far behind." But then she added, "Every step we come handier to the men who are now ahead of us and it will not be long before we send you word that we have overtaken all the other hikers." In spite of their best wishes for Burkman, bad news involving him and the Behans was good news for them.

AFTER A GOOD night's rest, the Behans put in one of the busiest days of the hike. They called on the mayor, the city clerk, Premier T.C. Norris and one of his MLAs, the Hon. Thomas Johnston. Then they delivered a card to Captain Penhale of the Royal Canadian Horse Artillery. It had been signed by his father at the Windsor Hotel in Montreal. After the hikers were fitted out in new breeches, they were escorted first to Camp Quarters and then around the city by Neil Wilson, a corporal at the Princess Pats Hospital with Jack Behan during the war. "He sure gave us a good time," Jack said.

The men toured the big Eaton's Store, with its new $3-million addition that spanned six city blocks, and delivered a letter to J.D. Dodd, of the Canadian Textiles Company, from E. McCoy of Montreal. The proprietor of the Russell Lang bookstore gave them a hearty welcome and hoped that they would call again on their return home. Then they called on Mr. Maitland, manager of the Ashdown Wholesale Sporting Goods Store, who fitted Jack out with a new raincoat.

The hikers took advantage of opportunities to speak at both the Garrick and the Dominion theatres in Winnipeg, and the dimes came rolling in. "I will consider my oratorship complete when this race is finished," Jack admitted to the newspaper. "I was a little timid at first, but now the more opportunities to raise money the merrier."

Eaton's Store, Winnipeg, ca. 1900–1925. The Behans were treated to tours of the T.E. Eaton Store, Ashdown's, and the Garrick and Dominion theatres.
Library and Archives Canada, PA-031548

Jack and Clifford reflected on the wonderful time they'd had in the city with friends old and new. They were tickled to receive a letter from L. Graham, president of the Dartmouth Athletic Club, who sent "congratulations on the courageous trip" on behalf of club members; and they thanked Capt. H.A. Young for the handsome balance pole nicely painted and lettered. The brass ferrules made to join the pole in the centre were the design inspiration of Charles Herman, chief engineer of the Dartmouth ferry, and were engraved by Birks.

The Behans planned to leave Winnipeg at 9 a.m. for Brandon. "Both were feeling 'jake.'"

Burkman reached Ingolf, Ontario, that day and was now close to the Manitoba border. He hadn't left Kenora until after 10, stopping briefly at Keewatin for dinner. Sixteen miles along the way, Burkman was startled by three young deer that darted out in front of him. "These are the first I have seen. I could have easily shot one, but the fine is fifty dollars, so I left them alone." He stopped at the section house in Kalmar for supper and decided to bed down for the night.

"The rain was so intense this morning that I held off leaving until ten thirty and didn't arrive at Ingolf until dinner. Now I'm waiting for the rain to let up."

Burkman still hoped to reach Rennie that night—weather permitting: "Twenty-four miles yesterday; twenty-eight to Rennie."

THE BEHANS LEFT Winnipeg in a heavy downpour, accompanied by N. Wilson, a friend who followed them to the city limits before wishing them "God Speed" and leaving them to hike in peace. It rained "cats and dogs" on their 29-mile jaunt to Marquette. Because there was no operator on duty at that station, Jack sent the night news from Meadows.

After putting away a good mess of boiled bacon, fried eggs and cups of scalding coffees the next morning, the hikers set off for Portage la Prairie. "Fine day from time we left," Jack told readers, "could see fields on either side of the track and swamp water covered with thousands of blue winged ducks swimming, and we saw two big flocks of geese this morning. The Americans are sure settling around here now, draining the lowlands and making some great farms."

They ate dinner at a boarding car on the tracks. As they walked, the car moved 10 miles west, so they ate supper there as well. "We are feeling like 'regular boarders,'" Jack joked.

Arriving at Rat Portage (the name favoured by early settlers of Portage la Prairie) at 8 p.m., the weary hikers were happy to call it a day. "Twenty-six miles," Jack noted.

The Dills, who were battered by fierce hail and rainstorms 17 miles outside of Dryden, described April 24 as their worst day since leaving Halifax. "We were drenched thru to the skin," Jenny complained, "and the mud was bothersome as well."

The storm marred the effect of the successes they had chalked up: 28 miles on Saturday and 35 on Sunday. When you are still in third place after 63 miles of hiking, and you are soaking wet to boot, who could blame you for feeling out of sorts, especially after reading of the generous treatment given the Behans in Winnipeg? The thought of the Behans' shopping spree in Winnipeg left her feeling petulant, and it was hard to hear about the network of friends that both "returned men" enjoyed—and the gifts they were receiving—and keep her perspective.

Besides, the Dills hadn't succeeded in beating the Behans to Winnipeg as Jenny had predicted. "Frank is still confident that we will pat the other hikers on the back before Regina is reached," Jenny admitted, "but I am not so optimistic as that—although I expect to overhaul them all before we arrive at Vancouver. We will try for 30 miles tomorrow—but we hardly expect to beat that mark with rain expected."

On that wet, miserable night in Dryden, Jenny could not even take solace in news of Burkman rallying in his attempt to beat the Behans, because the young maverick didn't send in a dispatch. Burkman had disappeared, yet again, into the wilderness.

THE DILLS MAY have been damp and down in the dumps, but they were still the most popular hikers on the rails, as evidenced by the oranges and candy thrown to them by passengers on a speeding CNR train only a few miles out of Dryden. "It was the greatest time of our trip, despite the stormy weather," Jenny said.

As expected, the downpour was steady as they left the city, but it gave purpose to their hike and helped them resist the "good people" who thought they should stop. "I guess the storm just made us travel faster," Mrs. Dill said.

Mr. Armstrong, the agent at Vermillion Bay, offered to entertain the couple that evening. "He is a great sport and has put himself out to be kind to us," Jenny said before forecasting: "Prospects for a clearing in the weather are not very bright at present. But we will be off bright and early in the morning regardless, as we know the good people along the way will be willing to let us dry our clothes by their fires."

The Behans arrived in Austin that night after a pleasant day of hiking from Portage. They had dinner at Burnside with Reverend Paul Langille, B.A., originally from River John near Pictou, Nova Scotia. Jack said that the reverend had the distinction of building a church at Hampton, Ontario, several years earlier and was in the party of Presbyterian ministers who travelled through the Rocky Mountains on mission work in the 1890s. "He gave us a good cheer, and we started toward Bagot."

THERE WAS STILL no report from Burkman on page three of the Herald, and his unpredictable behaviour had begun to annoy even his staunchest backers, including an ex-lieutenant of the British navy, who was supporting Burkman for $1,000 to win the transcontinental hike. The Herald editors hadn't heard from Burkman, so there was nothing they could say, but his fans believed that although the young man was disappointed with his performance to date, he could still catch up with the Behans and win the race.

The steady, reliable Dills reported a 38-mile hike to Kenora; they had even taken the time to visit a fish hatchery at Vermillion Bay. "Down in Nova Scotia we often heard of the fish hatcheries where they allow little trout to swim around unmolested, and have always craved to see the inside of one," Jenny wrote, not mincing words. "And at Vermillion Bay today, we went through the famous Gilbert Hatchery, and got the opportunity to see the operation first hand." Before leaving the hatchery at 10 a.m., the superintendent treated them to a wonderful fish dinner. Then, to their delight, the day turned out to be fine and they "decided to walk at least 30 miles or die in the attempt."

The Dills intended to reach Winnipeg—120 miles distant—within two days. "We are making big gains on the other hikers, but it is the Behans we are anxious to catch as I feel kind of sorry for Burkman who has been travelling in hard luck of late," Jenny said, finally clarifying their intentions for the readers.

Jack Behan told the Herald that he and Clifford had stayed at the Argyle Hotel in Austin and enjoyed a good rest, but the settlement's hospitality came in for a bit of snide commentary. "We had a good breakfast at nine a.m. and the good lady let us off very easy with four dollars and fifty cents! Austin is not a city, just a small town, but it keeps up with the city prices."

After dinner at Sidney, the hikers shaved and headed for Carberry, noting that it was Prime Minister Meighen's constituency. "There is a lot of rolling prairie on either side of the line, but the soil is very sandy, so it's not much good for wheat, but good for ranching," Jack said. "All along the line sheep ranches are plentiful with thousands of young lambs frolicking about."

He added that the homebrew popular in the area was "jake," and that it tasted of potatoes.

EVEN THOUGH THE Behans had taken two days off to sell postcards and relax with old army buddies in Winnipeg, Burkman was still a week behind his rivals when he finally reached Winnipeg on Tuesday April 26, after a week of silence.

The unpredictable lone hiker brought his followers up to date, reporting that he had made Kalmar, 24 miles north of Kenora, the previous Thursday, April 21. It rained Friday morning, so he holed up until noon and then hiked 21 miles to Telford. On Saturday, despite the heavy mist and rain, he bolted down a lunch at Rennie and finished a 28-mile jaunt at Whitemouth. It rained so heavily on Sunday that Charles stayed put in Whitemouth, but the despondent young hiker plugged 23 wet and miserable miles to Lydia on Monday, and the next day he steeled himself and did a 30-mile hike to Winnipeg.

Clifford Behan gave his father a break and wrote the night letter from Brandon. He reported that Tuesday had been cool and a good day for hiking. Father and son had enjoyed walking through the thriving agricultural landscape, admiring stands of winter wheat, sown the previous fall, that were already three inches tall; beautiful farms scattered around the countryside; and a train track that ran so straight you could see the grain elevators of Brandon 10 miles in the distance.

They stopped briefly at the station in Douglas, where the locals gawked and some bought postcards. Clifford noticed that nearly all of the small towns they passed through had nice skating rinks, even those half the size of Dartmouth.

At the Brandon CPR station, the Behans were the happy recipients of a new batch of postcards and four more suits of summer underwear, compliments of Stanfield's in Truro.

There was no news in the *Herald* from the Dills.

BY ALL ACCOUNTS, the great transcontinental race had turned into a serious battle of hide-and-seek by April 30. And when the *Herald* received only one dispatch on the last day of the month—and that from the chastised Burkman—a sympathetic editor took up his pen to champion the cause of its weary heroes.

"The Great Trans-Canada Hike," he wrote, "has settled into a gruelling contest... The remarkable interest which has been aroused throughout Canada and particularly in the Maritime Provinces is intensified by the close positions now held by the contestants. While this is a race of six or seven months' duration and the course is more than 3645 miles, the matter of a mere hundred miles or so does not seriously enter into it. The gains made on one or the other of the contestants is three or four days."

Of greatest relevance at the time, the editor pointed out, was the remarkable gain that Charles Burkman, the lone hiker, was making against his foremost rivals, the Behans. "Closely followed by the remarkable performance of Mrs. Frank C. Dill, who with her husband, is actually gaining on all the other contestants in this terrific grind to the Pacific."

In his latest dispatch, Burkman reported that he had completed 55 miles in a 24-hour hike to Melbourne—the longest recorded hike since the pedestrians left Halifax. He was now about 82 miles behind the Behans.

When the Behans had reported from Virden Thursday night, it was Clifford Behan's turn to be suffering from sore feet, and the duo was only able to make one mile during the day. The editor assumed that, since no report had been received Friday, they had been unable to continue, which was giving Burkman a chance to make a further gain on them.

There was no doubt that the Dills, too, were gaining on the Behans. Although the couple had failed to report the previous evening, when last heard from, they had recorded an impressive 41 miles to the Behans' meagre 16-mile effort.

With both Jack and Clifford dealing with sore feet, Burkman struggling gallantly along the railroad tracks to catch up, and the Dills consistently chalking up the best daily scores, the *Herald* predicted that, come Monday May 2, there would be a considerable change in the positions of the hikers.

Slings and Arrows

POSITIONS OF HIKERS MAY 1

Dills—At Winnipeg, Man.; 2,170 miles; out 90 days; rested yesterday

Burkman—At Melbourne, Man.; 2,238 miles out; 105 days; did ??? miles yesterday

Behans—At Elkhorn, Man.: 2,351 miles; out 97 days; did 31 miles yesterday

Halifax—0 miles; *Regina*—2,528; *Calgary*—3,004; *Vancouver*—3,645

When Frank and Jenny Dill reached Winnipeg on May 1, they were surprised to hear that Jack Behan's feet had gone bad, and that he and Clifford were about finished as competitors.

"Hard luck for the Behans but good news for the Dills," Jenny said.

"If it's true!" Frank muttered.

"And if it is, we'll just add another few extra miles a day to our itinerary," Jenny chirped, "until we greet the men with a pleasant, 'How are you, boys?'"

Frank wasn't so sure they had the stamina to add another couple of miles a day to an already punishing schedule, and for the first time in the journey he sounded more like an adversary than an advocate of winning.

"We'll find a way," Jenny snapped.

"You realize the state of our finances, don't you?" Frank asked. As keeper of the family purse, he was aware that by adding even a couple of hours to their hike day, there would be less time to stroll about selling postcards in order to meet mounting expenses. But the question was rhetorical. Dill knew his wife; when she got an idea in her head, there was no stopping her.

At the start, Jenny had been the centre of attention because of her gender, but now the possibility of winning the race called for a more aggressive strategy. "They cannot keep away from us much longer, as we have made better time than any of our rivals," she said. "Every place we go, people now tell us that they are wagering on the Dills to reach Vancouver first; and if humanly possible, we won't disappoint."

A new earnestness crept into Mrs. F.C. Dill's speeches: "The 'Peg is over 2,000 miles from Halifax and pedestrians should think twice before tackling it," she lectured an admiring crowd at the head of the wide, clean streets of the great western city. "It requires a stony but flexible resolve to deal with all the unexpected issues."

A sharp-eyed journalist was certain Jenny intended the statement as much for her husband as the crowd.

The Behans had sent their dispatch from Elkhorn, Manitoba, just 20 miles east of the Saskatchewan border. In Virden the previous night, they gave a travel lecture at the local movie house and sold cards to theatregoers during the intermission. When the Behans found out that most of the locals were attending a dance, they went along there as well and did a fairly brisk trade.

Jack and Clifford left Virden at 10 a.m. and stopped at Hargrave for dinner.

"The store keeper gave us some treat—two bottles of orange pop and some cake," Jack reported. Hardly a proper feed for ravenous hikers, readers agreed.

The Behans arrived in Elkhorn at 3:30 p.m. and were met at the train station by Mr. and Mrs. J.W. MacPherson, a couple from New Glasgow, who introduced them to the mayor and other important businessmen in the community. "This is a trip when one feels at home when they meet their own Bluenoses from Nova Scotia," Jack said. "Mr. MacPherson is an operator on the Canadian Pacific Railway. His brother runs three picture theatres in different western towns, and tomorrow night he has invited us to speak at Wapella Theatre and sell cards, so we expect a big night."

Jack was moved by the generosity shown them, admitting with some guilt, "I hope we don't meet any more Nova Scotians before reaching the coast, because they never stop doing for us, even though they are down and out themselves."

The Behans planned to push through to Fleming, Saskatchewan, the next day, leaving Manitoba behind for the Dills to worry about.

It was rumoured that Burkman was laid up in Melbourne; whatever the case, the lone hiker was silent May 1.

BURKMAN BROKE HIS silence on May 2 and continued to be optimistic about his chances of winning the race. "Winnipeg was a goal of the past; Vancouver is of the future," he said. "I arrived at Brandon tonight after doing 36 miles and am still close on the heels of the Behans. If I continue to make such gains, I will easily make the coast ahead of my greatest rivals."

Although he was respectful of the steady progress the Dills were making, Burkman continued to see them as non-threatening. Only when taunted by the locals about the prowess of Jack and Clifford did Burkman suggest to the public that it was the Dills to watch. "If the reports coming out of Winnipeg are true," he said, "the Dills are making the best times of all the hikers; they had already beaten me by seven days and the Behans by a good margin as well."

Now acknowledged as serious contenders in the Great Trans-Canada Race, the Dills took to reporting hiking mileages in two-day totals, which were impressive but misleading. "We travelled 63 miles in two days," Jenny wired the *Herald* from Portage la Prairie late that night. "Our mark today was 34 miles, which was traveled in excellent weather." This total was intended to instil fear in their rivals and awe in the public, but the 29-mile balance was not mentioned.

The couple continued to extol the charity shown them in Winnipeg, where they stopped with Frank's friend Fred Serry. "He was awfully glad to see us. Frank and Serry chummed around together in Halifax and other places in Nova Scotia," Jenny said.

A moving-picture photographer was now a regular feature of the race in larger centres and was on hand to snap footage of the Dills leaving the city. The photographer said that Pathé planned to release the newsreel footage to the public in Halifax come June.

THE BEHANS PULLED a vanishing act on May 2, leaving family and friends more curious than concerned. "Just resting up for my forty-fifth birthday!" said Jack by way of explanation when he checked in the next day.

JACK BEHAN CELEBRATES BIRTHDAY
AT SASKATCHEWAN

By Jack Behan

INDIANHEAD, Sask., May 3.—...This is my birthday: 45 years old and feel like 21. We are going through to Qu'Appelle, so sending message from here. Farmers along points today are re-seeding owing to terrible gale yesterday blowing the seed out. One man lost forty acres, great loss.

Mrs. F.C. Dill sent a saucy letter to readers from Sidney, Manitoba, on May 3. "We made only a slight gain on the birthday boy and his son," she said. "Intended to do twenty-five miles—but then, lulled by the delights of the day, we walked 31 miles instead."

They left Burnside at 8 a.m. after spending the night with Reverend Paul Langille—the same Presbyterian minister who had given the Behans dinner a week earlier. The reverend's generosity extended to lunches and bottles of milk for the road as well.

Jenny was very pleased to read that Burkman had been making big gains on the Behans. Her birthday greeting for Jack Behan was less kind: "With the lead that the Behans had last month, I thought that Burkman would never catch his rivals—now it looks as though the Behans will soon be behind Charlie." Jenny no longer hid her admiration for the handsome Burkman from her husband.

There was no report from Charlie in the *Herald* on May 3. Were his feet holding him up once again? Friends and family wondered but tried not to worry.

CHARLES BURKMAN WAS the only hiker to report back to the *Herald* on May 4. He was enthusiastic to describe the 48-mile hike he had accomplished from Brandon to Virden in 24 hours.

Aggravated by unseasonably warm weather and record-breaking dust storms, Burkman admitted that he had taken to travelling by night—even though he had been strongly advised against it. "Travelling by the light of the moon is dangerous," he admitted, "but it's the only way to beat the heat and make gains on my rivals."

After resting up at Alexander, the lone hiker requested a prepared lunch from the kitchen of the local hotel to eat along the tracks, then off he strode in the direction of Virden. Judging from the fact that he covered 48 miles in 24 hours, night walking agreed with him.

ALL THE HIKERS sent reports to the *Herald* on May 5.

Clifford penned the dispatch the day after his father's birthday celebration. Father and son left Qu'Appelle at 8:30 a.m. in fine, clear weather but ran into a "peach" of a sandstorm around 12 noon. Fortunately, the wind was blowing from the east, so the hikers were still able to make good time. "It sure was depressing to pass the 15 miles of pock-marked bush and burned short grass between Qu'Appelle and Balgonie," he wrote. "Dad claimed that all those nice hotels in the nice prairie towns we passed were built on pie-in-the-sky CPR dreams, and reflected an ailing Canadian economy. It sure was disheartening."

Luckily, the men also saw some prosperous Saskatchewan farms around Balgonie, which suggested that a good lunch could be had without guilt. They were not disappointed.

Jack and Clifford arrived in Regina late that night, exhausted and plastered with sand. "We looked like Japanese sandmen," Clifford joked. Feeling expansive after a long hot bath, another free meal and a 33-mile hiking feat, he wasn't above kidding Burkman: "While we were at Port Arthur with Burkman, we saw a card he received from Mrs. Dill. 'Go to it Charlie, the Dills are with you,' it said. It's our opinion if he don't soon get a move on, they will be with him."

The Dills arrived in Brandon on May 5 in fine spirits. Frank and Jenny felt like schoolchildren off on a holiday. "Train men, who passed us today, waved their greetings and threw candy to us, which tasted great. One kind-hearted engineer threw Frank a box of cigarettes and a package of matches, which was accompanied by a note wishing us luck. Frank helps me eat the candy," she said.

Outside Brandon, several cowboys shouted greetings to them, and one of the wild and woolly characters reared his horse and indulged in a bit of rope play for Jenny's entertainment: "I don't mind admitting it left me feeling giddy—for all of two minutes."

Forty miles was the longest hike the husband and wife had done for several days, and Jenny felt that they were entitled to a reward. "We can now afford to take our time in going after the men hikers ahead of us," she taunted. "They seem to be tied to a post the way we are gaining on them."

Mrs. F.C. Dill had no intentions of resting, and as soon as they'd posted their cards the next morning, they were hell-bent for Wapella—in pursuit of Burkman, the Behans and Vancouver.

AFTER WRITING A short communication to the *Herald* on May 6, Jack and Clifford treated themselves to a day of relaxation as guests of Mr. MacCarthy, proprietor of the Paris Hotel in Regina. They enjoyed a good tramp around the Royal city, home of the famed Royal Canadian Mounted Police training depot; gathered an impressive collection of autographs and a city seal from dignitaries such as

Premier William Martin, the Hon. Mr. George Lanley (MLA for Redberry), His Worship Mayor James Grassick, and the city clerk; and then tucked into a good spread at the hotel.

Jack wrote to folks back home that he and Clifford "were well." He was a gregarious fellow, and the communication sounded flat—possibly written by someone in dire need of more dimes, fewer parties and a proper break from the unremitting pressure exerted by Jenny Dill.

Burkman had planned to walk 52 miles on May 6 and make great gains on the Behans, whom he claimed were "paling [sic] around Regina with friends"— but it didn't happen. After stopping briefly in Virden to buy a new pair of hiking boots and to take supper with C.J. Casey, son of the late T.W. Casey, a former Dartmouth post office official, Burkman left the village at 10 p.m. and found that he could only hobble a dismal 17 miles to Elkhorn on his blistered feet. "Too bad; I expected to make up for it tonight, but the old feet in the new boots let me down." He vowed to make Whitewood, his birthplace, 52 miles away, in the next day or two. The innocent optimist could always find a new resolve.

As for Mr. and Mrs. F.C. Dill, they became furtive and disappeared underground. There was no column from them, but loyal followers had heard rumours and anticipated a big announcement the next day.

THE BEHANS HAD put their time in Regina to good use. Jack visited the *Regina Leader* newspaper to thank the writers for their support and was amused to find the typesetters out on a 44-hour strike. "The entire staff from the editor to the messenger boy was rushing around setting up type in order to get out a one sheet edition," he said.

Jack was interested in politics and was acquainted with the increasingly influential populist style of politics in the west that was riling easterners. Out here, embittered union men called for better conditions for the working classes, and angry farmers were joining in to speak with them in one voice. It was small wonder that striking newspapermen had little time to spend with the hiking stalwarts.

Canada had emerged from the Great War with a slumping economy and a federal government that was divided and at odds with the rest of the country. In the east, the two traditional parties, the Liberals and the Conservatives, struggled to hold on to power, while in the west, the Progressive Party was emerging as a voice for the farmer's movement and planned dramatic changes in Canada's political landscape. Farmers who saw the hikers striding along the railroad tracks were full of distrust and envy of people who could dismiss the discontent of a nation to walk cross-country on a lark, and the hikers frequently found themselves out of step with the earnest prairie farmers and unemployed labourers.

Sensitive to western politics, the *Herald* engaged Nova Scotians across Canada to rally in support of the hikers. And so, once again, Maritime transplants Mr. and Mrs. N.A. Donaldson, now living in Penz, Saskatchewan, treated their fellow bluenosers to a big supper.

From Regina to Grand Coulee...Penz...Pasqua...41 miles to Moose Jaw the Behans trudged. The burning haystacks of protesting farmers lit up the night skies and ensured them safe passage along the rails. Temperatures were unseasonably warm for May, so the Behans, like Burkman, had taken to treading the ties at night.

Brandon... Alexander... Virden... Hargrave... Elkhorn... Kirkella... Fleming, Manitoba... on to Moosemin, Saskatchewan—trading one prairie province for another—the determined Jenny and her Frank strode on until at last they reached Wapella, Saskatchewan: 77 whopping miles, one filthy dust storm, two days later. "I wish the Halifax people could have seen our dirty faces after the sandstorm," Jenny said. "We looked a real mess. It took nearly an hour to dig out all the sand from our skins."

The only major disappointment the Dills faced was the scarcity of Halifax newspapers, which served as a lifeline to friends and family at home and informed them of the movements of their rivals. No news led to idle speculation and senseless worry.

"Tomorrow should be a good day for us," Jenny said. "If we don't make 42 miles we will be very disappointed. We passed the point where Burkman telegraphed from this afternoon, and if he is not able to carry on because of his feet, who knows what will happen?"

Of course, even if your feet were fine, there was always the weather to hold you back.

And where was the elusive Burkman anyway? Even his staunchest fans were tired of his shenanigans—especially since a woman and her husband were lurking in the wings, threatening to overtake him.

MOOSE JAW...MORTLACH...Parkbeg...Chaplin...on their way to Ernfold, the Behans struggled against north winds through the dirt hills of Saskatchewan. It was a tough country, this land the government had staked out for returned soldiers from the Great War, although they saw little evidence that anyone had taken up the offer.

The hikers reported feeling good about their 26-mile hike to Ernfold but complained that the Dills' relentless nipping at their heels was taking the fun out of the race.

On Monday May 9 that competition intensified as the Dills moved into second place.

DILLS OVERTAKE BURKMAN AT BROADVIEW, SASKATCHEWAN
Husband and Wife Hikers Make Wonderful Showing and Continue Pursuit of Leaders.

"In our last telegram to the *Herald*, we said that we hoped to be with Charlie Burkman shortly and our statement has come true; as of 6:45 this morning we talked with Charlie by telephone from a small village some 20 miles from where he was resting, suffering with sore feet. That's where we caught him," a jubilant Jenny told readers.

When the Dills reached Whitewood—Burkman's birthplace—the operator was waiting to connect them with the lone hiker. "After reluctantly conceding second place to us, Charlie told us that the Behans were only a short distance ahead of us. This was cheering news to us, and we will set an even faster pace after those Dartmouth hikers, because it is now our one ambition to catch them before they reach the steps of city hall in Vancouver."

It was true, Burkman told the ecstatic couple: John Behan was having trouble with his feet as well and was only able to complete a small daily mileage.

"One could never hope to meet a better sport than Charlie Burkman," said Jenny. "He has carried on without complaining during the past two weeks—barely able to walk. It's only his great nerve and gameness that kept him going forward. With feet raw with blisters, he is only able to manage a few, feeble miles a day."

After their 28-mile hike to Broadview, Jenny proclaimed that they had started out 15 days behind Burkman, six or seven days behind the Behans, and were now only 160 miles behind the front runners. Winning never looked more possible, and she wanted it more than anything.

"Everything and everyone is splendid!" Jenny gushed: the weather, the real western farmers—some originally from good old Nova Scotia—the trainmen and, of course, all those friendly supporters who had succoured them along the way.

MAIN ST., WHITEWOOD, SASK.

Main Street in Whitewood, Saskatchewan, ca. 1913. When the Dills reached
Whitewood, Burkman's birthplace, they learned that they had taken over
second place. U of S Library Special Collections LXX-49

Burkman may have suffered "the slings and arrows of outrageous fortune," but
the Behans felt it was a little premature for Jenny to deliver such an enthusiastic
victory speech to the public.

Hell Hath No Fury
Like a Woman Scorned

POSITIONS OF HIKERS MAY 11

Burkman—At Broadview, Sask.; 2,435 miles; out 115 days; rested yesterday

Dills—At Indian Head, Sask.; 2,486 miles; out 100 days; did 51 miles yesterday

Behans—At Herbert, Sask.; 2,652 miles; out 107 days; did 28 miles yesterday

Halifax—0 miles; Calgary—3,004; Vancouver—3,645

REAL TEST OF STAYING POWER OF HIKERS STARTS TODAY
Dills Set Record By Making 51 Miles In One Day
Leaving Burkman Nursing Sore Feet.
All Canada Watching What The Western Papers
Call Most Gruelling Contest in History.

HALIFAX, May 11.—The great hike from Halifax to Vancouver which started from The Herald Building four months ago, and in which there has been no break of even one day, has now entered into the last lap...

The *Herald* would have been hard pressed to produce a more gripping sporting event than the one unfolding in front of the country with its stellar cast, inspired narrative and dramatic timing:

One hundred and twelve days ago, almost mid-winter, Charles Burkman and Sid Carr left Halifax, determined to reach Vancouver. Shortly after entering New Brunswick, Carr quit and returned to Halifax. Burkman went on alone. One week after Burkman and Carr started, Jack Behan and his son Clifford, of Dartmouth, went after Burkman, who at that time, was nearly across Nova Scotia and still travelling with Carr. Six days later, Mr. and Mrs. Frank Dill left Halifax in pursuit of Burkman and the Behans... Most people doubted that any of the hikers would last until they reached Moncton, and the idea that a woman could walk as far as Truro was scoffed at. Interest in the hike continues to spread. From Halifax throughout the province, then into New Brunswick, sweeping through Maine, growing in Quebec, and spreading like wild fire in Ontario, and on to...Manitoba... Saskatchewan...Alberta...

Editors rushed journalists to sites for exclusive interviews with the hikers: Manitoba was taken by storm, particularly by Mrs. Dill, and Saskatchewan citizens were now falling all over each other to pay homage to the hikers. Western papers referred to the event as a marvellous exposition of patience and endurance, and journalists spoke about the contest in superlatives: "In addition to being the most unique event ever attempted, it is also THE MOST GRUELLING CONTEST."

References to Mrs. Dill as one of the most wonderful women in the world were common, and writers claimed that words could not express Canadians' admiration for this plucky little Nova Scotia woman who had forsaken a comfortable home in midwinter to brave the elements and travel almost TWO THOUSAND FIVE HUNDRED MILES!

"Another remarkable thing about the Dills," the *Herald* said, "is that to date they have averaged better time than the Behans and Burkman."

In an attempt to hang on to second place, Burkman had reached Wapella after a late-night marathon from Elkhorn. He had passed through Kirkella at 3 a.m., rested until 6 a.m., arrived at Fleming in time for breakfast, struck out for Moosemin at 3 p.m., rested until 6 p.m., and with a final burst of energy arrived at Wapella at 11 p.m. to spend the night. The next day he met with the Dills at Broadview.

"The bottoms of my heels were so raw that I decided to rest up a couple of days with relatives in the country," he said, but those plans went awry. "On Sunday, I got a telephone call from the Dills at Wapella, and they wanted me to meet them there, but I said I would meet them at Broadview instead. And I did."

"Burkman is the best sport, but his feet are troubling him," Jenny maintained. "He will make up for lost time as his feet improve."

Solicitations and interviews over, Frank and Jenny Dill said their good-byes and set out in energetic pursuit of Jack and Clifford Behan. That night they reached Indian Head, completing the longest hike in any single day by any of the hikers—51 miles.

"The hikers all have their friends, but there are few who do not, way down in their hearts, hope that Mrs. Dill will be the first to reach the Pacific Coast," said the Herald. "The fact that she reaches the Pacific at all will place her achievement high among the laurels won by the greatest women in the world."

Such fine praise for the achievements of a "little woman" can't have done much for the Behans' egos. They had enjoyed baiting earnest young Burkman, but with the Dills now in second place—pushing hard and gaining fast—the race had a new undercurrent, with Jenny pumped and determined to win, and Jack tired but equally determined not to be beaten.

The disgruntled father and son left Mortlach, Saskatchewan, on May 10 with few good things to say about either the prairie communities or the people they passed. "Mortlach is a small town but with big ideas," Jack growled. "The town is near the CPR station and has a population of 900. We pushed from there at 9 a.m. in a downpour of rain, which continued all day. We had dinner at Ernfold at a 'Chinks'—same old menu." Not even the efficiently run Mennonite village of Herbert, Saskatchewan, cheered them up. The race had gone flat. Every day started early and ended late. The Behans were left with the reality of mounting debts, Jack's bad feet and the charge of the firebrand Dills at their heels.

Increasingly excited by the dynamics of the event it had created, the Herald once again ran postcard photographs of all the hikers.

FIVE PLUCKY CANADIANS ENTER LAST LAP OF GREAT COAST-TO-COAST HIKE.

Careful to appear fair in its coverage, the Herald assured readers on Thursday May 12 that it was much too early to declare a winner. "The Behans gained one mile on the Dills while Burkman, who says his feet are almost well, made a 31 mile 'hop' and gained three miles on the Behans and four on the Dills," it reported.

The day started poorly for Burkman. Shortly after he left Grenfell, it started to rain and he was forced to stop at Summerberry and take an early dinner. He didn't reach Wolseley until late in the afternoon, and after sending a short dispatch to the *Herald* he pushed on to Indian Head, ending with a spectacular 31-mile hike. Not too shabby for a hiker with sore feet! Playing catch-up appeared to agree with him.

When the Dills reached Balgonie, Jenny complained that it had been Frank's idea to make the 51-mile hike the previous day—at the expense of her own feet. "My feet were rubbed so raw that we abandoned the train tracks in favour of walking 27 miles barefoot, on hot dusty roads. Walking barefoot is no joke, even when you make good time like we did."

The Behans left Herbert for Swift Current and managed to enjoy a day of big sky and prairie landscape awash with spring. "Passed some of the finest sheep and cattle ranches in Saskatchewan," Jack said. "Thousands of sheep were being herded by boys on ponies. At Rush Lake we saw ducks and geese swimming about in the sloughs. The agent told us that in the fall the nature preserve is a hunting ground and sports from all over Western Canada come here to shoot."

At Waldeck the hotel was boarded up, forcing the hikers to accept dinner at a local home. "Further indication of the sagging prairie economy," Jack remarked to the fellow Nova Scotian who took time to "jolly them up." After doing justice to the meal, the Behans called on N.C. MacDonald, manager of the Royal Bank and formerly of New Glasgow. "He took what cards we had left and soon sold the lot."

Despite the tone of the Behans' night letter, the men had found the day just another slog. And all work and no play made Jack a sullen boy. "First shave we paid for since we left Halifax," he grumbled, "so we decided to allow our hair and whiskers to grow until we finish our trip—which I hope will be soon... Twenty-eight miles today."

Jack and Clifford decided to rest until noon the next day to avoid the heat wave sweeping the province.

THE GROWING SUPPORT for the Dills resulted in an increasingly brisk sale of their postcards. Everyone, it seemed, wanted a souvenir of the hiking husband and wife. "Thank goodness the post cards were at the Moose Jaw Station when we pulled in to town after a 43 mile journey, ending our financial troubles," Jenny sighed in relief. "When we let people know that we had souvenir post cards of ourselves, there was a wild rush at us and it only took a few minutes to dispose of several hundred cards."

It had been a day full of surprises: five miles out of Regina, when trainmen threw them money—accompanied by an encouraging note that the western people were behind them to win—even Frank smiled. At Pasqua, where the ghosts of thousands of crocuses still graced the short-grass country, the hikers were greeted by Frank's brother Blake and A. Cann of the CPR, who escorted them into the city. They covered the last seven miles of the route in one hour and 20 minutes: "A pretty good time for long distance pedestrians," Jenny said.

There were other compliments as well: "Blake said a lot of nice things about The Halifax Herald, which he perused many times during his last six month stay in Moose Jaw...He says that it is Eastern Canada's greatest newspaper."

That evening, while the Behans brooded over their mounting misfortunes in Swift Current, the Dills were entertained at a lavish garden party in Moose Jaw, where generous doses of optimism were dished out and 15 dollars' worth of postcards were sold, leaving Jenny feeling expansive. "We feel that the Behans have 'about shot their bolt, an expression Frank uses," she explained to guests. "And if our health holds, we should catch them in the next few days. Calgary is drawing nearer every step we take, and then the real race will start for Vancouver."

At the mention of Calgary, Jenny cast a worried glance in her husband's direction. He lowered his head. "Frank has many friends in Calgary," she explained, "but that shouldn't present any problems."

Along with their social coup in Moose Jaw, the Dills managed a "Special" in the *Moose Jaw Evening Times.*

MR. AND MRS. DILL LEFT FRIDAY NOON ON LONG HIKE
Man And Wife From Halifax Who Are Hiking
To Vancouver Visited Relatives Here Today

HALIFAX, May 14.—Mr. and Mrs. F.C. Dill, of Halifax N.S., two of the contestants in the Halifax Herald coast to coast hike, arrived in the city at 8:20 p.m. Thursday on their way west.

While in the city the trans-Canada pedestrians visited the home of Mr. E. Blake Dill, 264 Stadacona Street West.

Coming west from Regina, they approached Moose Jaw by the Pasqua road, and entered the city from the south-east. They were met at Pasqua by Mr. A. Cann and B. Dill who accompanied them in...After Mrs. Dill made her report to The Halifax Herald, they were taken to the home of Mr. B. Dill, where about forty friends and admirers were present to welcome them. After listening to many tales of adventure on their long hike they were entertained with music and song, the Misses Edwards and Mrs. D. Currie presiding at the piano.

The hikers left at noon Friday on the next link of their long journey. Mr. and Mrs. Dill are about fifty miles ahead of C. Burkman, one of the other contestants in the race. Ahead of Mr. and Mrs. Dill are the Behans, father and son, who are journeying together.

TELEGRAPH WIRES HELD UP NEWS
FROM HIKERS LAST NIGHT
No Word From Travelers On Account of
Wire Troubles East and West Last Night

Owing to the Aurora Borealis interfering with the CPR wires last night, many important dispatches intended for today's Herald were delayed...

It wasn't until Monday May 23 that the *Herald* finally caught up with Burkman. The cagey, if not duplicitous, hiker wrote from Swift Current that he had reached Regina the previous day. Despite sore feet, he had covered 42 miles and was now only one day behind the Dills. Charlie's friends still believed that he would reach the coast first, and western papers claimed that he was the freshest of the hikers.

Burkman took time to drop into the *Regina Morning Leader* office to drum up business and present his version of the hiking adventure.

REGINA MORNING LEADER
★ *special* ★
Transcontinental Hiker Is in City on Way to B.C.
Charles Burkman Has Many Adventures
on His Way Across Country

May 14, 1921, p. 17—Charles Burkman, one of the contestants in The Halifax Herald coast to coast hike, arrived in the city yesterday and is visiting with Mr. and Mrs. MacGachen, 2022 St. John Street. Burkman, who was born in Whitewood, Sask., entered the race with Behans, father and son, who were in Regina a few days ago, and traveled with them as far as Port Arthur where he stopped to visit with his family. Burkman paired with Sydney [sic] Carr, but his partner left him at Petitcodiac, N.B. owing to illness. Burkman kept on travelling with the Behans and during their journey along the CPR track they had some hard times, being forced many times to sleep in cold stations and bunk with section crews north of Lake Superior.

Burkman has been troubled with his feet during the past week but stated last night he was all right and would start to catch up with the Behans who are two hundred miles ahead of him. Mr. and Mrs. Dill, the other contestants, are about 50 miles ahead of Burkman... Along the whole route, the people have been very kind to Burkman and he declared that had it not been for the CPR section men, station agents and operators he would have starved to death.

Jack and Clifford Behan had left Swift Current on May 14 after an uneventful break. "We rested at Swift Current yesterday," Jack said. "Called on Deputy Mayor Bell and had a look around town. Business is very quiet. This, without a doubt, is the highest priced town we ran into yet. Met W. Croft, a former Dartmouth boy, who gave us a good time. We left the place at ten this morning."

During the 35-mile walk over the rolling prairie to Gull Lake, the dispirited Behans battled a freak spring storm with icy northeast winds and driving snow. They stopped briefly to warm up at Beverly and took lunch with a generous section foreman.

"Like in other towns we passed through, the hotels were closed," Jack said.

At Webb the hikers encountered a real "sporty Chinaman" who gave them a free meal. "The first of course," said an ungrateful Behan Senior, "as there has to be a first in everything,"

The men arrived at Gull Lake at 9:20 p.m., surprised to learn that they were 2,960 feet above sea level and pleased that they had suffered no ill effects. By now totally fed up, Jack and Clifford Behan decided to quit Saskatchewan—and the Dills. They disappeared for two days, turning up at Medicine Hat, Alberta, 32 miles later.

Monday May 16, 1921

HALIFAX HIKERS REACH MEDICINE HAT

John Behan and His Son Clifford Left Halifax Jan. 25th with Intention of Walking to Vancouver.

John Behan and son Clifford, both veterans of the Great War, reached the city last night on the transcontinental hike from Halifax to Vancouver, and to a News representative said, "We haven't spent a monotonous moment, but enjoyed every mile of our trip and expect to reach Vancouver by June 10." The travelers left Halifax on January 25, and their competitors in the race were Burkman and Carr, who left on the 17th, having had an eight day start. After a few days, Carr dropped out, returning to Halifax, but Burkman carried on and was overtaken at Chelmsford, Ontario. The Behans accompanied him around Lake Superior and as far as Port Arthur, where he rested.

Spending a couple of days in Winnipeg, they pushed on across the Prairie Provinces leaving Burkman still further behind. The average made was 25 miles a day; as the weather grew more spring like, more hiking was done at night and less by day. Yesterday, they made the longest run of the journey, coming from Hatton to Medicine Hat, a distance of 45 miles, and getting put up at the Assiniboia by 10:30 p.m. "Go To Green Lantern." A wire was waiting for them from W.A. Hart, proprietor of the Green Lantern, Halifax, to the effect he had arranged their meals with Mr. Murphy, of the Green Lantern, Medicine Hat, and there the news scribe found them, looking hale and hearty and ready, after meeting the Mayor and prominent citizens, to hike to Calgary.

On their trip they have met and received in a little book they carry the signatures of His Excellency, the Duke of Devonshire, Hon. Arthur Meighen, Hon. F.B. McCurdy, Hon. Peter Martin (Halifax) Hon. W.M. Martin, of Saskatchewan, Hon. Geo. Langley, Hon. James M. Caldwell, and many other prominent citizens of Canada.

The Halifax Herald is keeping in touch with the Dartmouth men, who guarantee to beat out Burkman and complete the Halifax-Vancouver hike in six months. No one seeing their cheery optimism will doubt that Clifford and his father Jack will make good.

The Behans pointedly made no mention of Frank and Jenny Dill.

The *Herald* also made contact with the lone hiker, who once again blamed his inability to overtake the Behans on his sore feet. "I am continuing on task and at my own pace," he said. Burkman left Regina Saturday afternoon, stopping frequently to rest his battered extremities. He ate supper at Grand Coulee, then pushed on to Pense, where he spent the night. "Left Pense at ten on Sunday for Belle Plaine and then on to Moose Jaw—another twenty-eight miles done." Burkman hit the rails at 7:30 Wednesday morning in the rain, ate dinner at Fauna and reached Swift Current minutes before 8:30 for supper: "My feet were so bad; I couldn't do a longer hike. Sorry didn't get this to you earlier."

The Dills raced 41 miles from Mortlach to Ernfold on May 15. They had bolted down a quick dinner at Parkbeg en route and then, too preoccupied to enjoy the generosity of the host—or to appreciate the admirers dogging their steps—tore off to Ernfold. There was a marked change in Mrs. Dill's behaviour. She was no longer content to accommodate people who wanted her to stop and chat or pose for pictures. The Broadview takeover had given her a purpose, a responsibility to win the race for her gender. The Behans were already in Alberta, close to the Rocky Mountains: time was running out.

The couple left Ernfold at 6:30 the next morning, ate a quick dinner at Herbert, wolfed down supper at Waldeck, and then stumbled into Swift Current at 10 p.m., dog-tired but able to boast 44 miles. "You looked like a sick jack rabbit," Frank told his wife. Jenny admitted that covering 85 miles in two days had taken a toll.

The Behans were still in Medicine Hat on May 17, relieved to be separated from the competition by "an entire province." They enjoyed taking time to relax, tour the city and sell postcards. "This city is lighted day and night," Jack said. "There is some fine manufacturing going on because gas is so cheap."

"While we were at breakfast today, Mr. Murphy [their host] phoned The News," Jack recounted. "And a pleasant looking lady appeared, expecting, as she said, a pink tea party. She gave us a big write-up in The News." After which the Behans were shown around the city and introduced to many by Mr. Murphy. "We are lecturing at the Monarch Theatre tonight before hitting the road to Calgary." Walking at night had replaced daytime hiking in the heat.

Content now with all the attention the *Herald* could muster, rested and grateful for the good grub received, and soothed by a favourable press release, Jack regained his combative stance. "We read in the Herald," he said, "where the Dills say we must be tied to a pole by the way they have been catching up to us. For their information they will consider they are trying to stand on the equator if they think they can over haul us."

JENNY DILL WAS all business when the *Halifax Herald* finally caught up to her and Frank at Hatton, a whistle stop on the Alberta/Saskatchewan border. "Hell hath no fury like a woman scorned," the sports remarked after reading the daily spreads by the feisty little woman racing to close the gap between herself and the Behans.

"We left Piapot at eight thirty... had dinner at Hatton at nine-thirty... Now we will rest up for our hike to The Hat tomorrow; made thirty-six miles today," said the "scorned" woman.

Now only a day and a half behind the Behans, Jenny admitted to driving a grim and relentless pace, with Frank attending the rails close behind. The *Herald* relished every moment of the event it had created.

THE DILLS LEFT Hatton at 6:30 the next morning in a hard rain. "We got wet and dried in the sun," Jenny wrote. "Stopped in Irvine for lunch at the Great West Café."

A correspondent to the *Medicine Hat News* described the Dills' visit in a roundup of events from Irvine, Alberta, a typical CPR prairie town, 20 miles east of the Hat.

MEDICINE HAT NEWS
★ *special* ★
Baseball is still going strong. Friday evening, May 20th, there was a game between married men (Has Beens) and single men (Would Be's) of the town...

During the past few days of the week, the weather has been beautiful but the sky is clouding again and in the next twelve hours it will most likely be raining. The farmers are all well satisfied that crops are looking favourable... Mr. and Mrs. Dill, the transcontinental pedestrians, who are on a walking tour from Halifax to Vancouver, are in town at present.

The couple also took the time to ensure that readers got their version of the hike before they raced through the Gas City.

Three pictures of Irvine, Alberta, a typical Canadian Pacific Railway prairie town, ca. 1920. The Dills ate breakfast at the Great West Hotel on South Railroad Street (bottom left). Esplanade Archives, Medicine Hat, Alberta (top); Irvine and District-20 Mile Post Historical Society, Irvine, Alberta (middle and bottom)

MR. & MRS. F. DILL REACH MED. HAT
Halifax Hikers Slowly Gaining on the Behans
in the Race to the Pacific

May 20.—Looking fit and well, Mr. and Mrs. Frank Dill, of Halifax transcontinental hikers left Medicine Hat this morning on the last stage of their trip to the Pacific Coast.

The Behans were in Medicine Hat on Monday last, so that it can be seen that the Dills are slowly but surely gaining on their rivals.

"We are only a day and a half behind the Behans now and are confident of catching them before they reach the coast," Jenny told the sports reporter.

"We have a better daily average and are doing better than either Burkman or the Behans," Frank added.

"And we have never rested a day excepting in the larger cities where all the hikers spent an equal amount of time," said Mrs. F.C. Dill, concluding the interview.

To the Hikers

From Halifax there went on hike
   Three teams with publication
To walk the ties or turnpikes...
   It's the Herald's sole creation.
Burkman, Behans and the Dills;
   All rush on in manoeuvre
To pass each other o'er the hills
'Tween here and old Vancouver.

Burkman first out, lost his pal,
   The Behans next out started,
Then young Dill, with his old gal
   The last four never parted.
But on they went day after day,
   Along the road they're fete'd
In towns and cities on their way,
They're welcome and well treated...

But should there be another race,
   We'll all be there once more
To start from the old Herald's place,
And tramp from shore to shore.

        ➤ M.P.

in *Halifax Herald*, May 23, 1921, p. 6

18

Within Striking Distance

POSITIONS OF HIKERS MAY 22

Burkman—At Swift Current, Sask.; 2,680 miles; out 126 days; did ??? miles yesterday

Dills—At Brooks, Alta.; 2,894 miles; out 111 days; did 40 miles yesterday

Behans—At Gleichen, Alta.; 2,952 miles; out 118 days; did 31 miles yesterday

Halifax—0 miles; *Calgary*—3,004; *Vancouver*—3,645

Individual dispatches from the hikers to the *Herald* were increasingly erratic after May 22 and occasionally resulted in incorrect information posted at the top of page six, where hiking news was reported. The sometimes irrational behaviour of the combatants frustrated readers and created suspicion among the loyal factions—even though the editor accepted the practice, confident that the signatures of officials acquired along the routes were a safeguard to hiker integrity: "This makes it absolutely impossible for the hikers to make progress any other way than by walking, even if they felt so inclined to do so; a thought which no one would harbour for a moment against the hikers who have day in and day out, for weeks and months, bravely struggled along in their effort to complete the tremendous task they set for themselves." Inconsistencies, the newspaper argued, were most likely the result of time-zone variances or the absence of telegraph offices in rural communities.

While the public waited for accurate hiking results to tumble in, reporters entertained readers with journalistic flair: "The race is now more thrilling than ever. The Dills, with a week to make up on the Behans at the start, are now within striking distance of their rivals. Even if they are not the first to actually reach Vancouver, they could drop back three days and still have a margin on the Behans for the RECORD in actual time taken to cross the continent."

"Interest in the hike has boiled over into the United States," claimed the *Herald*, "as high and rapidly mounting as the interest taken in the hikers in Canada." According to the newspaper, the cross-country adventure was the success it had hoped for, and everyone wanted a piece of the action, including poets, who made regular appearances in the newspapers of the day. On May 20, the *Medicine Hat News* chose such a rime to commemorate the great cross-country event.

By Monday May 23 the *Herald* was able to give readers accurate updates on the front-runners: "The Dills and the Behans were in Alberta both making a feverish run for the Rocky Mountains."

Frank and Jenny had not lingered in Medicine Hat. After a short rest they made a quick visit to the *Medicine Hat News* and then set off at a good clip west toward Calgary and the Rocky Mountains.

"We left Medicine Hat yesterday morning, Saturday, May 21st at nine o'clock, sorry that we were not able to visit the Green Lantern," Jenny said. "We thank Mr. Hart for the interest he has taken in us and we hope to visit there on our way back, as we feel now as if we can't afford to lose a day."

After completing a 26-mile hike from Medicine Hat to Suffield, and a 40-mile hike from Suffield to Brooks, the Dills were feeling fine. They had cut the Behans' lead to 58 miles, leaving no doubt that Jenny, the pacesetter, was out to win the race to the Pacific coast.

Jack and Clifford spent the weekend travelling through some of the flattest country imaginable. On Saturday they got as far as Alderson, about 35 miles from the Gas City, and discovered a community that was only a shadow of its former promise. Most farmers had given up trying to make money and moved on to more lucrative opportunities; as well, two massive fires and the Great War took away many of the town's young men. The war also led to the community renaming itself. Ashamed of its original German-sounding name, Carlstadt, the townspeople changed it to Alderson.

Between Alderson and Tilley, the Behans were overcome by heat and mosquitoes and took refuge in the shade of an old barn off the tracks. They reached Tilley in time for supper, and over a meagre prairie meal of boiled beef, watery gravy and lumpy potatoes, served up at a no-name cafe—at their own expense—

they tried to sell postcards. Instead, they learned a lot about the irrigation district from the local customers: "The CPR has men here to work the farms and have one thousand acres under cultivation. This is the irrigation district and demonstrates the wonderful way that the CPR has dams and water chutes for miles all running from Bow Lake eight miles away. Canals are arranged so that each farmer can control and work his irrigation by the turning of a wheel to suit his own farm."

"Very ingenious," Jack and Clifford agreed, trying to be attentive when their minds were miles away and focused on hiking survival.

On their way to Bassano, Jack and Clifford were caught in a dramatic prairie rainstorm; thunder and lightning crackled and lit up the skies for hours, and rain fell in torrents, pooling between the ties. A local farmer they met manuring his barn attributed the storm to Mr. Hatfield, an itinerant oddball and self-proclaimed rainmaker.

The Behans arrived in Brooks that afternoon and spent several hours strolling around town, hawking postcards. "Brooks is an attractive prairie town," Jack said. "Business is good, and the farmers expect a good fall harvest."

The mayor, from Antigonish, N.S., was another good sport. He told Jack and Clifford a yarn about the rainmaking wizard, Mr. Hatfield, who was presently in Medicine Hat setting up his magical chemicals. Having enjoyed considerable success locally, the infamous Hatfield had been invited to the Gas City and was promised a dollar a head to relieve the drought in southern Alberta. The locals expressed their admiration for the eccentric rainmaker in various ways, rhyme being one:

To Rainmaker Hatfield

E's a man wot's never seen,
Is Mr. Hatfield.
But I've heard a lot about,
Mr. Hatfield.
No reason to ask for why,
E's 'ere 'cause it's dry,
And 'e's focused in me eye
Is Mr. 'Atfield...

(With apologies to
Mud yard Ripling.)

— GUMBO JIM, Alderson

in *Medicine Hat Daily News*, May 19, 1921

Gleichen, Alberta, ca. 1908. The hikers found that walking at night when it was cool was the best way to make time in Alberta. Glenbow Archives NA-1633-6

That night the Behans carried on to Bassano. "We arrived at 4 a.m. this morning," Jack said. "The mayor looked us up, and along with the editor of the *Mail*, took us around town and out to Bow Lake where the CPR irrigation begins. Bassano's chief claim to fame was the big irrigation dam built by the Canadian Pacific Railway on the Horseshoe bend of the Bow River, 4 miles from town. 'Best in the West by a Dam Site,' is the way the town puts it." The Behans enjoyed themselves and learned a lot.

"We leave tonight for Gleichen," Jack said. "Put in a thirty-one mile day. Walking at night sure beats walking in the heat."

Having had little success building a nest egg with the sale of their postcards between Medicine Hat and Gleichen, the Behans agreed to leave the Palliser Triangle and put on a burst of speed for Calgary, communicating their whereabouts to the *Herald* but wasting no dispatch space on either the Dills or Burkman. Their strategy seemed to be: let them amuse and irritate each other.

The Behans may have found it easy to ignore Burkman, but the public didn't. A desolate image of Burkman struggling along at the back of the pack, scarcely able to keep up to his modified schedule, tugged at every mother's heartstrings. While the front-runners were racing across southern Alberta toward Calgary and the Rocky Mountains, Burkman was still in Saskatchewan.

MOOSE JAW, Sask., May 16.—Left Regina, Saturday afternoon last week. Stopped at Grand Coulee for supper and pushed on to Pense for the night. Sunday left Pense at ten o'clock, stopped at Belle Plaine for dinner, and made Moose Jaw, for the night—forty-two miles from Regina…

SWIFT CURRENT, May 19.—Arrived Mortlach late Monday night, twenty-six miles; Tuesday left at eight and had dinner at Secretan. Made Chaplin in time for dinner, made twenty-eight miles; Wednesday left there at seven o'clock made Herbert at seven-thirty—twenty-eight miles; Dinner at Fauna and made Swift Current at eight—twenty-eight for the day… Feet been bad; couldn't make long hikes. Rain held me up a lot, yesterday. Sorry didn't get stories in before.

The unusually hot temperatures continued to distress all the hikers. Even so, the Dills were able to creep up on the Behans. Jenny's euphoria over their consistent gains, however, was compromised by the niggling fear that Frank had plans to waste time visiting his pals in Calgary.

"We hope to be in Calgary either late tomorrow night or early the next morning, and then the climb over the Rockies begins. I have heard so much about them that I feel like walking all night and day now until we get there," she said. "Frank has a great many friends in Calgary but I hope we will not stay there any longer than to get a bit to eat. I tell him that we have lots of time to see our friends on the way back, and that we should devote every minute of the time now to the hike. I am taking this hike very seriously."

The couple left Bassano at 8:20 p.m., had dinner at Crowfoot and arrived at Gleichen at 5:45—calling it a day after 27 miles. The *Herald* claimed that the Behans were spending part of their day touring Calgary, so Jenny felt they could relax a little. A short break in their punishing schedule might placate Frank.

In Calgary, the legendary western cowtown, Jack and Clifford glad-handed their way through the dirty streets, predicting a comfortable win over all rivals, boasting that they would reach Vancouver in 15 short days and it would all be over.

Father and son were treated with great courtesy by the editor of the *Calgary Herald*, who introduced them to dignitaries J.M. Cameron and Mr. Finn, general manager and assistant manager of the CPR. "We were greeted like old pals," Jack wrote, "and for the first time presented with a permit to walk through the Connaught Tunnel, which we appreciated as the greatest Honour conferred on us in our whole trip."

The hikers received permission to speak, and sell their cards, to the audi-ence at Allen's Theatre, but then ended up footing the bill for their room and board. "Called at a Café, and presented our card written by Charles Murphy, but the good proprietor did not 'compre,' so we paid full price," Jack admitted. "Outside of this little co-incidence, Calgary is a great City with great, good-hearted people; very fine buildings too. On our arrival, we went to see the 'Y' and found the doors open, but nobody home, so we went over to the Depot House and put up for the day. Good clean beds and lots of fresh air."

Jack was in good form: one more lap and they'd be home.

The hikers yarned away a pleasant evening with R. Moore and his daughter, Mrs. Chisholm, both from Dartmouth, sharing commentary on the journey. After hiking more than 3,000 miles from Halifax to Calgary, the additional 650 miles to Vancouver was not viewed as a significant challenge—although the climb would take them to 3,539 feet above sea level.

The hapless Burkman reached Medicine Hat on May 24, protesting that he was still very much in the race. True, the other hikers had passed him, leaving him to plug on alone, but it was important to remember that the trek across Canada wasn't just about winning; it was also about getting to know the country. He assured readers that he had learned more about Canada walking cross-country than he could have in six lifetimes spent in one place.

As it did for the other hikers, the *Medicine Hat News* ran a story on Burkman's hike.

"I've been walking on the railroad,
All the livelong day;
I've been walking on the railroad,
Just to pass the time away..."

Charles Burkman, Halifax to Vancouver hiker, footed into the Hat on Monday, spent the holiday here and slipped away last evening for the long climb over the mountains and then down again to the Great Pacific Ocean. He isn't exactly hitting the ties "just to pass the time away," but is the last of the several sturdy easterners who are accomplishing the big idea of using "shanks mare" to go from ocean to ocean across the great Dominion. And he is having the time of his youthful life. Burkman left Halifax scarcely six weeks after he celebrated his twentieth birthday...the young hiker

Calgary, Alberta, ca. 1920. The Palliser Hotel is at the right, the Canadian Pacific Railway Station is right beside it.
Glenbow Archives, PA-3482-2

has since crossed the northern part of Maine and passed through Quebec, Ontario, Manitoba, Saskatchewan and part of sunny, Southern Alberta. His weight is practically the same—141 pounds now, 147 then—and he looks the picture of health. He ships the main part of his luggage from each of the larger centres.

Along the way he has received the autographs of many prominent citizens: Mayors, Officials, just plain Canadians...Premier Meighen signed it at Ottawa, and the Duke and Duchess of Devonshire added their signatures when he met them a short distance west of Schreiber, Ontario.

He had a great time at Port Arthur, where his father and mother and other members of his family live. He is the eldest of the children and his welcome home was worth the walk from Halifax.

At all the larger post offices the transcontinental tramp gets many encouraging letters. Two that were posted at Halifax were easily what the postal authorities would ordinarily reject for "insufficient address" but both were delivered to him months later, when he was in the heart of Northern Ontario. One was addressed to "Charles Burkman, Ontario," and the other to "Charles Burkman." He has quite a batch of letters from mayors of various cities for Mayor Gale of Vancouver, and he has dozens of letters of introduction to Vancouver friends of people whom he has met along the line. He is given many cards to mail back to people who are interested in his trip and he is running across a number of personal friends.

It was raining hard on the day Burkman left Halifax and he has run into all kinds of weather, the coldest day of the trip being the one on which he walked to Moncton. On his poorest day he covered only nine miles: He was leaving Quebec and entering Ontario on a day when snow and rain caused great clumps to form on his boots. His best record for a 24-hour day was 63 miles, bringing him to Ottawa where the blue nose members of Parliament gave him a hearty welcome.

"Take it easy," is the young hiker's tip to anyone who sets out on a cross continental trip. On this jaunt he has learned much that would make another good, long stroll easier. "It's surprising," he says, to discover that just a little bit of thread can give one a decidedly sore foot. And when he next doth walk abroad, he will have three or four pairs of boots already broken in. Sore feet and a slip on a rail have delayed him.

AFTER AN ASTONISHING, record-breaking, 52-mile hike from Gleichen to Calgary, the Dills were only 41 miles behind the Behans. Mr. and Mrs. F.C. had stopped briefly three times: once at Namaka to visit Mr. Johnston from Halifax; again at Cheadle, a pit stop; and at Sheppard, where they decided on a midnight dash for Calgary, arriving at two o'clock in the morning, bushed but euphoric.

"In a few hours, when day breaks and if we ever awaken, we will see the snow-clad peaks of the famous Canadian Rockies," said Mrs. Dill. "I hope I'll be able to move a foot so we can start off today, for we had an awful long hike yesterday and part of the early morning of today. We are sending this wire and then, as Frank says, 'we shall hit the hay.'"

Quick to anticipate disbelievers, Jenny told the doubting Thomases to check out the mileage on a CPR timetable. "We walked every step of the way," she said defiantly. "52 miles is nothing to us now; when we get to the top of the Rockies and start to slide down those mountains to Vancouver, do not be surprised to hear of us making sixty miles an hour—I mean a day."

Frank, Jenny claimed, would have been quite happy to stop at the 40-mile mark. "'No, Frank,' I said, 'I'm hungry to win this race; and remember there are BEANS ahead.'

"'Alright, girlie,' he replied. 'I am after the BEANS if it takes all the PORK off me.'"

Jenny was dead beat—they both were—but the end of the journey was near, and soon Mr. and Mrs. F.C. Dill would be back in Halifax, and the public could witness for themselves what hiking had done for poor, frail, little Mrs. Dill—and Frank, of course.

Clifford took up the pen for the family at Morley that evening. Father and son had left Calgary at 7 a.m. amidst flapping flags and colourful displays of bunting in honour of Victoria Day but soon found themselves in the foothills, gazing at the magnificent snow-covered Rocky Mountains in the distance. The hikers laboured upgrade all day, parallel to the mighty Bow River below, which had been enlarged by the melting snow on the mountaintops rushing down into the river bed at a terrifying speed—"sometimes as fast as several hundred miles an hour," Clifford wrote.

After eating dinner at the Alberta Ice Company's dining hall, they pushed through to Morley but arrived too late to reach an operating station. The Behans accepted the operator's invitation to spend the night. "Lots of good eats and milk to drink," Clifford wrote in the dispatch. "Like all Montreal people, he knows how to treat hikers. We learned a lot about the Stoney Mountain Reserve Indians."

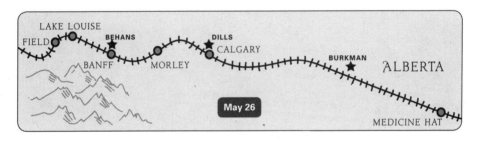

THE DILLS ENTERED Morley the same day the Behans left the town for Banff. After hiking the taxing 41 miles from Calgary, a disgruntled Jenny tried to enjoy the rousing reception prepared for them.

"The hiking fever is running at high pitch here following the departure of the Behans this morning," Jenny said before making a provocative statement. "We feel that the race is really won by us anyway, if only by the fact that we are ahead of the Behans in terms of days out. Besides, I am still confident that in a short five days time we will be the first to arrive at the coast."

Hundreds of confused Canadians called newspaper offices across the country wanting to know, "Who's ahead now?" and "How far did they go?"

Throwing caution to the wind, Jenny added, "We hope to report on Sunday that we are spending the day with the Behans—and then we will show them what our heels look like."

Things had not gone well in Calgary for the Dills, where Jenny's worst fears were realized. The boys from Halifax had succeeded in whisking Frank away to the Kiwanis Club for a publicity stunt—just as the couple was about to leave Calgary. "Mr. Conolly took Frank to the club," she told friends. "So we didn't get away until three-thirty. Then we had the bad luck to encounter snow and hail-storms and were forced to take shelter in a station house ten miles out. Had supper in Cochrane and arrived in Morley at six-thirty." Everything, it seemed, had conspired against Mrs. Jenny, and despite an outward show of civility, she found it hard to suppress her anger with Mr. F.C. Dill in private.

"We lost nearly a day and allowed the Behans to get out of our clutches for the time being," she pouted.

Feeling depressed and irrational, Jenny spent the night brooding over Frank's lapse of judgment. It could cost them dearly, and she knew it.

Men of Iron

As the five stalwarts of the Great Trans-Canada Race faced the final gruelling challenges of the event, tempers flared, frustrations surfaced and cruel accusations were fired, making it difficult to determine who were friends and who enemies. Jenny Dill—a little woman in a man's world—took more than her share of the undermining and name-calling.

"Crucial test for woman hiker begins as they reach high altitudes," the *Herald* reported on Saturday May 28. "Doubts that Mrs. Dill will be able to keep up the pace she and her husband have been setting in the great race across the continent were expressed...by friends of the Dills in Halifax and Dartmouth. The hikers are now on the up-grade, and a heavy grade at that, and at an altitude of more than 4,500 feet above sea level. It is well known that this high altitude has a weakening effect on the heart during heavy exercises, and with the steep grade the Dills are likely to be slowed considerably."

Mindful of Jenny's stellar performance throughout the race, loyal friends from home were quick to defend her. "She can withstand hardship as well as any man

OVER THE ROCKIES WITH THE HIKERS

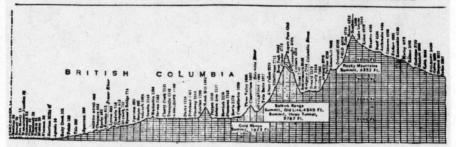

Halifax Herald, June 1, 1921, p. 6

can," they said. "If she reaches the crest of the Rockies as fit as she was in Calgary, people can expect an awesome spectacle down the mountainside to Vancouver."

No word had been received from the couple that day, so it was all idle speculation. The Behans, however, had reached Lake Louise. Jack was overwhelmed by what he saw but completely drained by the physical exertion it had taken to achieve it. "It is impossible for anyone to accurately describe the power and majesty of the beautiful scenery, the snow covered mountains and trees—some growing at the top of the mountain," he wrote, but "the climb up the mountain is a critical test that only men of iron can endure."

He and Clifford had been impressed by the abundance of wildlife along the route through the national park. A spectacular herd of very tame mountain sheep left them speechless as they passed through the Stoney Mountain Reserve, and the sight of a herd of sure-footed elk scaling a steep access to the famed Three Sisters mountains in the late afternoon was the most memorable experience of all.

The hikers had arrived at Banff around midnight the previous day—"so tired that they could hardly step over a match." They had hiked 40 punishing miles, and despite passing through some of the most stunning scenery in the world, Jack admitted that the trans-Canada hike was growing stale: "The walking is getting heavy and telling on the legs, so much so, we find it hard to make mileage. I will be glad when the hike is over…I weighed myself today, one hundred and forty-two when I started, and have lost fourteen pounds."

The *Herald* realized that the men were in need of some serious pampering and suggested that they take a few hours to relax and unwind, so the next morning the men enjoyed a Canadian breakfast for the small sum of 75 cents, took a pleasant stroll around the park, observed buffalo, deer and lots of mountain sheep, and ended

Cave and Basin Sulphur Pools, Banff, Alberta, ca. 1920, where the Behans relaxed and had a good bath.
Glenbow Archives NB-50-18

up at the famous Cove and Basin "sulphur springs," where they had a good bath. In the afternoon the men skimmed through the mail waiting for them at the CPR station—postcards and several back issues of the *Herald*—then attempted to loaf away the afternoon, trying not to worry about the progress being made by the Dills.

Something Jack had read in the newspaper niggled, however. "The Dills are blowing about catching us," Jack said. "Any hiker who walks fifty-one miles in one day beats the world record which is held by a lady in the States. Her time was forty-seven miles in one day." Since Whitewood, when the Dills slipped into second place and began their aggressive drive to take over first spot, Jack had tried to maintain a stony silence about the couple. He had enjoyed the rivalry with Burkman, but the Dills were different—Jenny in particular irritated him. The real threat of being beaten by *this* woman and her mewling husband was hard for him to stomach.

Late afternoon found the pair packed and headed for Lake Louise, more resolved than ever to end the race. They found themselves battling a strong headwind from the north and were eventually pitted against a driving snowstorm that obscured their view of Squaw and Sulphur mountains. After inching along the CPR tracks, they finally arrived at Lagan Station, Lake Louise. "Thirty-five miles today," Jack crowed to the folks back home.

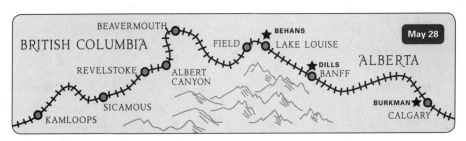

You're Bound to Pick a Winner!

The Cross-Canada Hike has gone so far it is practically certain that the Dills and Behans will be the first two teams to finish. So if you select either of these teams you are safe to qualify for our free ticket offer.

Further, you can take it for granted that at least two teams will reach the Coast. That means that

Two Customers Are Bound to Win $460

For we are giving two return tickets for as far as the two leading teams reach, or the equivalent in cash.

You have just as good a chance to win as if you had entered two months ago — but you have only a short time to enter now as the contest is closing. Every dollar spent here for new glasses or repairing the old gives you a chance to win. You'll be ordering glasses within a year — why not order them here and now when you may win a ticket to Vancouver and back?

T. J. Wallace
OPTOMETRIST AND MFG. OPTICIAN.

Final T.J. Wallace
advertisement.
Halifax Herald,
May 28, 1921.

Burkman did not report to the paper May 27. There was no reprimand from the *Herald*. The newspaper and his loyal following were now used to his quirky ways.

Thrilled with the way the race was shaping up to a dynamic finish, the *Herald* gave the public a final opportunity to get involved in the Cross-Canada Hike competition, sponsored by T.J. Wallace, Optometrists and Manufacturing Opticians. "You're Bound to Pick a Winner!" the half-page ad promised. "Two Customers Are Bound to Win $460." The hikers were now too preoccupied with reaching the end of their ordeal to protest this exploitation.

THE DILLS REPORTED from Field, B.C., on Monday May 30. "We left Morley Saturday morning and made Banff at eleven p.m.—forty-two whopping miles later," Jenny said. "We were so tired that I couldn't talk. It was the hardest day of the hike."

The couple left Banff on Sunday at 10 o'clock and spent the night at Castle Mountain. They left early the next morning, gulped down a dinner at Lake Louise and reached Field at 6:30 p.m., completing 37 miles. Mrs. Dill declared that it had been the most wonderful day of the entire hike: both were well and intended to make a few long hikes soon. "It is all down hill now." Jenny could hardly wait to get back home and tell some stories about this amazing trip.

As the race tightened, leaving competitors muscle-sore and foot-weary, with nerves frazzled and minds bitter, the levity in Jack's night letters was much appreciated.

"We had a very comfortable time at Lake Louise," he wrote. "Took the soft side of a board to lie on, and the rats and gophers whistled 'Home Sweet Home' all night. It is a long time since we have had to sleep out of a bed, but after all, this is the life. We would not change it to be the mayor of Dartmouth." What else was there to do this far into the race but grin and bear it?

Father and son had spent an uncomfortable day. "The altitude played havoc with us today," Jack said. "We bled at the nose a bit as we had been climbing for two days and reached the Great Divide, altitude 5,380 feet."

Jack (left) and Clifford (right) Behan at the Great Divide.
Courtesy of Donnie Behan family

Jack and Clifford stopped at Camp Carr for dinner and then, to their blissful relief, were told that the tracks were downhill to Field.

To get there the men had to negotiate the two Spiral Tunnels, which wound through Mount Ogden and Cathedral Mountain. "It was quite a sensation—one and three quarter miles long each," Jack said. "Lots of mountains on either side of us and beautiful cold springs running everywhere from the mountains. The water is the best in the world."

At Field the Behans were guests at the YMCA. Mr. Depew, the secretary, not only refused their money but also arranged an entertainment on their behalf with the resident guests. Jack was humbled and grateful. "We will never be able to pay back any of the hospitality shown to us here." He described Field as a fine place, a railroad centre with nice lawns and good people. "They all try to do something for you to make your future journey more comfortable," he wrote in his night letter.

As the Behans readied themselves for an early start and a final heave through the Rocky Mountains in an attempt to unload the Dills, who were close on their heels, people wondered where Burkman was. Was the lone hiker still in the race?

The answer was yes! Burkman was in Calgary on May 29 and was still very much in the game. No longer hounded by the public's expectation, he felt comfortable nipping at the other hikers from third place. He took a cut-off for Strangmuir at Gleichen and completed a 42-mile jaunt.

"Left Bassano, Friday at seven," he wrote. "It was a cold night for hiking." Left there [Gleichen] on Saturday at 8:30 and had breakfast at Shepherd, then started for Calgary, a 40-mile hike in all. I am feeling in the pink of conditions and in great spirits as I can see the foothills of the mountains in the distance."

Burkman didn't intend to stop in Calgary; instead he would push through to Radnor and reach Banff in two hikes. Farmers working in their fields and townsfolk going about their business could hear the fine tenor of Brukman as he sang one of the new tunes being circulated on 10-inch 78 RPM records. He strode along the CPR tracks with his head in the clouds, perhaps, but his eyes firmly fixed on Vancouver and the finish line in the distance.

JACK AND CLIFFORD Behan left Beavermouth, B.C., on the eastern boundary of Glacier National Park, at 8:30 a.m. May 31. It was a glorious spring day, and notwithstanding the upgrade climb toward the great Connaught Tunnel, they enjoyed the vast panorama of scenery along the route. The hikers were treated to a "great feed" by the CPR operators at Studer before continuing on to the famous Stoney Creek Bridge, which towered more than 200 feet above its footings. In the late 1800s this spectacular feat of engineering was reputed to be the tallest structure of its kind in the world.

When the men reached the Connaught Tunnel at 3:30 p.m., a train had just passed through its five-mile length, fouling the air with smoke and gases, and they had to wait half an hour for the air to clear before tying on handkerchief masks and setting off into the dark passageway. Jack's flashlight did little to counter the thick clouds of smoke locked inside the tunnel, and for the first two miles they stumbled along the ties, aided by walking sticks. A prick of light grew in circumference as the men navigated the final three miles to the mouth of the tunnel. They were happy to escape into freedom and fresh air.

One of the two watchmen inside the tunnel, whose job it was to report the progress of the trains back to the CPR main stations from telephone boxes posted every half mile along the tunnel wall, was happy to sign their books.

The Behans arrived at Glacier Station covered in soot and grease, and were met by Mr. Junkins, whose company had been awarded the contract to line the tunnel with concrete.

Burkman reached Banff the same day. His feet were now fully recovered, and he claimed to be at the top of his game. "The altitude caused me no problems as it did the Behans—in fact, mountain climbing seemed to agree with me," he said. Burkman still had two weeks left to overtake the Dills and the Behans, and he professed the noble resolve to do it.

Looking west at Connaught Tunnel, Rocky Mountains, ca. 1920. The Behans' trek through the tunnel after a train left them covered in grease and soot.
VPL Special Collections #31536

CPR train at Glacier
Station, Alberta,
ca. 1916–1930.
Glenbow Archives,
NA-4572-3

"Some I suppose criticize me because I let a woman pass me," he said. "Few know what I have gone thru since I left Halifax. It has been a hard, long, lonesome grind, and many times I felt like chucking the whole thing up. I would have felt different if I'd had company, but I decided to stick and I will until I reach Vancouver."

At Lake Louise, Burkman checked in with the *Herald* before pushing off for Field, venturing gamely through the spiral tunnels in the dwindling daylight.

The *Herald* also ran a contribution from J.A. Irvine, former Haligonian and now resident of Calgary, who had seen Mr. and Mrs. Dill when they passed through that city. "The Dills seemed to be in the pink of conditions," he wrote. "In Calgary they were entertained at several places, Mr. Dill going to the Calgary Kiwanis Club luncheon with George Connolly, a brother of J.L. Connolly, M.P.P. of Halifax. Everyone wished them success."

Poor Jenny must have winced when she read the article, knowing what Frank's social hobnobbing in Calgary was now costing them.

Albert Canyon Hysteria

Fuelled by adrenalin and bouts of anger, Mrs. F.C. Dill was too obsessed with beating the Behans and winning the race to Vancouver to concern herself with the latest musings of Charles Burkman. "We have gained back at least half of the lost time on the Behans," she mused, "and I hope that by Sunday, June 5, we will have gotten the other half day... They are only a few miles ahead of us, and we can almost feel the heat of their breath as they pant toward Vancouver."

Even though the Dills continued to do well, making significant gains on their rivals, Jenny refused to forget her husband's behaviour in the infamous Alberta cowtown. "I do not think that I shall ever forgive Frank for the long stop he made in Calgary when he went out with the Boys. I know the Club is a charming place—but no place for a married man," she said. "I told him not to stay more than ten minutes but he stayed almost that many hours, and we lost almost a day."

The Dills reported from Beavermouth on June 1, and the next day they seemed to fly from there to Golden, following the tracks of the first transportation route that the CPR had established through the harrowing Kicking Horse Canyon.

MEANWHILE, THE BEHANS had fallen uncharacteristically silent. This remote wilderness of the Canadian Rockies, with its stunning views, spectacular glaciers and remarkable waterfalls, was also home to a multitude of wildlife, including herds of robust elk, humpbacked grizzly bears and wary cougars, all known to attack when provoked in the spring while they were protecting their babies. When the *Herald* finally tracked down the father and son on June 2 with the help of telegraphers at Revelstoke station (a CPR western divisional point) the news, as feared, was not good.

"We will never forget the last day of May," Jack told the newspaper. "We got an early start THAT MORNING and figured on making a big day... Three miles east of Albert Canyon, Cliff took severe pains in the muscles of his back." He vowed he could manage to the Canyon station, and if he were worse there would take the train as far as Revelstoke, which he ended up doing. Clifford's sobering account of his trials, from Taft, B.C., headlined page six of the June 3 *Herald*.

CLIFFORD BEHAN IS FORCED TO TAKE TRAIN AFTER GREAT HIKE OVER CANADIAN ROCKIES
Son of Hiker Admits That Pace of Dills is Too Strong and Obeys Doctor's Orders.

Albert Canyon Station,
B.C, ca. 1900.
Revelstoke Museum
and Archives #1174

YMCA, Revelstoke, B.C.
ca. 1910. The YMCA
supported the hike
across Canada.
Revelstoke Museum
and Archives #1093

In Revelstoke, Clifford saw a doctor who diagnosed "a cold in his back" and advised him to "lay up for a few days," but, according to Jack, "he said nothing doing." The spunky 24-year-old took the No. 4 train going east from Revelstoke station at midnight, got off at Albert Canyon station, and started walking back to Revelstoke in the pitch dark. "It was the most lonesome walk I have had since leaving Halifax... I arrived back at Revelstoke at seven a.m. tired but feeling better," Clifford claimed.

After a joyful reunion, followed by a few hours of sleep, the shaken father and son headed west toward Taft, where they stopped with CPR agent J.W. Maloney long enough to share a feed and send a night letter to the *Herald*.

"I am so upset," Jack admitted, "that I can't think of anything more now."

Despite their adversities, the intrepid Behans continued on to Malakwa, where they bedded down for the night with the station agent, having covered an astonishing 42 miles.

During that last segment of their walk, the Behans hiked close to Craigellachie Station, where the last spike of the CPR was driven home in 1885. This symbolic link, which helped unite the Dominion and promoted settlement throughout the country, went unobserved by the two men, who now wanted nothing more than to reach the west coast and be on their way home.

No updates from the Dills or Burkman reached the *Herald*.

INDESCRIBABLY WEARY AND footsore, the Behans trudged from Malakwa to Salmon Arm on June 3. With the sun beating down on the ballasted track beds, and waves of heat bouncing off the iron rails, the world-class scenery of the Shuswap was all but wasted on the hikers. Pursued by clouds of hungry mosquitoes, and dehydrated beyond description, father and son felt no incentive to sight bald eagles posed like sentinels along the Eagle River. "We drank water at every stream and at times could imagine we were floating along, but our speed was limited," Jack said. "At times it was almost unbearable."

The Behans reached Sicamous too early for supper so continued along the tracks to the camp where Ralph Ross cooked for the Annis Bay Lumber Company. The ex-Lunenburg man listened to their adventures while preparing them a hearty meal of freshly caught rainbow trout and fried potatoes. After the top-up, the Behans hobbled to the Salmon Arm suburb of North Canoe. "We were so exhausted that we gratefully put up for the night with a Mrs. Sweeten," Jack said. "Twenty-six miles completed."

THE BEHANS WERE up bright and early June 4, and, after a fitful sleep, they were more determined than ever to get back to the tracks and end the race. "Hard to believe, I know, but we travelled from Salmon Arm through Notch Hill to Kamloops in a fifteen hour, fifty mile marathon—our longest junket in the race," Jack claimed. After posting a few letters at the station in Salmon Arm that morning, the Behans had left for Notch Hill and carried on to Chase, arriving there at 11:20 p.m. "There were no accommodations to be found in the village, so we decided on a pleasant evening hike to Kamloops."

Following a short breakfast stop at the Ducks Divisional House, they hiked along the South Thompson riverbank and into Kamloops—too bleary-eyed to note the changing physical landscape as it shifted from lush mountain greenery to semi-arid desert sagebrush and majestic sandstone hoodoos, and too afraid to rest lest they fall asleep.

The *Herald* finally located the Dills at Albert Canyon. After leaving Beavermouth at 5:30 a.m. and stopping only briefly for lunch at Glacier, the couple sprinted 42 miles in nine hours. To avoid having to go through the Connaught Tunnel, they enlisted the help of the Bear Creek game warden, who guided them over the mountain trail. The route was snowy and longer, but the novelty of exchanging boots for snowshoes appealed to Frank and Jenny, as did the spectacular view of large glaciers.

"Both," Jenny told the paper, "were O.K." So she wired the newspaper from

Sicamous at 8:15 p.m. the next day, saying "We stopped only once. For dinner at Taft; covered thirty-nine miles."

Burkman took the time to visit fellow Maritimers at the Hector Divisional Point before completing the terrifying walk through the Spiral Tunnels. He didn't reach Yoho Provincial Park and Glacier Station until dark. "I chalked up a startling NINTY-EIGHT MILES in two days," he bragged. The betting public admitted the stats were impressive. The lone hiker was still in the race, and sports continued to play at "what if?"

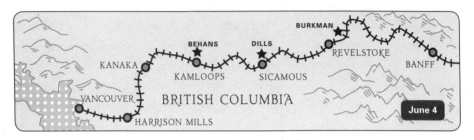

KAMLOOPS, AT THE junction of the North and South Thompson rivers, was surrounded by a parched wilderness of sagebrush and hoodoo outcroppings, where Bill Miner, the gentleman train robber, had carried out several bold train heists. Miner and his legendary gang had slaked their thirst at the city's Dominion Hotel, and local raconteurs still exchanged stories of his escapades for a pint. After treating themselves to a good soak and a decent meal, Jack and Clifford visited this very watering hole and found themselves at home in the environment, possibly sensing that one day they too would be part of the folklore.

The Dominion Hotel in Kamloops, where John Hugh Gillis, the very first man to walk across Canada, also stayed.
Kamloops Museum and Archives #574

John Hugh Gillis, the first man to walk across Canada in a non-competitive capacity (travelling from North Sydney, Nova Scotia, to Vancouver), had lived at the hotel for several months after he was discharged from the provincial tuberculosis sanatorium in Tranquille, 10 miles outside the Kamloops city limits, on September 12, 1912. The ravaged giant of the Canadian track and field scene, who had hoped to compete in decathlon at the 1912 Olympic games, died at home in Cape Breton on July 4, 1913. Charles Henry Jackman, Gillis's companion on the cross-country journey in 1906, had helped the Behans set up a serious cross-Canada hiking schedule when they stopped in Moncton way back on February 1.

Inspired by tales of Gillis and Jackman, the Behans eagerly pushed on to Walhachin early the next morning, stopping only for short dips in the swollen Thompson River to gain relief from the sweltering heat.

Fixated on getting to Vancouver, they showed little interest in the serried ranchlands they passed. Only the novel interplay of tracks and trains, which raced along opposite embankments of the river before changing sides and disappearing from sight, caught their attention. Jack, preoccupied with food, continued to worry about their dwindling funds. Eastern hospitality had been to his liking, but western grub was only adequate. Outside Walhachin, he grumbled, "We had dinner with an Italian section man—Black tea and toast were served us by him and we *relished* it fine."

They arrived at Walhachin, the land of the round rock, late in the evening and were much impressed. "This is a nice town, all English Earls, Dukes, and Lord's sons have ranches here," Jack told readers. "Before the war an English syndicate bought up this land and sold it to these fellows. Some were sold for six hundred dollars an acre. When the war broke out the majority of these gentlemen became majors and cornels in reserve regiments and were called home. Some never returned, being killed overseas."

Two million dollars had been spent to irrigate the extensive orchards, and flumes pulsing with water lined the hillsides. In early 1921 the community was still optimistic about its future—even though 97 of the 107 men in the community had enlisted in the Great War with Canadian or British forces, and many of those who weren't killed were reluctant to return. The operator at the CPR station, Mr. McLaine from Sydney, Nova Scotia, fed the hikers and made them comfortable for the night.

On June 6 the Behans struggled 32 miles along the CPR track, too exhausted to notice the steelhead trout making rainbow leaps in the Thompson River. They

Once a freight depot for the Cariboo goldfields, Ashcroft played host to the Behans, who could now almost taste the end of the race. Courtesy of Ashcroft Museum and Archives

arrived in the prosperous town of Ashcroft, known as "Mile 0" because it had been the major freight depot for supplies being transferred from train to stage as they headed north to the Cariboo goldfields. The Behans spent the evening reporting to friends and family. They were well, they said, but longing for Vancouver and home.

The Behans were now less than 200 miles from the west coast finish line, but according to the lone hiker, the Great Trans-Canada Race was far from over.

BURKMAN MAKES STRENUOUS EFFORTS
TO WIN BIG HIKE ACROSS CONTINENT

Chipping away at the competition from the rear, Charles Burkman was enjoying his best runs in the hike. He had covered an astonishing 95 miles of mountain terrain, immersed in winter conditions, over two days, crossed stretches of desolate countryside and treacherous railway bridges, and suffered the stress of daily warnings of bear maulings.

"I am prepared to apply every ounce of energy into the finish of this gruelling race," he vowed to reporters in Revelstoke. Readers were impressed, but although they cheered enthusiastically, they had to ask "Is it good enough to win the race?"

Gruelling Finish

POSITIONS OF HIKERS JUNE 7

Burkman—At Sicamous, B.C.; 3,821 miles; out 142 days; did 45 miles yesterday

Dills—At Cherry Creek, B.C.; 3,409 miles; out 127 days; did 31 miles yesterday

Behans—At Spences Bridge, B.C.; 3,475 miles; out 134 days; did 31 miles yesterday

Halifax—0 miles; *Vancouver*—3,645

Reporting from Spences Bridge on June 7, Jack Behan struggled to be objective. "It has been very hot all day with the sun dancing on the rails," he said. "You can see for miles ahead of you. Still in the dry belt but we hope to be out of it tomorrow." Flanked by the beautiful Thompson River to their right, the Behans could see only dry, clean hills, but 300 feet up the trail, past the dense stands of silvery sagebrush, hundreds of flourishing Chinese market gardens and thousands of potatoes in white bloom were fed by a waterwheel harnessed to the river below.

Rather than pay for a night's rest, the Behans curled up in a hillside burrow outside the village for a few hours of uncomfortable shut-eye. Weary as they were, a cacophony of coyotes, encouraged by the howling of scattered village dogs, kept them tossing and turning.

Morning light found them limping southward toward Spuzzum, stiff, hungry and with mounting resolve to put a finish to the race. At Lytton, where the swollen Thompson River joined the mighty Fraser, the Behans had a chance

Cisco Bridge over the Fraser River. Despite B.C. being the hardest part of their journey, all the hikers were awed by its beauty.

VPL Special Collections #8373B

meeting with the superintendent of the CPR and several other officials who were interested in their stories but, to Jack's consternation, didn't want to buy their postcards.

"British Columbia is not at all as liberal as the other provinces," Jack complained. "There are not many places to sell cards to pay our expenses; therefore we are putting up with every imaginable hardship as we near our finish."

After begging what turned out to be a depressing fried breakfast from the cook at a CPR workman's car outside Lytton, the Behans crossed the Fraser on the magnificent CP bridge at Cisco, with hordes of mosquitoes "thirsting after their bloody vitals."

Jack and Clifford stopped briefly to share dinner with the section men at Kanaka and ate a modest supper with a farm family outside North Bend. It was late evening when they finally arrived in Spuzzum and successfully roused the postmaster from his bed to pick up their mail.

Free breakfast at Lytton, free dinner at Kanaka and a free supper outside North Bend—all in all not a bad haul of free meals, but unfortunately for the Behans they had no hotel bed to look forward to and spent another night in a mountain burrow wearing all their clothes.

The same day the Behans reached Spences Bridge, Burkman completed a spectacular 45-mile downhill run from Revelstoke to Sicamous, making a gain on both his rivals. With the accomplishment came a renewed sense of commitment. "If it lies within my power to catch the other hikers before they reach the west coast I shall do it," he promised. "There is a great rivalry between the Dills and the Behans. And if I do not get to Vancouver first, I want to see that plucky little woman make it. She is receiving all kinds of praise in this part of the country, and people marvel at the endurance and pluck she has shown.

"This is a wonderful country," he said. "No one can imagine how beautiful it is, but despite all its beauty, I will be glad when I reach Vancouver. It has been a great hike, but I guess we will all be glad when it is over." Nearly five months into the trans-Canada adventure, it seemed that the challenge had lost its innocence even for a romantic like Charles Burkman.

"All" may well have included Burkman and the Behans; as for Jenny and her errant Frank, they still had much to prove, and a public show of their resolve and determination was demonstrated from Kamloops on June 7 in the anger that sizzled across the wires to Halifax after Jenny learned that the Behans claimed a 50-mile walking feat from Chase to Kamloops on June 4.

"The Behans said they were going to have the day they lost to us back," she said. "They claim to have walked thirty-three miles in four hours: Some walkers! If they had walked it all—as I have done—we would now be ahead of them. Besides," she smiled, "we will have days gained over the Behans to our advantage"—a reference to their staggered starting dates of January 25 for the Behans and February 1 for the Dills.

Frank and Jenny left Sicamous at 8:30 a.m. on Sunday June 6, taking time to have their pictures snapped with the mayor of the community. They bolted down a small dinner in Salmon Arm and then snatched a few hours of sleep in the section house at Carlin after completing 30 miles.

The couple left Carlin at 6:30 the next morning, ate dinner in Chase—where hurried repairs were made to Frank's boots—made an 8 p.m. pit stop at Ducks and then, driven by clouds of mosquitoes and gloating images of the Behans, pushed on in the growing dark to Kamloops.

After picking up their mail at the CPR station and skimming through the hiking news in the Herald, Frank and Jenny left the city, with renewed urgency, for Cherry Creek and the Behans. The front-runners were 47 miles ahead of them, while Burkman was 88 miles behind them. The cross-Canada event promised a gruelling finish.

PAST CHERRY CREEK ... Spences Bridge ... Kanaka ... North Bend, stumbling along railroad ties and weaving across narrow bridges built over the turbulent Thompson and Fraser rivers, the indomitable Jenny and her Frank charged into Spuzzum on June 8—only to make a sickening discovery.

"For the second time since we left Halifax, we today pulled into a town that the Behans had left the same morning," Jenny said. "We made 47 miles today and if we have to walk all night tomorrow, we will be within reach of the Behans." They had gone through a terrible ordeal that day but had survived it. After a short rest, they would again take to the trail in honest pursuit.

Anxious, exhausted, and psychologically frazzled, Jenny was no longer certain they could beat the Behans across the finish line. But it was almost impossible for them to be beaten in terms of days out, so with 180 miles yet to cover, Jenny Dill remained optimistic: "Tomorrow, we hope to make the big day of it, but tonight, I am mighty tired."

WITH THE DEAFENING roar of the Fraser River in their ears, the Behans were sometimes so distracted by the noise that they scarcely had time to leap from the tracks to safety as an iron horse thundered past. The sleep-deprived father and son were tortured by visions of a relentless Mrs. F.C. Dill cracking her whip at their heels, and so took to walking night and day. They wanted the ordeal over and they didn't intend to be beaten by the Dills.

Finishing first was synonymous with winning in Jack Behan's vocabulary, yet here he was, near the end of a race that had begun with a promise of high adventure and expectation, almost certain to win it, but facing a crushing reality: hiking was a sport that could bring you notoriety, but he had a family to feed. There were eight children back at Tufts Cove in North Dartmouth, Nova Scotia. Clifford, the eldest, was with him, and he was glad of that. Then there was Bertha, Frances, Rhodasella—*Rhoda*, he thought of her nickname fondly—Roy, John, Marguerite, Florence and finally Bernard. There! He could still remember them all. Catherine was a good mother and an undemanding wife, and she deserved something in return for the faith she had in him.

As Jack stumbled on down the track with his number one son, his self-pity gave way to a bright new idea, one that included money. He stopped suddenly to get Clifford's take.

"Run it by the *Herald*, see if it has legs," the lad replied. "Folks across the country will be sorry to have an end to this race, that's sure."

"Frank will go for it. Fella with a wife can always use a little money—but I'm not so sure about that highfalutin Burkman."

"Get the *Herald* to convince him."

"Could do that."

Father and son continued to jaw over Jack's money-making scheme, and that helped to hold them together until they reached Haig on June 9, barely able to stand up and just 89 miles short of Vancouver.

"We will arrive in Vancouver at noon Saturday, if we do not give out," Jack said. "The trip is wearing us both down. We are suffering hardships, for there are no towns here in which to sell our cards. Folks are not as kind in British Columbia as in the other provinces and we are not nearly so well revered ... Two more days and, God willing, it will all be over and then we shall turn our faces homeward, proud of the fact that we have accomplished what we set out to do."

Haig ... Kent ... Agassiz ... Harrison ... onward the Behans struggled, barely conscious of where they were, and too worn out to give a damn. Waterfalls gushed off the Coast Mountains, overflowing with spring runoff, and gave way to lush flooded meadows. But who noticed?

The same day, Burkman made it as far as Kamloops and put a new spin on the outcome of the competition. "While in Kamloops, I heard rumors of flooding in the Fraser valley," he said. "And if the reports are true and the flooding is near to where the Behans are camped, it is still possible to catch them this side of the finish line."

No one knew exactly where the Dills were that day, but Jenny Dill would almost certainly not have appreciated being disregarded in Charles Burkman's hiking equation.

He continued, musing about what might have been if not for his earlier misadventures. "I nearly equalled my best performance today when I hiked 49 miles," he said proudly, "but I left in the morning at three o'clock to enable me to make it to Kamloops tonight—strange to relate—I didn't feel a bit tired. I only wish that I had not had that accident ... and that I had felt as good all the way as I have the last few weeks. I would have been in Vancouver long before this." However, he was still going strong, and if walking his best would help, he might yet reach the coast first. "Tomorrow," he said with renewed confidence, "I will try for 60 miles."

On Saturday June 11, newspapers across British Columbia expressed concerns about the flooding Eagle River, and when the hikers had not been heard from by late afternoon, it was assumed their progress had been hindered by the spring floods.

"This means that it will be impossible for the Behans to reach Vancouver today," the *Herald* noted. "And if they do not reach there until early next week, the chances are that they will be overtaken by the Dills."

The Saturday *Halifax Evening Star* came forward with a bold prediction and a dramatic summary of the Great Trans-Canada Race. The language showed that the paper was intent on squeezing as much drama as possible from the final days.

GREATEST CONTEST IN HISTORY OF
PEDESTRIANISM WILL CLOSE MONDAY
"Will the Dills steal a march on the Behans?
Will Burkman make one last spurt and head off his rivals?"

No event of human endeavour has so captivated the imagination of Canada to the extent of this race. It has presented, in every detail, the marked contrasts of the Behans, forceful, resolute and dashing; the Dills, calmly determined—the strangest pedestrians that ever trod the soil of Canada; a young man, in the prime of his life, and a frail, unassuming, but courageous little lady... [But] it is to Charlie Burkman that the heart goes out. This boy has plodded along through the vast silence of this enormous country, his sole company his own thoughts, has slept alone in the impenetrable woods of Ontario, has faced the loneliness of the prairie lands, climbed the steepness of the Canadian Rocky mountains, the sole company [on]his long trudge the echo of his own voice as he sang his way through the gorges."

Whatever the outcome, the hike would soon be over, and the eyes of the entire Dominion were now concentrated on the last stage of this remarkable, heroic and splendid journey. The public held its collective breath and awaited the outcome.

Winning By a Nose

And then it was all over. The great trans-Canada adventure, which started as a simple concept of a walk across the Dominion, ended as a proverbial barnburner of a competition five months later, when Jack and Clifford Behan appeared on the outskirts of Vancouver on Saturday June 11, wobbling between the rails of the CPR line, half-starved and near collapse. Hundreds of well-wishers, on the lookout for the hikers, met them and walked with them to the downtown CPR station on Cordova Street, where a well-deserved celebration was organized.

BEHANS, BY ALL NIGHT HIKE, NOSE OUT DILLS
FATHER AND SON TRAVEL 61 MILES IN 22 HOURS
Dartmouth Hikers Reach Vancouver First,
But Will Likely be Five Days Behind Dills in Time.

HUSBAND AND WIFE HAVE LEAD IN AVERAGE
Vancouver Welcomes Halifax Hikers: Ready to Give
the Dills and Burkman a Wildly Enthusiastic Reception.
Newspaper Men Getting Stories Of The Long
Tramp From The Behans—The City Threatens to
Go Wild Upon the Arrival Of the Dills and Burkman,
the Lone Hiker.

The newly built Canadian Pacific Railway station in Vancouver was the last station for the 1921 hikers. VPL Special Collections #31536, Fred Spalding Photo

A jubilant Jack Behan wired the *Herald* from Vancouver the next day: "We have done it and done it first. We arrived here at 2:30, Saturday afternoon Pacific Time. We are grateful for everyone's support, and we're sure looking forward to returning home shortly—this time by train."

Addressing the crowd in front of the CPR station, Jack revealed that when he and Clifford heard from a private source that the Dills had reached Spuzzum the same day the Behans left the town, they made a snap decision to walk non-stop to Vancouver. "To be absolutely certain of reaching the balmy shores of the Pacific first, we actually walked for 22 hours on our last drive without a rest—making 66 miles," Jack said.

A ripple of derisive laughter passed through the audience as people quickly calculated the miles into an hourly average. Could anyone walk three miles an hour for an entire day? But Jack didn't back down. "I don't know how we did it, and I doubt if we could do it again," he said, silencing the doubters. "I guess we figured it was a matter of life or death."

It didn't take Mrs. F.C. Dill long to react to the Behans' winning claim. She wired from Harrison Mills late Saturday, blazing mad. "We won anyway, from a time standpoint," she argued. "We are only 61 miles from Vancouver, and it is like a step to us now after hiking all the way from Halifax."

There were other issues that she felt compelled to address. "I was thinking today of those people who laughed at us when I started out from Halifax last winter: She who laughs last, laughs best. I think I have proved that a woman can do any athletic stunt that a man can." (In her heart of hearts, Jenny probably knew that the *Herald*, her great benefactor, was one of the doubters.)

Burkman also wired Halifax from North Bend on June 12. "The race is officially over, and I have been beaten," he admitted. "But I intended to finish in a sprint, making better time on the home stretch than any of the other hikers have done. I'm now 3,504 miles along the way and only 109 miles from the finish line. You can tell everyone in Halifax, and others who have been following the hikers, that I will finish, or be finished. Vancouver or bust has been my motto from the beginning—especially since I was left alone and the hike turned into a race."

AFTER VISITING MAYOR Robert Henry Otley Gale and handing him letters from the mayors of Halifax and Dartmouth, Jack's official business was completed, and the father and son gave over to having a well-deserved wonderful time. As Jack saw it, their chief enemies to having fun were the newspapermen.

"We have been throttled in the street, in hotels, at our baths, at breakfast, dinner, and supper, by everyone from junior reporters to newspaper proprietors." Jack beamed. "We've told our life stories a hundred times and the scribblers have sat at our feet in awe as we described minutely and vividly every feature of the hike."

The Behans may have been out to relax and slough off the last five months of hiking dust, but now that the race was over, Jack was confronted by his real-life responsibilities of mounting debts, here and at home. This need for money was never far from his mind, and with the help of the *Herald* and his broad base of support across the Dominion, he intended to create an even greater marathon racing challenge from Montreal to Halifax. He would have his cake and show them all. Jack could picture his final heroic dash into Halifax: *Down Barrington Street—clearing a screaming mob of local fans—then a victory circle around the grounds before bounding up to the podium erected on the Commons, the Canadian Red Ensign, symbolic of every man's hopes and dreams, snapping in the crisp Atlantic breeze behind him, and finally accepting the $1,000 reward in front of the hushed crowd of admirers. In front of everyone, Catherine and the children, his drinking buddies— almost all of them returned men—the Herald …* Jack's mind faltered, then refocused on the fantasy. He would show Mrs. F.C. Dill just who was the best hiker in the land.

FRANK AND JENNY Dill reached Vancouver on Wednesday June 14, and newspapers across the country announced their arrival with great enthusiasm. They were content to finish the race in 134 days to the Behans' 138. The citizens of Halifax and Vancouver went wild.

Mr. and Mrs. Dill Arrive in Vancouver from Halifax
WOMAN SMASHES HIKING RECORD

"The hikers arrived in the city just after 5 o'clock tonight, Pacific time, completing their walking trip across Canada from Halifax in 134 days—a world's record," reported the *Herald*. "The couple walked every step of the way and refused the aid of autos on their arrival at the outskirts of the city."

Dozens of questions filled the air at the CPR station.

"Are you glad you went?"

"How did you enjoy the adventure?"

"We enjoyed the race and we are glad we went," Frank said above the confusion.

"Would you be willing to do it again?"

"Any time," Jenny said.

When met by a delegation from the Kiwanis Club, consisting of President Archie Teetzel, J.R. Sigmore and Ed Knowlton, the first thing the

"Woman Smashes Hiking Record"
Jenny and Frank Dill arrive in Vancouver 134 days after starting out.
Vancouver Sun, June 15, 1921, p. 4

Dills did was praise the sportsmanship of the *Halifax Herald*.

"It civilized the event for us," Jenny said, "ensured us eats and a place to nod off along the way."

"Well, some of the time," Frank laughed. The crowd laughed with him.

After the delegation had offered congratulations and hands were shaken all round, eager reporters hounded the Dills with another round of questions.

"How many pairs of shoes did you wear out?"

"This is our sixth pair."

"How many suits of clothes?"

"Two."

"What were your worst hardships?"

"Sleeping in a Maine bed with frost sticking on the comforters and wading in snow, waist-deep, also in that state—also sleeping on the station floor at Yale, B.C."

"The most thrilling experience, madame?"

"When I watched a goose chase my husband for 150 yards near Winnipeg."

"Your first western experience?"

"Going up a grain elevator at Cheadle, Alberta. The owner sent me up the lift and being a lightweight I went up like a helicopter."

"Was it easy walking across the prairies?"

"Yes, we did 1,033 miles in 33 days."

"What route did you follow?"

"The Canadian Pacific all the way. We walked through 40 tunnels and over high bridges."

"Did you carry a pack?"

"I carried a 40-pound first aid kit, and my husband carried the one with our clothing, which weighed 50 pounds."

"Mrs. Dill, have you any other record?"

"Yes, that of having written my name on every provincial and state boundary line monument on the route gone over between here and Halifax."

Giving in to fatigue and a need for privacy, the couple finally concluded the interview. After stopping at the post office to pick up their mail, the Dills went straight to their hotel.

The Behans observed the scene in silence.

His Worship John S. Parker, mayor of Halifax, sent a telegram to Mrs. Dill. "Congratulations on behalf of the citizens of Halifax on your wonderful accomplishment in walking from Canada's eastern gateway to the Pacific coast," he wrote. "You are the only woman who has ever performed such a feat and in record time, an honor which carries its own reward. You have won the admiration of all for your wonderful pluck and dogged determination."

Not to be outdone by the Halifax mayor, Premier G.H. Murray of Nova Scotia also sent congratulations to the Dills. "The feat you have accomplished shows the stuff of which Nova Scotians are made," he said.

Frank and Jenny Dill were treated as celebrities throughout their week-long stay in Vancouver. With her limited wardrobe, it wasn't easy for Jenny to be scrutinized by all the glamorous women and their well-heeled husbands, and her emotions were often conflicted. But though she longed for the safety of Halifax and the sanctity of home, she felt proud of her accomplishment, a pride shared by many of the people she met... and there were even times when she felt angry with herself for being so hard on Frank.

Charles Burkman arrived in Vancouver at noon on June 16, 151 days after leaving Halifax. The hard-luck hiker was happy to answer the barrage of questions posted by the jovial crowd. He gave several reasons for his poor showing:

The Dills were treated like celebrities in Vancouver after the race. *Halifax Herald,* June 1921

his bad feet, a three-day visit with his parents at Port Arthur and his lone status. "I would not advise anyone to start out alone if he wishes to make time," said the 20-year-old hiker. "When one is alone he will rest when he feels like it, but if he has a partner then one urges the other along."

"How do you feel about spending five gruelling months battling the wilds without being paid?"

"Haven't had much time to think about that."

"What about collecting on the wager put up for you in St. John?"

"Yeah!" shouted an indignant sport in the gathering.

"Five hundred dollars if you completed the trip on foot within six months? You remember that?"

"Barely," Burkman replied, "bit fuzzy about that one."

"I'd say you qualified, hands down. Right, boys?"

"Don't let the piker renege on that offer!"

The boys from the Press Club gave a hearty cheer, making Burkman feel good right down to the toes of his callused feet.

"I feel that a prize for winning the race is unnecessary."

"You do?" The man sounded disappointed.

"Really."

"How's that?"

"I have learned more about Canada from the hike than I would have known in 60 years—and that is prize enough for me."

"So how come you signed up for Jack's race from Montreal to Halifax then?"

Burkman raised his eyebrows. "I'll have to give that question some thought…"

"What was your best time in the race?"

Burkman was grateful for the change in subject and shot a smile at the young fellow holding up the shiny new Bentley cycle. "I walked 63 miles in 24 hours to reach Ottawa."

"What's Ottawa like?" asked a reporter.

"I received a great reception from the bluenose members of parliament, like R.H. Butts, M.P. for Cape Breton. The new parliament building is wonderful…"

"Give us a memorable moment?"

"At Peninsula, east of Schreiber, Ontario, the Behans and I met the Duke and Duchess of Devonshire who were en route east. They autographed our books and the Duchess gave us enough fruit to last a week," he told loyal followers.

"The Behans never mentioned you were there."

"Can't think why."

"Tell us about your ingenious invention for whipping along the rails," a newsy interrupted.

"Simple, really—I just attached a pair of roller skates to a pole that I leaned into. It was a novel way to get from Sudbury to Moose Jaw. At Moose Jaw the rails became too hot for walking, so I hiked along the ties."

"What about your most *humbling* day?"

"My most humbling day in the competition was a nine-mile hike."

"How was that loss received?"

"I am not ashamed of the showing... and hope that my friends in Halifax and other parts of Nova Scotia are not disappointed in my hard-fought fight either," Burkman said, picking his words carefully.

The lone hiker was suddenly tired of the reporters, the crowds and all the questions. He wasn't a hero and resented being treated as one. He had grown up during the past six months, and he didn't have to suffer fools. It had been exhausting, and he needed time to unload the burden of the race and reorient himself. With a dazzling smile, his new confidence intact, Burkman terminated the interview.

THE ELDER BEHAN didn't need to be asked to take on the official role of host for the hiking team. Besides speaking on behalf of their sponsors, the *Halifax Herald* and the *Evening Mail*, it provided him with a chance to seek out opportunities for employment and to promote Jack Behan. In his few remaining days in this west coast metropolis, Jack intended to shake the right hands, promote his latest scheme and enjoy himself.

"This is an ideal day for hikers," he said on June 17:

One we will never forget. The people of Vancouver can not do enough for us, and to complete our visit, Deputy Mayor Owen and Chief of Police Anderson, with their wives, gave us a trip all around Vancouver. We visited Stanley Park and saw beasts and wild birds of all species. The beautiful walks, trees, and flowers made us think we were in Paradise. After seeing and enjoying everything possible, the party returned to the hotel, and... had a sumptuous dinner, nothing too good for us. The ladies were very much interested in our hike and thoroughly enjoyed our stories. The mayor gave a speech inviting us to return some day, also Chief Anderson, in which we had to respond on behalf of Halifax and Dartmouth and the *Halifax Herald*.

"After bidding farewell to his worship and Mrs. Anderson, we drove to the police station accompanied by his worship's wife," Jack continued. "The Chief took us all through City Hall and to his collection room… to make it clear to all that one's trip to Vancouver is not complete without a visit to Chief Anderson's museum, a collection of 20 years."

Voluble Jack Behan wandered around the city, faithfully carrying out all his remaining ambassadorial business and meeting with former residents of Dartmouth and Halifax to carry their greetings home to old friends.

Although the hikers enjoyed the hospitality shown them in the city, they were keen to move on. For Clifford and Jenny, that meant a short stopover in Montreal and then a train ride home; for the *Herald*, it meant promoting another hiking race. Jack and Frank were in full support, but Charles was having second thoughts, no longer certain that he wanted to be involved.

The *Vancouver Sun* snapped a group picture of the trans-Canada hikers shortly before they departed for the east. And at home in Halifax, Jack's wife, Catherine, cut one last poem about the Great Trans-Canada Race from the *Evening Mail* and pasted it in her scrapbook, something her children and grandchildren, maybe even her great-grandchildren, would have to remember John (Jack) Behan and their son Clifford.

Halifax Hikers At Vancouver

Frank Dill, Jenny Dill, Jack Behan, Clifford Behan and Charles Burkman, pose in front of the *Vancouver Daily Sun* offices, June 1921. The newspaper incorrectly counts Burkman's 150-day walk 10 days short. Library and Archives Canada NL-22182

Epilogue

As far as the public was concerned, Jack and Clifford Behan lost the Great Trans-Canada Race to Frank and Jenny Dill. The *Herald* tried to smooth over the reality of the win by crediting the Behans with being first over the finish line, and the Dills with winning the race in terms of days out, but Jack took the implication of defeat hard. Not that the decision came as a surprise or that any money exchanged hands, and it is clear Jack already had a "save face" proposal in place before June 11, when he and Clifford entered the city. Few *Herald* readers missed the boxed notice placed next to the front-page hiking headlines in the newspaper:

BEHANS WILL MAKE BIG ANNOUNCEMENT TOMORROW

An important announcement from Jack Behan the first of the hikers to reach Vancouver will be made in the *Herald* and *The Mail* tomorrow.

Owing to the late hour this morning at which it was received, it was impossible to set the letter in type.

The letter is the most astonishing and most interesting that has been issued for months and promises to create the greatest sensation ever known to the Maritime Provinces.

Jack Behan is a man who has wide experiences in peace and war, and his announcement in the *Herald* will be of the most extraordinary character.

Jack Behan may have quit school after grade four, but his sense of the dramatic was a match for any *Herald* journalist.

The announcement, as promised, appeared the next day—along with news of the Dills' arrival in Vancouver.

$1,000 PUT UP FOR HIKE TO HALIFAX
Group Of Business Men Back Jack Behan's Challenge
To Frank Dill And Charles Burkman.
MEN WILL ONLY WALK FOR 10 HOURS DAILY
To Leave Vancouver By Train This Week
And Go To Starting Line At Montreal.

HALIFAX, June 14.—The acceptance of Jack Behan's challenge by Charlie Burkman and Frank Dill to hike from Montreal to Halifax makes one of the greatest athletic events ever staged in Canada a certainty…A group of Halifax business men, who have taken an interest in the hikers ever since they left Halifax, have put up a fund of One Thousand Dollars, in order to create a greater interest in the great contest. The prizes will be as follows:

First Prize, $500
Second Prize, $300
Third Prize, $200

There was a good deal of dissatisfaction over Jack's proposal, and at least one reader of the *Herald* said so, and more:

First off, I think Jack owes Charlie Burkman the palm, due to the fact that when Charlie left Halifax, he did not start out on a race, only a walk across the country. It was the Behans who set a challenge and made a race of it causing Charlie's partner to drop, leaving him to continue on alone.

Second, Mrs. Dill: Not only did she have the strength to stick out the race, but she won the hike! I say she won the race because even her husband admitted that she set the pace, and had it not been for her pluck, Frank Dill would probably not have finished in the position of the race where he did.

I presume that the Montreal to Halifax hike will be under the auspices of The Herald and The Evening Mail, so why not let them make the conditions or appoint a committee to do so?

Also on this individual hike, why are Mrs. Jenny Dill (The champion hiker of Canada) and Clifford Behan not invited to participate? Surely by walking across the continent they have earned the right to participate if they wish.

Trusting that this will be arranged so that not only one of the participants will get to name the condition of the Montreal to Halifax race,
I am,

➤ ONE VERY MUCH INTERESTED

The *Halifax Herald* agreed to appoint a staff correspondent to follow the hikers and telegraph daily stories of their progress back to the newspaper. The hikers would have an opportunity to take home some real money, thanks to Jack, and the concerned public would have the *Herald* monitoring the event. The only hiker to grumble over the terms was the idealistic Burkman, who continued to voice his concerns over money being offered in exchange for winning.

ALL THE HIKERS enjoyed the train ride back across the country to Montreal, and a sense of camaraderie developed among them within the confines of the passenger car as they passed through areas they had so lately vacated. In Montreal the now-famous trans-Canada foot racers were again treated to accommodations and meals by the *Herald* and were given additional opportunities to retell their stories, although Jack, in his role of promoter of the "most astonishing and interesting challenge," spent much of his time guying army pals and drumming up business for the Montreal-to-Halifax event.

On Wednesday July 6, conditions for the race were finalized, including one remarkable, although not entirely unexpected, surprise: Charles Burkman had withdrawn from the race.

DILL AND BEHAN BATTLE FOR SUPREMACY
CLIFFORD BEHAN AND MRS. DILL HOME TONIGHT
Burkman Backs Out of Big Race After Not Accepting Hike Terms and Remains in Montreal.

MONTREAL, July 7.—Behan and Dill will leave Montreal at ten o'clock this morning for Halifax in the contest for the One Thousand dollars cash prizes donated by Halifax and Dartmouth citizens. The first prize is for Six Hundred dollars, the second is Four hundred dollars.

The day before the race start, Behan and Dill put aside their differences to do the rounds of men's clothing stores in the city, though they had trouble finding ideal garments. At one store they each purchased a light sweater, Jack's being in the colours of the celebrated Lorne Aquatic Club of Halifax, and Frank's in some more gaudy combination of colours that it would be hard to find a club to sponsor. They also each selected green eyeshades.

"The race ought to be a record-breaker, judging not only from the physique and experience of the hikers, but from the care which they displayed this after-noon in the selection of equipment they consider necessary to enable them to take part in the race," wrote Roy Carmichael, special correspondent for the *Herald*.

Mrs. Dill arrived back in Halifax to a tumultuous welcome and a hiking con-test of her own: Two Fat Women challenged her to a walk to Toronto. "I want to look them over first," she said. "If they think hiking is a joke, then I'm willing to show them the way to Toronto. I want, however, to be sure of their sincerity. In all my walking I have never found a woman who said she would like to race me." Mrs. Dill had fought hard for her laurels, and she was ready to defend them under the right conditions. "I am afraid these challenges are mere bluffs," she said.

Frank Dill and Jack Behan left Montreal in the forenoon on July 7 and walked under a blazing sun all day, arriving at the Windsor Hotel in St. John's, Quebec, exhausted by their strenuous efforts in the torrid temperature.

The rivalry that existed between the men broke out afresh during the day when they passed through a village where Jack was well known. It was said by the special correspondent that a wager was made that Behan would best his younger rival by more than 100 miles before Halifax was reached. Dill said he resented this and stated that he would be willing to put up his share of the prize money to Behan's friend if he did not reach Halifax at least one day ahead of Behan. Several bets were then made on the outcome of the race. Unfortunately, the temperature was so great that night that the rivals forgot their differences and admitted to sitting up half the night fanning each other with bedsheets.

The next morning, Behan and Dill spent a pleasant enough time touring the town with Dr. Bouthillier, a member of the provincial parliament and jovial good fellow who abandoned his practice to act as host.

In order to avoid the heat, the hikers didn't leave the French community for Foster, 40 miles distant, until 7 p.m., intending to arrive before morning. The weather didn't co-operate, however, and the rain came down in torrents, while thunder and jagged flashes of lightning lit up the darkened sky for miles around.

Despite the challenges of the weather, Burkman and Dill arrived at Foster to a tumultuous welcome. But the next day, the race was called off.

HIKERS ARE OVERCOME BY HEAT WAVE
Dill forced to Abandon Walking When
Mercury Goes to 104 In Quebec

MONTREAL, July 10.—The hike between Jack Behan and Frank Dill from Montreal to Halifax has been declared off. On account of illness, which has overtaken Dill at Foster, Quebec. Owing to the oppressive heat, Dill has been forced to abandon the hike and been told by a doctor that his condition will not permit him to walk to Halifax. He will leave by train Monday night for Halifax.

Mrs. Dill said that she was not surprised as she had received a letter from Frank complaining of the weather. "I want to do it for your sake—and for the sake of the province in which I was born," he'd written.

The *Herald* reported that "great disappointment was expressed in athletic circles in Montreal...Although Behan was unaffected [by the heat] it was the general view here that he would have been unwise to continue in defiance of medical opinion."

Racing officials decided to postpone any further trial of long-distance-hiking supremacy until at least September, when cooler weather was expected to prevail.

Jack Behan and Frank Dill returned by train to Dartmouth and Halifax, respectively, on July 14. Dill, at least, was met by loyal friends and a devoted family.

Dills Followed By Big Crowds

Mr. and Mrs. F. Dill, the TransCanada hikers, were followed thru the streets of Halifax last night by large crowds. The crowds grew larger as the hikers neared The Herald building, where the hikers were called to give an account of their experiences during the evening.

To Jack Behan's chagrin, Frank and Jenny Dill remained the primary focus of attention wherever they went. Jenny received many challenges and said that she hoped to receive many more. "Unfortunately midsummer is not an ideal time for hiking," she admitted. "I prefer mid-winter. And I am willing to meet any challenges when the weather cools, and will walk any woman, any distance, at any time."

The Dills slowly wound down their public appearances. Jenny spoke to a gathering at Cornwallis Street Baptist Church, and at the Classic and Royal theatres in Dartmouth, she reiterated her intentions to write a book of their cross-country experiences—"perhaps this summer or early fall."

All the trans-Canada hikers, including Charles Burkman, took part in one last contest, accepting invitations to the championship meet, which was sponsored by the Halifax Wanderers Amateur Athletics Association and held at Wanderers Grounds, the city's official home for many sporting activities, including track and field. Races were open events, although, of course, women's competitions were run separately. When James M. Doucette, a much-decorated athlete from Cape Breton, accepted an invitation, levels of anticipation and excitement were raised. There was no purse for winners, but inside betting was rampant.

HIKERS WILL COMPETE HERE NEXT WEEK
Doucette, Who Claims Record to Vancouver, Has Accepted Challenge of Halifax Hiker.

HALIFAX, August 17.—Halifax and other Nova Scotians, who have been waiting for months to see the transcontinental hikers in competition against each other will have an opportunity on Wednesday of next week, when Jack Behan, Clifford Behan, Charles Burkman and J.M. Doucette will take part in a program of sports on the Wanderers grounds.

A huge crowd of more than 3,200 spectators, "the largest crowd that has ever turned out to a midweek sporting event in Halifax," watched the competitions on August 24. Everyone was interested in Mrs. Dill and her eight competitors in the two-mile hike for women. "The stands were crowded with females fully an hour before the opening of the event took place," said the Herald. "Mrs. Dill led practically all the way, but Miss M. O'Hearn of North Dartmouth, who had been trailing the leader, made a sensational spurt on the last lap and finished on even terms with the famed transcontinental hiker. In a magnanimous gesture, Mrs. Dill requested that Miss O'Hearn be given first prize."

Burkman had too much speed for his rivals in the men's race, and after passing the half-mile mark, he had everything his own way and won by 200 yards over Jack Behan. Clifford Behan and Frank Dill dropped out of the race after the two-mile mark.

"That should prove to them what Charles Burkman is capable of," the first-place winner said, showing only a thin line of perspiration along his upper lip. He had done what he came to do and proved what he needed to prove to his loyal fans, hoping, perhaps, that Sidney Carr was in the stands watching.

The much-publicized long-distance runner James Doucette was entered in the race but didn't start. "After learning that the event was advertised for the Championship of Canada," he told the racing committee the day before the event, "I had no intentions of competing, as I already hold the championship." Recorders found no official proof of his boast.

As the summer of 1921 slipped away, the last recorded race involving a trans-Canada hiker took place. On September 5, Jenny Dill competed in the "go-as-you-please hike for women around Onslo," a distance of about eight miles. "Mrs. Dill led the field of 13 contestants for a good part of the way, but Miss Guilda Lewis, who maintained the third spot for most of the race, passed Mrs. Dill at Jupiter Street, a little east of Robie Street cemetery, and thereafter was never headed." Miss Lewis, of Bible Hill, won by about 25 feet, in 85 minutes. Jenny said that she saved as much strength as possible for the finish.

What became of the contestants of the Great Trans-Canada Race of 1921? Not much is known about any of them after Burkman won the championship meet at Wanderers Grounds in Halifax on August 24 and Jenny lost the go-as-you-please hike for women.

The marathon event from the end of January to mid-June 1921 left none of the pedestrians rich or famous, but it did give them the distinction of being Canadian pioneers in long-distance exploits and stunts.

We do know that Frank Dill died in 1928, seven years after the race. We also know that Jenny Dill did not write the book she promised and that she remarried after Frank's death and died in Halifax in 1941. Frank's aunt, Kitty Landry, told me in a telephone conversation, before she too died in 2008, that she found a photograph of Frank and Jenny at the bottom of an old trunk containing scrapbooks compiled by family members in 1921. The photograph had been ripped in half. What could that mean? I asked her. "Possibly a heartbreak was involved," the old woman told me.

Charles Burkman, who hated patronage and sponsorship money equally, had a ticket from Montreal to Halifax but never used it. After winning the championship race so handily, he set out from Halifax in late October 1921 to walk around the world in three years for a prize of $20,000, subscribed by sportsmen in the Maritimes. It is not known how he made out. Rumour has it that the exceptional young man went on to be an RCAF pilot during the Second World War and later returned to Port Arthur, where he married.

At 80, Jack Behan still claimed that he and Clifford were the only ones who walked all the way across Canada, and he was sorry then that they had. "We came home broke, our families in debt, and we couldn't get work," he told reporters in 1956.

John (Jack) Albert Behan and Catherine Walsh were married in September 1895 at St. Peter's Church in Dartmouth; they had nine children between 1896 and 1912 and lived at Tufts Cove, in North Dartmouth, where he became Postman #2 for the town. Jack and Catherine moved their large family to Boston, Massachusetts, around 1926 to look for work and pay their debts. Catherine died in Boston in 1932.

In an email to me, Donnie and Carol Behan, Clifford Behan's great-grandson and his wife, wrote: "After his wife's death, Jack continued his gypsy life style across the States and Canada until his travels brought him back to his birth place, Dartmouth, Nova Scotia in the fall of 1962." Here, at the age of 86 and in failing health, he entered Camp Hill Hospital in Halifax in October 1962. John Albert Behan's famous travels came to an end on October 6, and he was buried October 10 in the Gates of Heaven Cemetery, Lower Sackville, Nova Scotia. In the end, Jack's family said that it was Burkman, the first man on the trail, that he and Clifford intended to beat, and they did. Nowhere do they mention the Dills.

And what about Clifford Behan, what is said of him? This quiet, battle-scarred survivor of Vimy Ridge, frequently in the shadows of his brash, outspoken father, went off to Boston with his parents in search of a better life but ended up with a drinking problem and with several failed marriages. Most of the Behan descendents live in the United States.

It might be argued that the big winner of the event was the *Halifax Herald*. Organizing and exploiting a novel cross-country sporting event has to be near the top of the list of the newspaper's many successes, even though it is doubtful that the *Herald* fully understood the ramifications of what it was doing. The fact it brought together such a unique cast of athletic personalities, who overcame the physical, psychological and emotional challenges that united them as Olympian athletes, can only be explained as calculated luck. Adding a woman to the mix was sheer ingenuity. No one could have predicted that Jenny Dill had the inner fortitude, the physical toughness or the social impudence to best her male competitors, or the psychological makeup to stand up to her husband in public—*or* to take on the formidable Jack Behan and his son. In order to accomplish this, Jenny had to give up caring what anyone, even Frank and his overly protective mother, thought of her, to discover her steely resolve and become the best athlete she could be. History suggests that it left an indelible mark on their marriage.

Acknowledgements

FOR THEIR HELP securing text and images, I'd like to thank Debbie Reid, librarian, The Halifax Herald Limited (publishers of the *Chronicle Herald* and the *Sunday Herald*). Thanks also to the Nova Scotia Museum and Archives, the Okanagan College Library, the Salmon Arm Library, The Vancouver Public Library, R.J. Haney House Village and Museum, the Kamloops Museum and Archives, the Glenbow Museum, Library and Archives Canada, the National Gallery of Canada, the University of Saskatchewan Library, Images Nova Scotia, the Revelstoke Museum and Archives, the Prairie West Museum and Archives, the Ashcroft Museum and Archives, the Esplanade. I also thank Elinor Barr of the Swedes in Canada Project.

Thank you to Heritage House Publishing Co. Ltd., especially publisher Rodger Touchie, managing editor Vivian Sinclair and editor Audrey McClellan.

I send special thanks to John (Jack) Behan's descendents: Donnie and Carol Behan; and Frank Dill's descendents: Kitty Landry and Nicole Landry.

About the author

SHIRLEY JEAN ROLL TUCKER is a theatre director and playwright whose works include *The Queen of the Shuswap*; *You're Loving, Kind and True, Jack Boy*; *The John L. Wilson Story*; *The Supper Waltz*; and *Sowing Seeds in Danny*, a musical adaptation of Nellie McClung's novel. A fine-arts teacher before becoming a writer, Shirley taught high-school art and musical theatre for many years. She also founded and ran an interior design company and owned an art gallery. She is an active member of Shuswap Theatre, where she has designed, directed and produced numerous mainstage plays, including six that she wrote. *The Amazing Foot Race of 1921* is her first book of non-fiction. Born and raised in Alberta, Shirley now lives on a heritage farm in the Shuswap region of British Columbia.